# WELFARE

As We Knew It

# WELFARE
## As We Knew It

*A Political History of the
American Welfare State*

CHARLES NOBLE

New York    Oxford
OXFORD UNIVERSITY PRESS
1997

Oxford University Press

Oxford    New York
Athens    Auckland    Bangkok    Bogota    Bombay    Buenos Aires
Calcutta    Cape Town    Dar es Salaam    Delhi    Florence    Hong Kong
Istanbul    Karachi    Kuala Lumpur    Madras    Madrid    Melbourne
Mexico City    Nairobi    Paris    Singapore    Taipei    Tokyo    Toronto    Warsaw

and associated companies in
Berlin    Ibadan

Copyright © 1997 by Oxford University Press, Inc.

Published by Oxford University Press, Inc.
198 Madison Avenue, New York, New York 10016

Oxford is a registered trademark of Oxford University Press

Library of Congress Cataloging-in-Publication Data
Noble, Charles, 1945–
Welfare as we knew it : a political history of the American
welfare state / Charles Noble.
p.   cm.
0-19-511336-5; 0-19-511337-3 (pbk.)
1. Public welfare—United States—History.   2. United States—
Social policy.   I. Title.
HV95.N53   1997
381.973—dc21        97—23704

9 8 7 6 5 4 3 2
Printed in the United States of America
on acid-free paper

# Contents

# Acknowledgments

All research, whether carried out in groups or by lone scholars, depends on the work and support of others. In this case, I have had the benefit of good friends and insightful readers. The following people have read all or part of the manuscript at one or another stage and provided invaluable advice: James William Gibson, Edward Greenberg, Jennifer Hochschild, Peter Hall, Joel Krieger, Michael MacDonald, Lawrence Noble, Bo Rothstein, Wendy Sarvasy, Ron Schmidt, and Michael Wallerstein. I owe special debts to two people. Frances Fox Piven provided invaluable comments on the first draft. Larry George read the entire manuscript twice. I benefited as well from the comments of the anonymous referees who evaluated the manuscript for publication. The editors at Oxford University Press were a pleasure to work with (Thomas LeBien's substantive suggestions were especially useful; Lisa Stallings' help during production was invaluable). As to responsibility for the final product, the usual caveat applies: I am sure I ignored too much sound advice; the blame for any errors that follow is entirely mine.

California State University at Long Beach, although not equipped to support scholarly research, and burdened by an inhospitable fiscal environment, has provided me with what help it could afford at critical junctures. My colleagues in the political science department have encouraged this work; my students in graduate and undergraduate courses have gamely tried to come to terms with every new literature I threw at them as I worked through these materials.

Finally, in different ways, my wife, Pamela Bottaro, my daughter, Rebecca, and my parents, Hyman and Jeanette Noble, have provided me with the emotional and psychological aid and comfort that a project of this sort requires. I thank them all.

*Santa Monica, California*                                                   C. N.
*December 1996*

# WELFARE

## As We Knew It

# Introduction

Careful observers of social policy have known for some time that the conservative complaint against America's welfare state—that it is too big and takes too much care of an increasingly dependent population—is, in international perspective, wrong. The U.S. welfare state is striking precisely because it is so limited in scope and ambition. Compared with governments in most other rich capitalist democracies in the West, from Sweden to Canada, U.S. public policy does *less* to change how markets, whether global capital markets or local labor markets allocate income and employment opportunities: the American welfare state is exceptional because it is so *market conforming*. After a hundred years of welfare-state building, Americans remain more vulnerable to the free play of market forces than do the people of nearly every other rich capitalist society.[1]

This book describes and, more importantly, offers an explanation for this condition. Contrary to many accounts, I do not believe that public hostility to the welfare state explains why the American government does less. As we shall see, public-opinion surveys regularly report that Americans support a wide range of social-welfare programs, from social security to public assistance for the poor. Nor do I think that Americans are better off with less government; in contrast to the free-market assumptions that now inform elite discussions of social policy in the United States, the available evidence suggests that public programs to promote economic security have substantially improved people's lives.

Rather, I will argue that the structure of the American political economy has profoundly limited what social reformers intent on building a welfare state have been able to accomplish.[2] Fundamental features of the political environment, principally the balance of power between business and labor, decentralized government and party institutions, and racial cleavages have prevented Americans from getting the more comprehensive welfare state that citizens of other Western capitalist democracies enjoy. If this is true, it follows that a successful effort to create a more just and generous welfare state must first change present conditions.

3

Reformers have, of course, expanded the scope of public provision—most notably in the 1910s, the 1930s, and the 1960s. But even progress during these watershed periods quickly ran up against limits imposed by the political environment. Lacking state and party structures that might have facilitated political mobilization by the economically insecure, and a well-organized, unified labor movement that might have better pressured government for public benefits and full-employment policies, American reformers were led to make substantial concessions to powerful financial, industrial, and occupational groups with vested interests in the status quo. And these concessions have short-circuited efforts to build a more generous safety net and frustrated efforts to solve the problems of economic insecurity that Americans face and that Americans *want* government to help them solve.

In emphasizing the impact of structure, I will not ignore what social scientists call "agency," that is, conscious decisions taken by political actors in pursuit of the their goals. In fact, I will argue that during two decades—the 1930s and the 1960s—social and economic forces and political events created conditions that allowed reformers momentarily to overcome political and institutional resistance to welfare-state building and act decisively. Unfortunately, because they made larger concessions to the opponents of reform than politically necessary, decisions taken by reformers proved strategic failures, exacerbating the constraints created by political structures. Yet even in these cases, I will argue, strategic failures made sense *in context*. Indeed, this is the real tragedy of American social policy: what reformers can do about economic insecurity in the United States remains deeply constrained by the political-institutional environment in which they must act.

My interest in the development of American social policy is not driven entirely by theoretical concerns. While I am convinced that Americans need and want a more just and generous welfare state, I also doubt that the dominant "liberal" approach to economic insecurity embodied in contemporary social policy can accomplish these goals; reformers need to rethink the very way they approach the role of government in the economy. It is not a question, however, of inventing new policies; there are already many sound proposals to improve public assistance, save social security, and restructure Medicare without seriously degrading the quality of public benefits.[3] The more pressing task is to understand how political structures and political strategies shape our policy choices: why liberals have been unable to better secure the political foundations of this welfare state and how reformers who want to build a better one might proceed.

On its face, my conclusion that structure matters so much would seem to make this sort of political guide irrelevant. But there *is* room for optimism: my analysis suggests both where different decisions might have been made, and, more important, where those who are interested in increasing the government's ability to tackle social and economic problems should focus their energies—on political-institutional reforms that can change the underlying political structures, thereby facilitating political action by ordinary citizens. Because Americans do not have the welfare state they want, structural changes that make it easier for the majority to express its desires are likely to change how government approaches the problem of economic insecurity. Political-structural change of this sort is admittedly an enormous project. But given the public's deep dissatisfaction with the political system, it is not beyond our grasp.

I proceed in four steps. Chapters 1 and 2 provide an overview of how the American welfare state differs from the welfare states of other rich capitalist democracies and survey alternative explanations for those differences. After rejecting single-factor approaches that emphasize political culture, class conflict, or state structures to explain American welfare-state development, I argue for a self-consciously synthetic approach that takes into account multiple determinants. Drawing on recent social-scientific and historical research (including cross-national quantitative studies of spending growth since 1950 and qualitative case studies of social-policy development since Germany's breakthrough in the 1880s), I suggest that interests, institutions, and racial cleavages best explain the development of American social policy in the twentieth century.

Chapters 3 through 6 explore this argument historically, focusing on four key moments of decision and the interplay of structure and agency at each point: three periods when events conspired to widen political actors' room to maneuver (the Progressive period, the New Deal, and the Great Society), and one (from the 1970s to the mid-1990s) during which liberals were forced to defend their accomplishments against a conservative backlash. In each case, I examine how structures shaped the opportunities available to reformers, how reformers chose among them, and the political and policy consequences of those choices.

While stressing the role of structure, I also identify two strategic missteps. In chapter 4, I suggest that President Franklin D. Roosevelt failed to take full advantage of the economic collapse of American capitalism to promote social change, accomodating instead business interests and southern conservatives in the early New Deal when he might have tried to build a social-democratic coalition. In chapter 5, I argue that President Lyndon B. Johnson might have done more to confront economic inequality in the mid-1960s. In these chapters we see how the weight of political and institutional obstacles and the concessions made to them combined to shape American social policy, from the turn toward "maternalism" in the 1910s (in the form of social policies designed to help women as actual or potential mothers), to the restricted scope of the social-insurance programs adopted in the 1930s, to the decision in the 1960s to stimulate the economy not by expanding social spending but by cutting taxes.

Based on this account, the final chapters examine the likely prospects for reform in the near and mid-term. Chapter 7 critically evaluates alternative proposals to reinvent liberalism, as well as the likelihood that conservatives will be able to remake the welfare state along free-market principles. I conclude that while conservative social policies are not likely to satisfy the public, liberal reformers who proceed without attention to the limits imposed on them by deep political structures are also likely to fail. The conclusion returns to the structure/agency issue and considers the future of reform in that light, showing why reformers must address structural obstacles to reform if they want to change social policy.

# ONE

# The Problem

In capitalist societies, welfare states exist to protect the public from the impact of unregulated market forces. That is their rationale and, to a significant extent, their principal effect. The poor receive cash and in-kind assistance, the elderly receive tax-subsidized pensions, and the jobless receive unemployment benefits because society has decided that individuals, families, and communities should not be asked to bear the brunt of economic change alone. But societies also vary in the degree to which they use government to counteract free market forces, and these differences matter enormously in people's lives.

The United States stands at one extreme: compared with most other rich capitalist societies, the American welfare state is more *market conforming*. America has a welfare state, of course; federal, state, and local government spending on social-welfare programs accounts for approximately one-fifth of the nation's gross domestic product (GDP).[1] Many of the things that other welfare states do are done here as well. But according to statistics collected by the Organization for Economic Cooperation and Development (OECD), the GDP share devoted to "social protection" in the United States is two-thirds of the average GDP share spent on similar purposes by members of the European Community and the lowest of *any* Western industrial society.[2] When the American government does act to shelter individuals and families from economic hardship, it is more likely to do so in ways that conform to market *principles,* that is, to the idea that an individual's life chances should be determined not by political decisions about where and how firms invest, or how income and wealth are distributed, but by that individual's ability to work, save, and invest, and to compete in labor, commodity, and capital markets.[3]

America's failure to provide government-guaranteed health care or universal family allowances is particularly striking. Unlike every other industrialized nation in the world, the United States guarantees neither medical services nor health insurance as a right of citizenship. Government-financed health care targets three narrowly

7

defined groups: the poor, the aged, and the military. In combination, they account for less than one-third of the population.[4] Family
benefits are also targeted: except for a small, standard income-tax
deduction and a tax credit for child and dependent care, only individuals in poor, single-parent families qualify. In contrast, Western
European governments offer a wide variety of family benefits to a
far broader clientele.[5]

The U.S. welfare state also treats the poor less generously.
Other Western welfare states typically provide a much richer set of
benefits for poor families, adding access to public preschools, more
generous housing allowances, and other social services to cash assistance. For example, measured as a proportion of the average production worker's wages, the value of all benefits available to single-
parent families is 222% higher in Sweden than in the United States,
184% higher in the Netherlands, and 41% higher in Austria.[6]

American economic and employment policies are also more
market conforming. Economic policies are designed to control inflation by restricting the money supply rather than promote economic
expansion and job creation by increasing public spending.[7] Even
those countries, such as Germany, that have also emphasized anti-
inflationary goals have compensated for their economic policies' deflationary effects by developing "labor-market policies" that educate,
train, and relocate displaced workers so that they might better adjust to changing patterns of economic development.[8] In the United
States, in contrast, educational and job-training programs are
poorly funded and coordinated.[9] In the late 1980s, the GDP share
devoted to education, training, and relocation services for displaced
and unemployed workers in the United States was less than a third
of the average OECD share; much of that was spent on job programs for the poor.[10] Consequently, most American workers have
had to find private solutions to, and absorb the costs of, economic
dislocation on their own.

The American government also imposes fewer obligations on
private firms to provide social welfare benefits to their workers. As
a result, American employers enjoy considerably more discretion
when deciding which fringe benefits to offer their employees. Unlike
its Western European counterparts, for example, the American government does not require that private employers offer pensions,
medical benefits, or paid vacations. Rather, these decisions are left
up to bargaining between unions and managers, or, in non-union-
ized environments, to negotiations between employers and individual employees.

Some observers who question the viability of comprehensive
public provision have suggested that these differences will narrow
because demographic changes, mounting tax and debt burdens, and

pressure from internationally mobile firms looking for friendly business climates will force all welfare states to cut spending. There is
some evidence in support of this view. Since 1973, intensified global
competition and changing demographic patterns have undermined
the social and economic foundations of the contemporary welfare
state. Increased competition has led firms everywhere to look for
ways to cut costs and governments to cut taxes. At the same time,
the relative decline of male-dominated, nuclear families, the growth
of single-parent households, and aging populations have increased
demands on public-benefit programs, particularly pension and health
care systems. The balance of political power has also shifted rightward throughout the West, making it harder for advocates of public
spending to defend previous gains. Economic integration is likely to
intensify the pressure on European welfare states to cut the scope
and quality of public benefits, if only to meet the requirements of
monetary union.

The result has been a slowdown in the rate of increase in social
spending throughout the West, and there have been some significant
cuts in means-tested income maintenance, health, and social-service
programs targeted on the poor and the long-term unemployed.[11]
Full-employment commitments have also suffered, especially on
the European continent where (in contrast to the United States)
they were once taken seriously by policy makers.[12] Based on this
evidence, it is not hard to imagine that American and Western
European welfare states will eventually converge on restraining
the growth of social spending and restructuring core social-welfare
programs.

But the American experience with retrenchment has also been
distinctive, and is likely to remain so. On the one hand, the scope of
European cutbacks is often exaggerated. While important changes
have been made in Europe (for example, more benefits are now
means-tested, patients pay more for health-care services, workers
are likely to have to postpone their retirement, and they receive less
generous disability payments) these welfare states are cutting back
from a far larger base and are likely to continue to offer their citizens a much richer mix of services and benefits. Moreover, as recent protests in France and Germany suggest, supporters of the
welfare state in Europe are likely to resist strongly even modest cutbacks.

In contrast, American opponents of public provision have
proved unusually effective. The backlash started earlier in the
United States and has lasted longer, and social spending growth
rates have tended to slow more dramatically than elsewhere. Indeed, the United States was one of only three cases where social
spending grew slowly in the 1970s *and* the 1980s (the other two are

Britain and the Netherlands), and the only one of these three cases to retrench again in the 1990s, even though it had already spent a smaller share of its GDP on public provision.[13] Perhaps most important, by cutting taxes and increasing public deficits, American advocates of retrenchment have also succeeded in re-engineering the rules of the game governing social spending, leading to enormous pressure on public officials to restrain the growth of social-welfare expenditures.[14]

Taking all of the evidence together, then, it seems more reasonable to conclude that the U.S. welfare state will remain distinctive, still leaving more of its population unusually dependent on the distribution of private property, education, skill, talent, and luck. What accounts for this curious situation?

### Beyond Culture

For much of the postwar period, the dominant explanation for the distinctive characteristics of the American welfare state rested on the influence of political culture on American public policy.[15] According to this view, some cultures are simply more comfortable with assigning responsibility for social-welfare needs to central political authorities, while others want families, the market, or local community organizations to retain control. The United States, it is argued, has a smaller, less ambitious welfare state because Americans—whether voters, social reformers, or public officials—have been motivated by deeply held, "classical liberal" values that argue against public provision.[16]

According to this theory, in each critical period of welfare-state building in America, public opinion constrained policy choice. In the 1910s, the Progressives were unable to sell European-style social insurance to a middle class fearful of a central state with European-style powers. Even as capitalism collapsed around them in the 1930s, New Dealers remained inhibited by most Americans' indifference to the kinds of radical solutions that found mass support abroad. In the 1960s, the Great Society offered the poor an equality of "opportunity" rather than of "condition" because that is what most Americans, even poor Americans, wanted. The conservative backlash against the Great Society since the 1970s has been so successful, it is argued, because it has resonated with the public's distrust of "big government," "bureaucrats," and "social engineers." Only in the case of public education, which conforms to cultural preferences for opportunity and social mobility, has American government kept pace with its European counterparts. As one proponent of the cultural approach has put it, *"the state plays a more limited role in America than elsewhere because Americans, more than other people, want it to play a limited role."*[17]

The underlying premise of the cultural account—that values and ideas shape people's perceptions of what is and is not appropriate— is unassailable. The situations in which actors find themselves are never transparent. Even social and political identities must be "constructed." Culture or ideology shapes how people "enter" politics, how they act to influence government, and what they think of public policy.

Public-opinion polling confirms that political cultures vary among the Western democracies and that these variations are related in a systematic fashion to differences in how governments deal with economic insecurity. Societies like Sweden, which have statist and solidaristic traditions, have built larger more egalitarian welfare states. Societies with more individualistic, antistatist cultures, such as the United States, have less active governments and leave far more to the family, the market, and voluntary associations.

Furthermore, Americans *are* unusual in their preference for nonstatist forms of public provision, in their celebration of individual initiative, and in their deference to market outcomes. Here, majorities consistently reject the idea that people have a *right* to an income and a job. It is not unreasonable then to conclude that classical liberal ideas about the appropriate relationship between the state and market have affected public policy, if only by conditioning how arguments for and against public provision are heard and understood.[18]

But while culture, values, or ideology cannot be ignored, there are good reasons to doubt their explanatory purchase. It is hard to support the claim that abstract public values *have had* to result in a particular set of policy choices at a particular time in a particular case. Abstract values must be translated into specific policy choices through the political process. As a rule, preferences for individualism, capitalism, or private property are too general, ambiguous, and self-contradictory to tightly constrain policy makers dealing with concrete problems. Does respect for private property require that employers be free to determine the working conditions of their employees? Or only that government give employers certain procedural protections before setting and enforcing regulations? Over time, government has moved from the former to the latter position, all the while claiming to respect the "inviolate" property rights of factory owners.

It is also hard to know whether or not the values, ideas, or opinions in question independently influence political structures and policy decisions (i.e., are "exogenous") or are the product of those structures and decisions (i.e., are "endogenous").[19] The political rhetoric of elites does not provide enough evidence to resolve the issue; elites often appeal to shared values when trying to justify decisions taken for other reasons, often in response to pressure from economic interests with a material stake in policy outcomes.[20] Indeed, over time, public opinion may actually fall in line with the policies being pursued rather than determine them.[21] Citizens of societies that have generous welfare states may come to believe in the efficacy of state intervention because the government works for *them*.[22] Conversely, it is not implausible that citizens in countries with small, ineffective welfare states have concluded that government cannot or will not come to their aid and, *as a consequence*, have grown skeptical of, and resistant to, politicians who promise to expand the state on their behalf.[23]

In addition, the differences between American and European values are not always as dramatic as proponents of the cultural view suggest. Europeans are much more likely to endorse state action and redistributional reform and agree that government has an "obligation" to take care of the poor and the unemployed. But cultural accounts exaggerate the importance of "social-democratic" values, in particular solidaristic values, to the development of even the largest European welfare states: Europeans do not always embrace them and Americans do not always reject them. For example, even though a smaller proportion of American than German or Italian respondents endorses levying taxes on the rich to produce greater income equality, *three quarters* of Americans still want that done. And even though Americans are *more* likely than Europeans to do so, *both* rank "freedom" over "equality of position" when asked to choose between the two.[24] Nor does Americans' greater reluctance to embrace the idea of state-sponsored economic security mean that a majority opposes it: as many Americans think that government should "provide a decent standard of living for the unemployed" as do not.[25] Indeed, a clear majority of Americans embraces the idea that "the state should guarantee every citizen food and basic shelter."[26]

Americans also strongly support social policies that transfer resources and spend money on the economically insecure. Americans want to strengthen social security,[27] spend more on the poor[28] and the unemployed,[29] guarantee universal access to medical care (without regard to ability to pay),[30] have more government help with child care,[31] and simultaneously increase taxes on the rich.[32] The only thing that Americans do not want is "welfare," and only because that is understood to consist of programs that help people who they think should work but refuse to do so.[33]

For these reasons, it is hard to be content with the political-cultural explanation of the limits of the U.S. welfare state. How else might we account for the particular trajectory taken by American social policy?

## Interests

Given the important role that economic conflict plays in politics, political competition among the various constituencies that might be helped or hurt by social policy provides one obvious place to look. That social policy might be shaped by interest conflict is not surprising. The expansion of public provision involves both taxing and spending policies which have immediate and long-term effects on different economic interests. Employment policies affect the balance of power between workers and employers. It is not surprising then that most contemporary models of politics and public policy rely, in whole or in part, on political struggles among economic interests to explain what government does.

The most popular version of the interest-based approach argues that class-based conflicts explain the distinctive character of the American welfare state: where workers are well organized, both in unions and leftwing political parties, they are more likely to force concessions from employers and from government. The U.S. welfare state is so limited and uneven, it is argued, because American workers have been so poorly organized and politically weak. America's failure to establish social insurance in the early twentieth century resulted from the inability of workers to form effective trade unions and an electorally successful socialist party, and from business opposition to policies that would have sheltered workers from the market. The New Deal was limited both by business power (most important, the direct participation of key business elites in policy planning during the Roosevelt administration) and the failure of workers and farmers to forge the kind of cross-class coalition that carried social-democratic reforms in Scandinavia. Big business participation in, and support for, the Great Society also explains President Lyndon Johnson's refusal to consider explicitly redistributional reforms. And big business's retreat from costly social reforms in the face of heightened economic competition explains the subsequent conservative backlash against liberalism.[34]

By focusing on the balance of power between the economic interests most immediately affected by welfare-state policies, the class-based account highlights real and important political relationships. The comparative evidence reviewed in chapter 2 indicates that popular unrest *was* a necessary precondition for reform in the late nineteenth and early twentieth centuries. Even though Western welfare states were not brought into being by leftwing parties, and mass unrest was not a *sufficient* condition for social reform, political mobilization by wage earners did help precipitate welfare-state building. And where organized labor clearly wanted government to redistribute income and wealth, and where proponents of state intervention into the economy were able to form independent political parties (or, through strong unions, decide the balance of electoral power between the existing parties), reformers who wanted to expand public provision, whether on the left or in the center, were more likely to succeed.

But there are also many things that class does not explain, including welfare states that are larger (e.g., France) and smaller (e.g., Australia) than the balance of power between business and labor would seem to dictate. Nor does the trajectory of retrenchment since the early 1970s precisely map variations in class organization.[35] The American experience in the early twentieth century appears particularly puzzling from this perspective. American workers were politically weak as were British workers, yet the British welfare state "took off" dramatically with the introduction of noncontributory old-age pensions in 1908 and unemployment and health insurance in 1911.[36] Nor has American business been alone in the capitalist world in opposing welfare-state building: business elites everywhere have lobbied against legislation to protect wage earners from the discipline of the market. The real question is why business opposition has been so effective here.

To answer these questions, we need to look at how political institutions have affected conflict among competing interests.

### Institutions

Scholars who focus on political institutions (i.e., the relatively permanent, routinized arrangements that organize formal political activity) suggest that government and party institutions have been the most important factors affecting social policy. Variously labeled "state centered," "polity centered," and "institutionalist," this approach suggests that we pay special attention to historically specific sequences of state formation, the "structural properties" of states, and "policy legacies" to explain what government does. According to this view, social policy has not passively *reflected* some already-established balance of power among competing interests. Rather, welfare states have been shaped by the organization and dynamics of political institutions themselves.[37]

Scholars working this vein have suggested, for example, that state actors have initiated reforms in advance of, and even in opposition to, societal pressures. They have shown how political institutions and public policies have shaped group demands and group identities, including the very "classness of politics," and influenced the ability of different interests to use state power to their advantage. They have explored how party systems have shaped interest representation, and have suggested how state "capacity" has affected what governments have done and can do to affect market outcomes. According to this argument, strong states—those that are centralized, administratively well developed, and well funded—have facilitated policy innovation. In contrast, weak and divided states have made reform difficult.[38] Both the institutional decentralization and bureaucratic underdevelopment of the American state, institutionalists suggest, help explain the slower and less comprehensive development of American social policy.[39]

Progressives, it is argued, were handicapped by an independent judiciary hostile to social reform, the underdevelopment of the public bureaucracy, and patronage politics in the early twentieth century; in combination, these caused middle- and upper-class reformers to reject wage earners' demands for public provision.[40] The New Dealers' ambitions were also checked by institutional underdevelopment. Where the government was unprepared to act, or the states were already involved, the Roosevelt administration remained passive; only where the federal government had already intervened successfully, as in the case of agricultural policy, or government had yet to intervene, as in the case of contributory old-age pensions, could new social and economic policies be adopted quickly.[41] In turn, the legacy of New Deal institutions and policies shaped the Great Society reforms. When reformers looked for solutions to poverty in the 1960s, they found ready precedents for and good ideas about new income maintenance and fiscal policies—areas of concern to reformers in the 1930s—but little precedent or institutional support for creating the kinds of labor-market policies popular in Europe.[42]

As we shall see, institutional factors have definitely mattered in this history. But institutionalist accounts have their own problems. Early efforts to "bring the state back in" also had the unfortunate tendency to push class back out, as if political structures and public policies resulted only from the decisions of state actors (who were *assumed* to be insulated from the play of societal interests) and the bureaucratic properties of existing institutions. In this way, advocates of a "state-centered" account succeeded in trading places with the "society-centered" theorists they had criticized, overemphasizing the state instead of class. Yet, as critics quickly pointed out, without taking class organization into account it was hard to understand the political conditions under which state actors might hope to act against the interests of business elites, or why government institutions developed more rapidly in some cases than others.[43]

Nor, on closer examination, were political history and political structure the complete bar to reform that this account seemed to suggest. The Progressives, for example, pushed past bureaucratic underdevelopment, as well as middle- and upper-class fears of political corruption, to build new institutions in several areas, including public education, workmen's compensation, and mothers' aid. Nor were all members of the middle and upper classes equally pessimistic about the state's administrative capacity to do good. The American Association for Labor Legislation, the National Consumers' League, the Women's Trade Union League, the settlement house movement—all were staffed by upscale reformers who were ardent advocates of European-style reforms, including public benefits to workers. The barrier to reform erected by the judiciary was also permeable: the Supreme Court proved amenable to laws regulating property rights throughout most of the period as long as those statutes did not protect the unions' right to strike, to boycott businesses, or to engage in other forms of direct action.[44] For its part, the Roosevelt administration acted in the face of institutional underdevelopment, inventing new institutions on several occasions, without always respecting the prior commitments of state and local actors. Similarly, the Johnson administration's decision to use social services to create economic opportunity required the creation of new institutions with new authority and new administrative capacities.

## A Synthetic Approach

Since several different factors have shaped the development of Western welfare states, we clearly would be better off with a self-consciously synthetic approach. This brief survey suggests how one might be constructed.

The first principle is that a theoretically coherent explanation must look at how societal interests and political institutions *combine* to shape the environment in which reformers act. Consider, for example, the question of business power. As we shall see, too much can be made of business's influence in politics, but once we also take political structure into account, we can better understand the institutional conditions under which business is likely to affect public policy. Business's political power, it turns out, has been greatest where the government has been decentralized. Decentralization has made it easier for business interests to veto unwanted social legislation and encouraged competition among subnational jurisdictions for investment. In turn, "competitive federalism" has given business interests "structural" power over social reform by discouraging governors and state legislatures from imposing high costs on geographically mobile firms.[45] Similarly, the structure of the American electoral system—including single-member districts and winner-take-all elections—has affected the balance of power among competing interests by discouraging demands for structural reform and penalizing the political forces that enter the political system from either extreme.

It is also clear that we need to look closely at the complex and contingent relationship between structure and agency.[46] Both matter. On the one hand, political actors are in some sense free agents. The historical record reveals a variety of ways in which reformers have used government and politics to maximize their opportunities, sometimes even changing the structural and institutional conditions under which they have acted.[47] It is fair to say that the most successful reformers have been precisely those who have been able to navigate past structural and institutional obstacles to create new paths where none previously existed. For example, the Swedish Social Democrats' decision to build a universal welfare state that also appealed to the middle classes helps explain that political party's success. The fact that the Australian labor movement, though relatively powerful, pushed for full employment and wage bargaining, rather than universal public provision, helps explain why that country's public safety net is relatively limited in scope. The decision by the Austrian Social Democrats not to build a universalistic or egalitarian welfare state helps explain the structure of social spending there.[48]

On the other hand, the circumstances under which people choose are vitally important, both to the actors themselves and to our understanding of why a particular choice was made at a particular time. To a large extent, political, economic, and social institutions and organizations define those circumstances, establishing the range of effective options and strategies that political actors are likely to adopt while attempting to realize their ambitions.[49] Structures are not only barriers, of course. They also provide opportunities, allowing some groups access to decision makers, for example, or encouraging alliances among societal interests who find themselves acting under similar circumstances. Nor are structures immutable; they can be changed, at least in the long run. But structures are relatively fixed aspects of the political environment, and, as such, they load the dice against certain decisions, making some options politically unfeasible.[50] In extreme cases, structures may so constrain choices that an actor's freedom is only nominal.

Put differently, reformers have not been able to invent social-welfare institutions and policies indifferent to context. Recently, historical institutionalists have tackled this issue head on. They have focused on how the same institutions that have shaped and constrained political actors' decisions have also resulted from those decisions, and how in periods of rapid change or institutional break-

down, political actors have been able to take advantage of new opportunities to radically alter the menu of politically feasible options
available to them.[51]

Finally, we need to look at these relationships in historical and
national context. The organization of interests and the arrangement
of political institutions have mattered in different ways at different
times and in different places. Though we must rely on generaliza-
tions developed from the observation of numerous instances, in the
end we have to pay close attention to exactly how these various factors have combined to shape the process of welfare-state building in
any given country. In particular, nations vary considerably in how
their social and political structures have affected the possibility of
using government to solve problems of economic insecurity. On this
assumption, the next chapter looks more closely at what recent research in the social sciences and history tells us about both the development of welfare states generally and the United States in particular.

# TWO

# An Unusually Inhospitable Environment for Reform

Three factors have proved decisive in the development of Western welfare states: the balance of power between business and labor, the organization of political institutions, and the nature and extent of racial and ethnic cleavages. Individually and in combination, these factors have determined whether social reformers have been able to build comprehensive welfare states. Where wage earners have been unified and well-organized; where labor, social-democratic, or socialist political parties have emerged to represent working-class voters; and where the state and party systems have been centralized—under these conditions, welfare-state building has proceeded apace. Absent these preconditions, social reformers have faced enormous collective action problems that have made only the most limited reforms politically feasible.

Seen from this perspective, the American political environment has been unusually inhospitable to social reformers. In the United States, workers have been weak and divided by racial and ethnic identities, business interests have been both powerful and resistant to reform, and the state and party systems have been highly decentralized. These factors have combined to create unusually high barriers for political movements that have wanted to use government to promote economic security, and have led to more market-conforming policies.

## The Class Struggle, American-Style

The role of class-based organizations in the development of Western welfare states is clear. The organization of business and labor, the resources that these two groups can bring to bear in political struggles, and the ways in which both have defined and pursued their interests have regularly influenced what governments have done to protect society from market forces. American unions' inability to organize a majority of wage earners—in particular, their failure

19

to combine organized workers into a broadly based, class-conscious
political movement—and business's ability to resist social-democratic reforms have both delayed and limited the development of a
more comprehensive welfare state.

## How Class Matters

That class-based organizations have mattered in social policy should
not be surprising. In every capitalist democracy, both business and
labor have had vital stakes in public policies toward jobs and incomes, and both have tended to act in predictable ways.

All other things being equal, workers have benefited when government has extended public provision and aggressively pursued full
employment. In contrast, business interests, particularly employers,
have had good reasons to fear the effects of public benefits and full
employment on wages, taxes, and labor discipline. Low-wage employers, employers in labor-intensive industries, and smaller and
medium-sized firms less able to absorb additional costs have been
especially concerned about the impact of welfare on wages and
profits. This has been as true of commercial farmers who have employed labor as it has been of manufacturers. But even large corporate interests have tended to oppose reform; indeed, business elites
have typically been the most important interest supporting conservative coalitions opposing welfare-state development. Where these
business interests have been well-organized, they have been able to
delay and distort welfare-state building.

Some businesses have supported the expansion of public provision and, at times, that support proved crucial, particularly when
organized labor and public officials were too weak or too divided to
initiate and sustain state building on their own. But when business
interests have participated in the development of social policy, they
have sought to direct innovation into channels that supplement
rather than supplant private corporate welfare efforts, and have
wanted major concessions from reformers for that support.[1]

Conversely, the willingness and ability of workers to form encompassing political and economic organizations (e.g., social-democratic or labor parties and centralized, industrial labor movements)
have helped social-democratic reformers by providing them with a
well-organized, more easily mobilized mass base, something vitally
important in democratic political systems.[2] This has been a two-step
relationship. Reformers have been more likely to try to build redistributional welfare states (and succeed at it) where social democrats have been powerful; and social democrats have been more
powerful where workers have been combined in class-wide organizations that have attempted to promote working-class interests.

The relationship between class power and public policy needs to be carefully specified. First, the impact of working-class organization has varied according to both how we measure that effort and the country and period in question. Studies indicate that working-class organization has affected both the size of the public sector in toto and direct government provision of goods and services, but not transfer spending (e.g., spending on old-age pensions).[3] Second, working-class organization has also affected government's economic policy choices: where workers have been organizationally strong, governments have been more likely to commit themselves to full employment.[4]

Workers have played different roles at different times. Variations in working-class organization do not explain variations in the initiation of Western welfare states in the late nineteenth and early twentieth centuries, for example.[5] Before wage earners had won basic political rights, and mobilized politically, working-class political parties were simply not in a position to govern, or directly challenge established parties. Social policy developed in response to the initiatives of conservative and liberal elites, not labor's demands.[6] In Denmark and Sweden, where social democracy eventually triumphed, universalistic social policies *preceded* the emergence of a politically powerful, socialist working class. The German state denied industrial workers independent political representation while the traditional conservative elites who were in control of the government took charge of welfare-state building. In Great Britain, liberal elites, not labor party representatives, took the first steps toward state-sponsored economic security.[7] In contrast, unionization and the political organization of workers played a far greater role *after* World War II, with the largest effects occurring after the sea change in economic conditions in 1973 when strong unions were better able to resist retrenchment.[8]

In some cases, large welfare states have developed without leadership from labor or its political representatives. In societies with conservative-corporatist traditions, Christian Democratic and Catholic parties also traveled the path to a large welfare state.[9] In Belgium, the Netherlands, Germany, Austria, and Italy, centrist governments under the control of religious parties expanded social spending by providing generous transfer payments to support working families rather than radically restructuring the capitalist market, as social democrats had wanted.[10]

Finally, even politically well-organized workers have needed help from other social groups: reformers were most likely to decide to build comprehensive welfare states where workers were able to forge political alliances with the middle class. Cross-class alliances with farmers were essential to the emergence of Scandinavian so–

cial democracy in the 1930s, for example, and alliances with white-collar workers were critical to its consolidation in the 1950s and 1960s.[11]

## Race and Ethnicity

Social heterogeneity has also affected what Western societies have done about economic insecurity. The existence of cleavages based on race and ethnicity (as well as religion and language) have affected reformers' calculations in several ways.

Contrary to the impression created by countries like the United States, with its small welfare state and extreme racial conflict, social heterogeneity has not automatically resulted in a limited welfare state. Rather, internal social cleavages have generated "contradictory pressures."[12] At times, political demands from excluded minority groups for remedial social programs have driven the expansion of public provision; the expansion of the public assistance rolls in the United States in the 1960s was caused in part by the mobilization of the black poor.[13] But social heterogeneity has also undermined reformers' efforts to expand public provision by dividing the potential beneficiaries of social-welfare programs from each other, encouraging separatist allegiances that have just as often discouraged collective efforts to use government to promote economic security.[14] Divisions based on descent have also encouraged workers to ally with their employers on the basis of race, ethnicity, and religion, thereby creating cross-class alliances between competing economic interests that have diluted expected support for social welfare programs.[15]

Some observers of American politics have suggested that social heterogeneity is *the* principal explanation for the underdevelopment of the American welfare state.[16] But evidence casts doubt on this proposition. It is simply not the case that all heterogeneous societies have small welfare states, as the Belgian and Dutch cases make amply clear: both societies are divided—by language and ethnicity in Belgium, by religion in the Netherlands—yet both have large welfare states. In these cases, political elites appear to have used public benefits to integrate otherwise divided societies. Conversely, some homogeneous societies (e.g., Norway), are relatively modest spenders.[17] Rather, the impact of social heterogeneity on the development of welfare-state institutions has depended on how political institutions have dealt with it. It appears that by giving "sharp expression" to them, political systems with decentralized government and party institutions have tended to magnify these divisions.[18]

## A Disorganized and Divided Working Class

In the United States, reformers' ability to expand public provision or impose obligations on employers has been sharply limited by the interaction of class and race. Reformers have been limited by American unions' organizing failures, by the absence of "encompassing" institutions, and by business's political power.

American unions' failure to organize a substantial portion of the working population is well-known, and the consequences have been predictable.[19] At its peak in the mid-1950s, organized labor had organized only a quarter of the American labor force, including only a third of nonagricultural employees. Today, fewer than one in six workers are in unions, leaving the American labor force by far the least unionized in the West.[20] Equally important, American unions have had difficulty coordinating their political and economic activities. Unusually decentralized, they have regularly fallen prey to internal jurisdictional disputes and to internecine struggles over the control of the labor movement itself. Lacking encompassing organizations to coordinate their activities, the unions' efforts to organize, bargain, and influence politics have suffered.

Many explanations have been offered for this condition, including the strength of employer resistance, government's failure to protect worker rights more effectively, and even the size of the American economy.[21] But racial and ethnic conflicts appear to have been particularly important. Both the forced importation of African slaves and voluntary immigration from Europe, Asia, and Latin America created an enormously diverse labor force subdivided by ethnic, linguistic, and religious group affiliations.[22] And because so many of the European immigrants and southern blacks who moved to northern cities in the late nineteenth and early twentieth centuries lacked the craft skills possessed by native-born white workers, racial and ethnic divisions coincided with and exacerbated differences based on skill. Deep antagonisms resulted, hindering the development of American unions during a formative period. Residential segregation, discrimination at the workplace, and voluntary patterns of communal association subsequently reinforced these divisions.[23]

This racial and ethnocultural segmentation resulted in the well-observed tendency of American workers not to vote their economic interests, as did workers in most other capitalist democracies, but their cultural identities instead. As one observer has noted, American workers voted for Democrats or Republicans "on the basis of cultural and emotional loyalties that reflected the fundamental concerns of family, church, tradition, and daily life."[24] This cultural skew moderated somewhat in the 1930s and 1940s,[25] but it re-

mained a powerful factor thereafter, as the Republican party's success in appealing to the white working class with racial appeals in
the 1970s, 1980s, and 1990s demonstrates.[26]

Racial conflicts have made it especially hard to enlarge the
union movement. Having failed to encourage abolition in the antebellum period and having failed subsequently to champion the cause
of freed slaves, the trade-union movement found it difficult to build
a southern labor movement at the height of industrialization. Even
after they had been absorbed into the industrial economy, blacks remained divided from white workers and were often pitted against
them by employers.[27]

There were exceptions. Both the Industrial Workers of the World
and the United Mineworkers tried to organize African Americans in
the early twentieth century; the Communist party tried again in the
late 1920s and early 1930s. Partly sparked by Communist gains, the
Congress of Industrial Organizations targeted southern textile mills in
the late 1930s and launched Operation Dixie immediately after World
War II to increase its presence in the South. But southern employers
and political elites successfully resisted these efforts. The racism of
many white workers also hampered union efforts.[28] Conflicts between
unions and civil-rights organizations over the War on Poverty continued to divide wage earners well into the 1960s. As a result, organized
labor was distracted and divided at a time when European unions
were successfully lobbying for even more comprehensive welfare-state
benefits and firmer guarantees of employment security.[29]

In limiting the unions' economic and political power, these divisions also narrowed reformers' political choices. Because they undercut support for liberalism and encouraged political appeals
based on racial rather than economic identities, cross-cutting cleavages made it doubly difficult for those who wanted to build a coalition of wage earners in support of an expanded welfare state. The
failure to directly challenge white racism left all social-reform movements vulnerable to divide-and-conquer strategies. Labor's failure to
organize the South also left northern liberals vulnerable in Congress. Indeed, until quite recently, the commitment of the white
South to maintain a repressive and discriminatory racial order
made it hard for northern liberals to use the Democratic party for
reform. Despite a respectable level of union organization in the
cities of the Northeast, Midwest, and West Coast, organized labor
was constantly frustrated by southern interests who used the "institutional leverage" given to them by decentralized political institutions to block worker-oriented legislation.[30]

The racial division of labor also created incentives to more
fiercely resist welfare. It was largely southern employers' determination to maintain their control over African American workers that

led them to oppose national welfare measures that could have benefited the South, heightening conflict over intergovernmental relations in the 1930s. More recently, white attitudes about blacks have
allowed conservative elites to develop political ideologies that simultaneously have demonized the poor and undermined majority support for the very social rights that labor movements elsewhere have
routinely defended.

### Business and Reform

Because political decentralization has favored those interests who
have wanted to stop government from acting, decentralization has
worked to business's advantage.

It is important not to overstate American business's opposition
to social-welfare programs. Certain firms and business elites have
been willing to see the welfare state grow. In each of the three watershed periods of state building in the twentieth century, some
business leaders stepped forward with proposals to expand government power, including recommendations to build a social-insurance
state. In the Progressive period, bankers associated with the financial empire of J. P. Morgan sought to develop a business consensus
on the need to use government to stabilize the market economy,
founding the National Civic Federation (NCF) and funding the
American Association for Labor Legislation (AALL)—two organizations that formulated reform legislation and lobbied the wider business community to support their proposals. Workmen's compensation legislation received widespread support from this group.[31]
During the 1930s, a small group of reform-minded business elites
took part in policy planning for federal pension and unemployment-
insurance legislation. They served on Roosevelt's Business Advisory
Council and on the Presidential Advisory Council on Economic Security, a tripartite group of employers, labor leaders, and independent experts created to help the Committee on Economic Security
(CES) write the Social Security Act (SSA).[32] In the 1960s, Lyndon
Johnson consulted regularly with corporate executives on the Business Council, who, like their New Deal and Progressive predecessors, believed that government could be used to promote economic
prosperity and increase corporate profits.[33]

Based on this record, some revisionist historians and social scientists have concluded that social reformism is best understood as a
political movement of American business led by class-conscious corporate leaders. They have wanted to extend government authority
over the market, it is argued, in order to stabilize an inherently disorderly market system, to undercut the power of labor militants and
the appeal of socialism to workers, and to protect their profits.[34]

Such an account is misleading in several ways. First, whatever their intentions, it is hard to argue that reformist business leaders have spoken for business "as a whole." To the contrary, American business has been very divided, and competitive market pressures—rooted in differences in firm size, location, industry, union density, and international competitiveness—have discouraged firms from cooperating politically.[35] For the most part, lobbying groups have been highly fragmented and decentralized, and businesses have lobbied through single-sector trade associations and firm-specific organizations, not peak associations of the sort found in Europe.[36] The trade associations themselves have often been divided between smaller and larger firms, which have defined their interests differently.[37]

Second, if there has been any consensus, it has been *against*, not for, government intervention.[38] Influenced by a tradition of anti-statism (itself reinforced by the not-illogical conclusion that reform would benefit  workers, consumers, and competitors), most business interests have preferred laissez-faire—unless government intervention could be shown *immediately and directly* to enhance their profits or market share. On most issues, the NCF was roundly opposed by the National Association of Manufacturers (NAM) and other employer groups who fought hard against, and helped defeat, most AALL-sponsored social legislation proposals in state legislatures.[39] Franklin Roosevelt's friends in the business community could not credibly claim to speak for business during the 1930s because most business interests remained deeply suspicious of greater state intervention into labor markets and steadfastly opposed to the higher taxes needed to pay for increased social spending.[40]

What business support there has been for reform has been highly contingent. Escalating costs and increased competition have often sent economic elites initially sympathetic to reform back to the other side. Many of the business leaders who initially supported Roosevelt, for example, turned against the New Deal in the summer of 1935, when Roosevelt turned toward the left.[41] And while Lyndon Johnson tried assiduously to establish a working relationship with Fortune 500 companies during the 1960s, it soon became clear that business support for state intervention depended on administration efforts to cap social spending and cut taxes.[42] Indeed, nearly every period of welfare-state building in the United States has been followed by severe retrenchment, typically led by business elites who changed their minds about the costs and benefits of an accommodation with increased governmental power.

Not surprisingly, these intramural conflicts have undermined efforts by economic leaders, however well-placed, to forge an all-business consensus on what a corporate-friendly welfare state might look like. As a result, when business leaders have participated in the development of reform legislation, they have usually done so to pursue fairly narrow, firm- and, at most, industry-specific interests. Bankers joined the fight over financial reform in the 1910s because the new Federal Reserve System promised to shape profoundly the relative power of Wall Street versus regional banking centers in the Midwest.[43] The executives who helped the CES draft New Deal legislation wanted to make sure that reform proposals brewing in the state legislatures and in Congress did not unduly burden *their* companies and industries and were modeled on the private, company-based programs *they* had developed in the 1920s.[44]

In crisis periods, these centrifugal tendencies within the business community have benefited reformers by increasing the odds that one or another significant business interest would support reform. However unrepresentative of business "as a class," the Morgan interests' support for Progressivism, the "House of Rockefeller's" sympathy for the New Deal, and the Business Council's support for the Great Society in the 1960s all helped reformers press their plans on Congress. But American business's inability to act *collectively* to fashion and promote a vision of how an active government might serve its interests has *not* meant that reformers could safely ignore business demands. As the next section makes clear, American reformers have still had to consider the fact that business elites who have opposed welfare-state measures have been able to use the decentralized political system to slow and stop reform.

## The State and Welfare

Like class and race, political institutions have shaped welfare-state building in complex ways. But this much is clear: efforts to build a comprehensive welfare state have been more likely to succeed where political institutions have been centralized and where electoral arrangements have favored multiparty systems. Conversely, decentralized institutions and electoral systems that have favored two-party systems have frustrated efforts by public and private actors who have wanted to build more comprehensive welfare states. In the United States, both a two-party system that has discouraged the formation of a social-democratic left, and decentralized state and party systems that have empowered conservative opponents of public provision and encouraged racial and ethnic conflict have undercut reform.

### Electoral Systems

The structural properties of electoral systems have shaped the politics of social policy in the West in several ways. First, multimember, proportional-representation systems have encouraged leftwing par-

ties to form and these parties have helped mobilize the demand
from wage earners, small farmers, and other groups for more ex-
tensive public benefits and full-employment policies. These electoral
systems have also made it easier for labor-oriented parties to wage
ideological campaigns for public provision. As a result, when the
public has been uncertain of the benefits of social policies, programmatic parties have been better able to focus public attention on
ideologically distinct alternatives, highlighting the differences between movements of the right and left and their impact on social
policy.[45]

In contrast, in the United States, a single-member district, winner-
take-all system has produced a two-party politics in which parties
have cleaved to the center in order to compete for power.[46] In
this system, politicians have been more likely to make relatively
vacuous symbolic appeals or offer "distributive" (i.e., easily disag-
gregated and highly individualized) benefits, rather than seek votes
with coherent, class-based programs.[47] Competition between parties
in a two-party system can lead to the expansion of social spending
when those parties seek to build electoral coalitions around patronage and particularism. But because it has burdened the Left, two-
party politics has not encouraged reformers who have wanted to
build a redistributional welfare state or one that aggressively pur-
sues full employment.

The *timing* of enfranchisement also appears to have shaped the
course of welfare-state politics. In countries where strong central
bureaucracies developed early and authoritarian governments resisted calls for political democracy, the newly mobilized lower
classes were led to take ideologically extreme positions in the competition for political access. Defenders of the ancien régime were
forced, in turn, to defend that system. As a result, political opponents tended to engage in a more ideologically coherent, programmatic party competition that helped reformers expand public provision in the twentieth century. In the United States, in contrast,
where democracy preceded the development of a strong state bureaucracy, politics developed differently: newly formed, mass-based
political parties competed for voters with patronage rather than organize the electorate into hostile ideological camps, thereby dampening demands for a social-insurance state.[48]

### Centralization

Whether or not public institutions are centralized has also influenced what reformers could do.[49] As a rule, political centralization
has been positively related to social spending.[50] The three paradig-
matic cases of government-led social reform—Germany in the

1880s, Scandinavia at the turn of the century, and Great Britain immediately after World War II—occurred in highly centralized states.[51] Conversely, all of the countries whose level of welfare is markedly lower than their level of economic development—Switzerland, the United States, West Germany (before re-unification), and Australia—are federal states.[52]

Studies of the impact of centralization on social policy suggest several explanations for this positive relationship. More centralized states have facilitated political and policy coordination.[53] They have also provided fewer veto points for conservative interests opposing reform.[54] In contrast, in political systems fragmented by federalism and/or the separation of powers, reformers have had to spend considerable resources coordinating supporters' activities across a wider range of institutional venues. In contrast, opponents of public provision who have been satisfied with market outcomes have needed only to take advantage of one or another veto point to block state action. Moreover, because it has made more credible investors' threat to "exit" unfriendly political jurisdictions, federalism has also increased business's "structural" power, that is, its ability to influence what government does from a distance, whether or not it also participates in the decision-making process.[55] Finally, the separation of powers has affected, if only indirectly, the nature of party competition by encouraging legislators to define their interests differently from the executive, encouraging the development of distinct presidential and legislative factions, and, thereby, increasing the heterogeneity of party coalitions.[56]

But the relationship between state centralization and public provision is complex. One comparative study of welfare-state development between 1870 and 1965 shows that centralization both promoted and retarded growth in social expenditures, encouraging welfare-state efforts in France and Britain but slowing them in Italy, where conservatives used a unified government to resist reform. In these cases, political structures appear to have been "a mediating rather than directly causative factor."[57] Exactly how power has been centralized has also made a significant difference in whether it has helped reformers' build new institutions. One recent study of health policy in Europe indicates, for example, that reformers have been more likely to succeed not only where the state has been centralized, but also where executive branch decision makers have been insulated from parliamentary and electoral pressures.[58] Alternatively, those interests that have wanted to maintain the status quo have been more likely to succeed where the state has been fragmented in more than one way—where, for example, federalism has been combined with presidential government and strong bicameralism, as is the case in the United States[59]—and where traditional representative institutions have played a large role. These state structures have provided the greatest opportunity for intensely interested political minorities to veto policies.[60]

Research on social democracy and corporatism in Europe also suggests that the precise impact of state centralization has depended on the nature of interest-group politics in the country in question: centralization has been more likely to be positively linked with social spending in societies with corporatist systems of interest intermediation. This is an indirect connection. Unitary states have been more likely to develop corporatist institutions because state centralization has both encouraged centralized business organization and facilitated economy-wide bargaining among competing economic interests. Corporatist institutions have in turn encouraged business support for universal public provision,[61] and, generally, higher social spending by involving business leaders directly in negotiations over the size and scope of the welfare state, and encouraging them in the belief that social policies could be crafted simultaneously to maintain corporate profits and reduce conflict between employers and employees.[62] In contrast, federated state structures have encouraged political factionalism and discouraged cooperative relations between business and labor.[63] States that have been both centralized and administratively competent have been even more likely to arrange and enforce the kinds of collusive arrangements that have encouraged cooperation among major economic actors, reinforcing the tendency toward corporatism and social spending.[64] Conversely, states that have been decentralized and administratively weak have been likely to use social policy to buy support directly from powerful constituents rather than appeal to wage earners with universalistic public programs.[65]

Finally, as noted earlier, decentralization appears to have slowed welfare-state building by stimulating conflict based on social heterogeneity. Political structures have not necessarily caused communal conflicts (though this has happened); nor has social heterogeneity precluded strong, comprehensive welfare states from emerging, as the case of Belgium with its division between Flemish- and French-speaking populations shows. But welfare-state development has been slowed when cleavages that have arisen from social heterogeneity were given expression by a decentralized polity. In these cases, by giving institutional expression to social-structural cleavages, political decentralization has made more difficult the kind of encompassing politics that has encouraged reform. In contrast, reformers working within centralized political institutions have been better able to overcome these effects, tempering the impact of social heterogeneity on politics and policy.[66]

## The State against Reform

The design of the U.S. electoral system has clearly encouraged American reformers to moderate their demands and undercut efforts to build a more substantial welfare state. In principle, one might imagine that by forcing party leaders to build majority coalitions in order to win office, American electoral arrangements have helped secure the social basis for reform. But in practice, the rules of the U.S. electoral system have made it more, not less, difficult to mobilize support for change.

First, restrictive rules and other practices that have discouraged registration and voting have disadvantaged social reformers. Personal registration and residency requirements and the frequent and often inconvenient scheduling of elections have made it more difficult for the less affluent and less educated, who might have supported public provision, to participate. Second, the combination of single-member, winner-take-all election districts and a presidential rather than a parliamentary system of government has strongly encouraged two-party politics and the formation of centrist political parties with moderate political agendas rather than programmatic parties with class-redistributional agendas.

In these ways, the rules of the electoral game have burdened political movements outside the mainstream, and this has slowed the spread of new ideas and the mobilization of new political forces that might have forced more substantial welfare-state building. Indeed, once established, mainstream parties have tended to discourage programmatic politics altogether. In this institutional environment, they have found it rational to compete for voters' loyalties on the basis of concrete benefits and particularistic appeals grounded on local, racial, ethnic, and cultural identities rather than gamble on building the kinds of working-class coalitions that by demanding class-redistributional policies might have alienated established political and economic èlites.

Even when voters have been drawn to more radical ideas and candidates, the American political system has made it difficult to translate that support into political power. The bias toward two-party politics was especially critical in the late nineteenth and early twentieth centuries. Even Theodore Roosevelt, enormously popular and well financed, could not overcome this hurdle, only succeeding in splitting the Republican party vote in 1912 and throwing the election to Woodrow Wilson, his Democratic opponent. Welfare-state builders have been particularly hurt by the firm grip of two-party competition on American politics. Already burdened by restrictions on the electorate, political movements that have attempted to mobilize the bottom half of the society have had to struggle against enormous odds to win support from voters reluctant to abandon traditional partisan loyalties—and afraid that in doing so they would only help their political adversaries win. At the same time, one or another of the two major parties has usually sought to coopt protest. Reformers who *have* decided to work within the existing parties have typically found themselves forced to moderate their views and negotiate with established elites, further reducing pressure on the system to make concessions.

Even after the Great Depression shattered the conservative political coalition that had dominated American politics since the 1870s, the structural dynamics of two-party politics continued to encourage moderation. The Communist and Socialist parties offered more radical policy agendas, but while both enjoyed significant local support, neither could compete with the two major parties at the national level. Without a major party to articulate its demands, social reformers found it hard to bring together the various constituencies that supported the idea of a more active, redistributional government. And because they were obliged to deal with the established Democratic party political brokers and conservative elites, especially southern conservatives, they remained sharply constrained. As a result, liberals found it extremely difficult during the 1930s (and subsequently) to construct political coalitions that could support proposals to plan the economy, use public spending to achieve full employment, or concentrate agricultural aid on the poorest farmers.[67]

Fragmented government institutions have further encouraged reformers to compromise with powerful market actors. Divided by federalism and then redivided by the separation of powers, the American state is the most fragmented among the capitalist democracies. The same institutions that have pitted, in James Madison's formulation, faction against faction in order to frustrate the majority's ability to govern, have discouraged reformers who have wanted to expand public provision. Fragmentation has burdened social reformers in several ways. It has increased the number of power centers that have to be controlled to make government work, creating enormous transaction costs for any group that has sought to use government affirmatively. At the same time, by creating multiple veto points, fragmentation forced reformers to fight and refight their battles in a multiplicity of legislative, executive, and judicial venues—often at both the state and national level—while devoting scarce political resources to coordination. In contrast, defenders of the status quo have had to succeed only at one place, making it possible for one or another group within an otherwise divided and disorganized business community to veto reform.[68]

Federalism has also facilitated the exercise of business's "structural" power. The "competitive federalism" that has resulted from economic competition among the states has proved particularly hard for social reformers to overcome. Because national corporations can locate and invest anywhere, state and local governments have been reluctant to impose higher costs on mobile corporations.[69] In the nineteenth century, railroad entrepreneurs used federalism as an escape route to avoid regulation, playing public officials in the various states against each other in an effort to avoid strict control.[70] In the early twentieth century, Progressive mayors and governors were discouraged from moving too far from national "norms" for fear of unsettling the local business environment.[71] The decentralization of the state was most burdensome to reformers before the New Deal (when social policy making was almost entirely confined to the states), but business was again able to take advantage of the implicit threat to abandon state and local communities during the 1970s and 1980s, as competition for business investment led states to cut taxes, regulations, and social spending. In this sort of institutional environment, the most liberal jurisdictions suffered, forced either to retreat from new social policies or pay the costs of breaking new ground.

A strong party system might have overcome some of these centrifugal forces, but American political parties have been notoriously weak, and the Progressive reforms made things worse. At that critical time, when reformers in Europe were attempting to use national political and administrative institutions to do something about economic insecurity, political reformers in the United States attacked the political process itself, encouraging institutional fragmentation and the separation of politics from policy making. This effort to eliminate political corruption and the rule of party bosses was not entirely misguided; the system was corrupt and dominated by party machines. But political reformers changed electoral institutions in ways that weakened the parties, depressed turnout, and made it more difficult to construct stable majorities in support of new legislation.[72]

Individually, and especially in combination, institutional changes since have further hurt the prospects for social reform. The spread of direct primaries in the 1960s, the post-Watergate reforms of Congress (diminishing the role of committee chairs and increasing the influence of junior members), the growing role of the electronic media, the explosion of political action committees (PACs)—all have further undermined the ability of party leaders to build policy-oriented legislative coalitions. These changes have also encouraged political actors to set themselves up as independent political entrepreneurs, seeking financial support from interested lobbies. As a result, congressional authority has been subdivided among overlapping and competing committees whose members have become highly dependent on the financial support of PACs sponsored by economic interests affected by legislation, and who have been highly resistant to party leadership except under extraordinary circumstances. The resulting combination of extreme fragmentation and PAC-oriented political entrepreneurship has made pursuing social reform even harder.

Fragmentation has also made it comparatively easy for regional political constituencies, particularly southern interests, that have opposed nationalizing reforms to block legislation supported by a national majority. From the late eighteenth to the mid-twentieth centuries, southern commercial farmers took maximum advantage of political decentralization to maintain tight control over black labor. In the late nineteenth and early twentieth centuries, state-level control over voter registration allowed southern elites to disenfranchise blacks and poor whites, creating a conservative, one-party system. Assured of reelection, southern congressmen then built nearly impregnable power centers on the most important legislative committees, and they used this institutional leverage to insist that new legislation include institutional arrangements that protected their interests. In the 1930s, fearing that the expansion of federal power would challenge the economic interests of large commercial farmers by promoting the interests of poorer farmers and share-croppers, southern representatives successfully demanded that social legislation allow local elites to tailor the implementation of new benefit programs to local labor-market conditions and employer demands. Even after southern Democrats had lost much of their institutional leverage, they continued to exercise tremendous influence over the shape of the party's legislative agenda, particularly regarding labor and social-welfare legislation.[73]

Fragmentation has not always been an enemy of reform. As we shall see, Democratic congressional majorities fought off Republican presidents who wanted to cut social welfare spending in the 1970s and 1980s; and a Democratic president resisted the most draconian cuts proposed by a Republican majority in the mid-1990s. Nonetheless, by creating so many additional veto points and increasing reformers' costs of political coordination, fragmentation has most often worked against those who have wanted to use government to impose public standards on the market.

### Choosing Liberalism

Taken together, class, state, and race have profoundly shaped the way political actors inside and outside of government have viewed the possibilities and limits of state action in the United States, more often than not leading them to make substantial concessions to the status quo. Organizational and institutional factors have not precluded the creation of a welfare state. Three times—in the 1910s, 1930s, and 1960s—crisis conditions upset settled political arrangements sufficiently to allow reformers to overcome institutional commitments and conservative opposition. In these periods, reformers were able to take advantage of popular mobilization and divisions among business interests to build new social-welfare institutions. In two periods—the 1930s and 1960s—reformist presidents put together liberal political coalitions in support of the expansion of the American welfare state.

But during all of these periods, structural obstacles both affected reformers' calculations about what was feasible and complicated their efforts to achieve even those goals deemed within reach. A divided and disorganized working class; powerful, antistatist business elites; two-party politics; and divided institutions all loaded the dice against collective action by workers, and the pursuit of more substantial state action by social reformers. Together, these limiting factors pushed political elites who wanted a welfare state to moderate their demands and drove reformist presidents to the center where they tried to build coalitions spanning business and labor rather than mobilize a mass-based movement in support of structural reform. In this way, American reformers have adapted to rather than changed fundamentally the environment in which they have acted. The next four chapters explore the consequences for welfare-state building in the United States.

# THREE

# *Progressives*

The transition from agriculture to industry, and from small-scale commercial enterprise to large-scale, corporate capitalism transformed the West in the late nineteenth and early twentieth centuries. Everywhere, reform movements emerged demanding that government tame these new social and economic forces. In the United States, Progressive reformers called for a variety of new institutions and policies. But class and state combined to erect insurmountable barriers to European-style welfare-state building in the United States.

Reformers were not entirely deterred from expanding public provision. Popular concern about the impact of laissez-faire capitalism on everyday life and democratic politics laid the foundation for a first wave of American social policy innovation. But the American welfare state took a different turn than that taken in Western Europe: rather than adopt social-insurance programs to support unemployed or aged male workers, the United States instead experimented with maternal social policies, notably mothers' aid (or "pensions" for widowed mothers) and protective wage and hour legislation designed to protect women and children from abusive working conditions.[1]

To be sure, no Western European government replaced private charity and poor relief with national social insurance all at once.[2] But by World War I, most had begun to institutionalize the old-age, health, and unemployment insurance programs that would become the core of the modern welfare state.[3] The United States did not, either at the state or national level. Publicly funded old-age assistance legislation failed when first considered by Massachusetts in 1903 and failed again when introduced into Congress in 1909.[4] Wisconsin established the nation's first state-level unemployment insurance program only in 1932.[5] National health insurance was roundly defeated. Only state-level workmen's compensation succeeded in the United States at this time.[6]

The cultural explanation—that public opinion explains the trajectory taken by the American welfare state in the early twentieth

century—is not supported by the evidence. Though it is notoriously
hard to know exactly what the public wanted in this pre-polling era,
the available evidence suggests strong overall support for social reform. The Progressives made repeated—and, if their success at the
polls means anything, popular—efforts to address the problems that
followed rapid industrialization and the spread of the modern corporation. With widespread public approval, Progressive mayors
fought to expand municipal authority to regulate housing and hazardous working conditions, and to clean up the slums.[7] Progressive
governors sought laws to protect workers from predatory employers
and to cope with threats to public health.[8] At the federal level, Progressives fought for a host of new regulatory agencies that could
impose public standards on private business conduct. Reformist
lobbying organizations like the American Association for Labor Legislation (AALL) called for public benefit programs that would have
transformed the Poor Law system into something much closer to a
European-style social insurance state.

But if culture does not tell us why American public policy developed differently from European public policy in the early twentieth
century, political and institutional factors do. Class played a large
part: except in a few instances, business elites were fiercely opposed to social-insurance reform and well positioned to defend their
views. In contrast, labor unions were weak, divided, and ambivalent
themselves about the role of the state. Government and party institutions, including an independent judiciary hostile to social reform,
an underdeveloped public bureaucracy, and the structure of the
electoral system also stymied reformers. As state-centered accounts
have pointed out, America was ill-suited for modern governance in
the early twentieth century.[9] Reformers might have overcome the
barriers imposed by either class or state, but the combination of the
two proved deadly. Taken together, the shallowness of the support
for European-style reform, the certainty of fierce resistance from an
antistatist business class, and the obstacles erected by unusually
configured political institutions led reformers to choose a different
road than Europe was taking to the welfare state.

## A Vacuum on the Left

That millions of Americans wanted government to do something
about the consequences of capitalist industry is not hard to demonstrate. As industrialism spread in the post-Civil War period, American farmers and workers regularly looked to government for protection from the market and for limits on what employers could
legitimately do in the pursuit of profit. Throughout the nineteenth
century and into the twentieth, popular movements and parties

arose demanding a larger role for government, including the Green-back party, the People's party, and the Socialist party. Each of these, moreover, had significant labor support.[10]

Nonetheless, American workers at this time *were* unusually divided and politically disorganized. Culture, race, region, and religion all competed with class for workers' loyalties, making it impossible to forge the kind of shared social-democratic political project that brought workers together elsewhere. In the end, ethnocultural motivations, not class, largely determined how workers voted.[11] And on this basis, American workers divided their political affiliations among mainstream parties that were reluctant to represent their economic interests against their employers'. Those that were class conscious moved from one third party to another, each with little chance of electoral success. In a truly competitive party system, third-party voters might have enjoyed influence beyond their numbers by throwing their weight behind one of the likely winners. But American elections had become decidedly less competitive after 1896 as the parties carved out regional power bases and then maintained their influence with cultural appeals and patronage politics.

Middle- and upper-class social reformers, though more ethnically and religiously homogeneous, divided in other ways—over principle and program. Anticapitalist radicals competed with "corporate liberals"; "good government" reformers with social-welfare advocates; equal-rights feminists with maternalists. The result was a vacuum on the left that deprived advocates of social insurance of both the mass base needed to carry out reform and a political party sufficiently powerful to force established political elites to act.

The AALL, founded in 1906 to research labor conditions and promote labor legislation, was the most ardent supporter of social insurance for workers. Although heavily dependent on wealthy donors and counting a fair number of old-stock, upper-class reformers among its leadership, the AALL positioned itself as the voice of new middle-class professionals and intellectuals and self-consciously sought (and arguably succeeded, at least in its early years) to develop a distinct view of social welfare independent of both business and labor. Most important, it publicized the progress that had already been made on the European continent, drafting model bills that Progressives might propose to Congress and state legislatures, lobbying for a wide range of contributory social insurance programs, including old-age, unemployment, health, and disability insurance.[12]

A second group, consisting largely of middle- and upper-class women, pushed not for social insurance, but for public policies that would help women and children, not as dependents of male workers, but as citizens, or potential citizens, in their own right. Led by the growing network of women's clubs and associations that had formed to educate and uplift middle-class homemakers, most importantly the National Congress of Mothers, the General Federation of Women's Clubs, and the National Association of Colored Women, these reformers called for government to take on the roles of caring and nurturing—work once done by women and mothers but that now had to be "passed on to the state."[13] Supported by millions of homemakers, the women's clubs helped "promote a nearly nationwide debate about the moral desirability of providing public aid to worthy widowed mothers and their children."[14]

Another group of women activists, including Jane Addams, Julia Lathrop, Florence Kelley, Edith Abbott, and Sophonisba Breckinridge, supported demands for mothers' pensions, but saw these as merely an opening wedge in a larger struggle for a universal welfare state. Based in and around the settlement house movement, they created a national network of advocacy organizations, including the National Consumers' League, the National Child Labor Committee, the Women's Trade Union League and the Women's Joint Congressional Committee. These activists, much closer in spirit and ideology to European social democrats, argued for "socializing democracy," in Addams's words, using state power to lessen social inequality.[15] Their hope, voiced by Julia Lathrop, head of the newly created Children's Bureau, was that mothers' pensions would be "an awkward first step" toward social insurance.[16]

In contrast, the most important labor unions—arguably the natural constituency for social spending programs to aid workers— opposed most forms of social insurance. Instead, the American Federation of Labor (AFL) argued for "voluntarism" (privileging organization building and collective bargaining) over efforts to establish new social rights through state action. Once organized and free to strike, the AFL believed that all but the most dependent workers would be able to win what they needed most: concessions from employers (in the form of private benefits and collectively-bargained limits on the hours of work) and union-managed unemployment-relief funds.

It is important not to overstate the case. The AFL supported noncontributory old-age pensions (paid for by employers or government rather than employees), and its wariness of statist reform was not exceptional. Other labor movements in the West were equally concerned that the state would compete with the unions for workers' allegiances, that public programs would replace union-controlled mutual funds with government-controlled insurance schemes, and that government would use its new powers to buttress the strength of employers, not workers. In Britain, the Liberal party introduced state-run, contributory unemployment insurance in 1911 *against* labor opposition. Led by syndicalists, the French labor movement was even more adamantly opposed to social insurance. Typically, European trade unions and labor parties supported social insurance only after it had been established by other actors and only on the condition that new programs would not tax workers, that is, that they be financed from progressive taxes and general revenues.

Nor did opposition to social insurance from the national leadership of American labor reflect the opinions of the average worker. The evidence suggests that many American wage earners were comfortable with the idea that government should help them in their struggles with employers. There were a fair number of socialists in the American labor movement in the early twentieth century, including a significant number within the AFL itself. In 1902, nearly half (46%) of the delegates to the AFL national convention voted for the Socialist party's platform; in 1912, a socialist challenged Samuel Gompers for the presidency of the federation and received one-third of the vote. Certainly, the delegates were more comfortable with the idea of European-style social insurance than were the more conservative union leaders.[17]

Many state-level federations and local unions were quite similar in impulse and instinct to European social democrats. They cooperated with supporters of social legislation, including working-class social clubs like the Fraternal Order of Eagles, and backed social insurance and regulatory protections, including health and unemployment insurance and old-age pension proposals. Local unions in the more industrialized Northeast and Midwest were very active in the struggle for social protection. According to Christopher Anglim and Brian Gratton, by the 1920s, the state federations provided "broad and consistent support" for public welfare proposals throughout the United States, despite the AFL's public position against them.[18]

Nonetheless, national trade union leaders resisted the expansion of the welfare state longer and harder than their European counterparts, and that undermined the movement for reform. As Gwendolyn Mink has argued, the AFL's "dogmatic opposition to social legislation concealed the context and constituency for social reform."[19] The AFL rejected calls for national social insurance, at various times criticizing health insurance, disability insurance, unemployment insurance, and contributory old-age insurance. Samuel Gompers was "unambivalent" in his opposition.[20] He told the United States Commission to Study Social Insurance that he would rather "help in the inauguration of a new revolution against compulsory insurance than submit."[21] In 1904, the AFL's national convention rejected old-age pensions as socialistic. The AFL also objected strongly to protective labor regulation for men. In 1914, the AFL re-

versed a 50-year-old campaign for maximum-hour laws, calling instead for collective bargaining to resolve even this issue.[22] Even
when it did not oppose the idea of increased state power, the AFL
took part in reform campaigns "selectively and suspiciously."[23] The
AFL reluctantly supported workmen's compensation only after failing to win wider support for a reformed tort system that would have
strengthened workers' hands in court suits. Even protective legislation for women and children did not excite organized labor's imagi-
nation. While state federations did take an active role at first and
the AFL officially endorsed the campaign for women's hours laws,
both the national and state federations ceded leadership of the
movement to women reformers and middle-class activists, preferring to spend their time and money on the organizational issues that
most concerned them.[24]

Whenever possible, the national union leadership preferred to
pursue workers' interests privately, by organizing, bargaining, and
controlling access to craft jobs. When the AFL did enter politics, it
did so with the goal of augmenting workers' bargaining power, most
significantly by exempting unions from court injunctions under the
Sherman Antitrust Act and restricting open immigration. As the
second decade of the century wore on, organized labor grew *more*,
not less, hostile to a European-style welfare state.

A variety of explanations have been proposed for the AFL's decision not to pursue an interventionist state actively. Early students of
the labor movement suggested that American workers were as influenced by classical liberal ideology as the conservative political elites
who opposed redistributional social reforms. More recently, others
have focused on how voluntarism served the interests of the labor
leaders themselves and the white male craft workers they represented. Institutionalists emphasize the impact of early democratization on the formation of working-class identities in the United
States and the hostility of an independent judiciary to labor-oriented legislation.[25] We will return to this issue in the conclusion.
Suffice it to say here that the AFL's stance profoundly affected the
political calculations of anyone interested in mobilizing popular support for more substantial public provision.

Quite possibly, neither fragmentation on the left, nor the absence of a successful, mass-based labor party, nor the AFL's preference for voluntarism would have been sufficient to turn the
American welfare state away from European-style reform. But in
combination, these factors mattered greatly. Together, they created
a vacuum on the left that made it all but impossible to build the kind
of cross-class coalition that was needed to force American political
elites to take social insurance seriously. Though the AALL prosely-
tized middle-class professionals and public officials, without support

from organized labor or the club women's movement its political influence proved limited. Apart from workmen's compensation reform, the AALL's social insurance proposals never reached the public agenda. The women's movement was more successful, stepping
into the political gap left by organized labor. But internal divisions
undercut its strength as well: while a fair number of women activists found their way into positions of authority (as members of
agencies and commissions, school superintendents, health officers,
social workers, and factory inspectors), the club women were uninterested in developing an interventionist state that might mediate
between business and labor or redistribute power, and they proved
indifferent to political alliances with organized labor or, for that
matter, with women activists with a more radical agenda.

In the end, only the most conservative version of maternalism—
protective legislation for women workers and mothers' aid—could
command support from all interested parties, and only because
these reforms cabined protection in ways that limited their impact,
as the settlement house activists feared. Nearly everywhere else
Progressives turned in social policy, conflicts over principle and
practice prevailed, undermining the ability of the left, however defined, to force political elites to commit to any particular path.

## The Defense of the Market

Like workers and the middle classes, American business elites were
also divided about the use of state power, enormously complicating
the effort of a small minority of capitalists who wanted to create an
affirmative state to solve business's own market problems. But most
business interests opposed the idea of a welfare state. More important, they were able to take advantage of the structure of the American state, notably its decentralized government and party structures, to resist the expansion of public provision.[26]

As a rule, business opposition to statist reform was widespread
and intense in the early twentieth century. Indeed, American business leaders were nearly united in their opposition to any attempt
by government to control wages, hours, or working conditions, or to
use public money to fund programs that (1) provided potential wage
earners with alternatives to the labor market and (2) threatened to
raise taxes.

The National Association of Manufacturers (NAM) took the lead
role in defending the market. Notoriously antiunion, NAM opposed
all forms of legislation that might aid workers or organized labor, including changes in the Sherman Antitrust Act that would have protected unions from prosecution, 8-hour bills for federal employees,
and most forms of protective labor legislation.[27] But while NAM was

particularly hostile to "class legislation," most business organizations shared NAM's outlook.[28] The Chamber of Commerce, for example, organized to provide business with a more "responsible" alternative to NAM's strident antilabor rhetoric, also denounced all efforts to protect wage earners from the market.[29] Put simply, American employers argued that workers who failed to secure their own futures should look to relatives and private charity, not to government, for help.

To be sure, because unrestrained market competition also threatened business profits and market shares, a small but influential group of bankers became interested in reform.[30] The Morgan interests helped found the National Civic Federation (NCF) and fund the AALL to help businesses formulate their own legislative proposals, and both organizations suggested ways to stabilize the market economy, while lobbying other business actors to support these proposals. Based on this evidence, some revisionist historians have concluded that Progressivism was a political movement of finance capital—class-conscious economic elites interested in extending state power to bring order to an increasingly disorderly capitalist system, to undercut the power of labor militants and the appeal of socialism to workers, and to protect their profits.[31]

But Morgan-style corporate liberalism was not as popular among American business, even the largest, most enlightened corporations, as is sometimes suggested. Partial business support for the AALL did not translate into widespread business support for that organization's programs. To the contrary, most business actors continued to oppose anything that threatened to disrupt private labor markets or increase public outlays and taxes. Indeed, most employer groups fought hard against and helped defeat AALL proposals in state legislatures. Even the NCF leaders who cooperated in the construction of new regulatory and banking institutions worried about social-welfare legislation, preferring self-regulation to state intervention.[32] Under the NCF's leadership, the most progressively managed firms experimented with private "welfare work" as an alternative to government, providing private, employment-based welfare benefits, including health care, insurance, pensions, schools, technical education, low-cost housing and recreational facilities to faithful employees—all programs that left firms with as much autonomy as possible.[33]

Business preferences did vary across issues. Business groups were likely to actively support reform when it promised to reduce business costs substantially. This was clearly the case with workmen's compensation legislation; many employers believed that the change from a tort to a no-fault system would bring certainty to increasingly costly and uncertain legal confrontations between workers and employers.[34] Business groups were more likely to acquiesce when reform provided benefits to the "deserving" poor (that is, those not expected to work), and did not impose large costs on public budgets. Business groups did not lobby against mothers' pensions because widowed women with young children could legitimately be exempt from work and because the specific administrative arrangements proposed to finance and distribute these benefits (i.e., funded by fiscally conservative county governments and often implemented by the same private charity organizations that worried about giving aid to the "undeserving" poor) assured business elites that the program would be administered austerely.[35] Likewise, most businesses had little to lose from maximum-hours laws and did not object to them. The Citizens' Industrial Organization, allied with the antiunion, antireform NAM, actually supported the Supreme Court decision that upheld state-level maximum-hours legislation for women.[36] Whenever possible, employers lobbied legislatures for amendments that would exempt as many employees as possible and/or make compliance less costly.[37]

When business interests anticipated that legislation might allow workers who should work to escape labor market obligations, substantially raise public outlays, or force higher taxes, they lobbied fiercely against reform. There was strong business opposition on these grounds both to social insurance (including programs for the unemployed, the sick, and the aged) and to minimum-wage laws for women because they gave government the power to order businesses to increase their wage bill. Even the NCF, the most progressive business lobbying group, opposed minimum wage legislation for women.[38]

Finally, in some cases, economic elites concluded that it would be better to channel the reform tide than to challenge it head on. With public opinion clearly on the side of women and children workers abused by long hours and unsafe working conditions, many employers decided to accept, or at least not to oppose, the passage of protective legislation for these two groups. Only those employers with an immediate and compelling economic stake in these labor markets, that is, manufacturers and retailers in highly competitive product markets who relied on these low-wage workers, appear to have been willing to risk taking the responsibility for killing this Progressive legislation.[39] Once state-level regulation had passed, one or another group of employers typically reversed direction and pressed for national reform legislation, seeking federal standards that would force their competitors in unregulated states to absorb these costs, too.[40]

In their struggle against Progressivism, business interests were helped enormously by the structure of the political system itself, which magnified the strength of conservative opposition to change while raising the costs of coordinating the movement for reform. Not that public officials did not want to expand the state's social regulatory powers. There was widespread support among actors at all levels of government for a more interventionist state. As president, Theodore Roosevelt had sponsored the 1909 White House Conference on the Care of Dependent Children, helping to build the movement for protective legislation.[41] Running as the standard bearer of the Progressive party in 1912, he broke decisively with laissez-faire, calling for a "New Nationalism" in which government mediated between capital and labor, providing European-style welfare-state solutions to class conflict. As a candidate, Roosevelt endorsed mothers' pensions, federal research into the working conditions of women and children, and state laws outlawing child labor. The Progressive party endorsed the minimum wage for women, the prohibition of child labor, and social insurance, including workmen's compensation.[42] Juvenile court judges, public welfare officials, and after 1912, the newly formed U.S. Children's Bureau lobbied hard for child-labor legislation. Even Woodrow Wilson, far more conservative than Roosevelt, saw the need to reorder the relationship between state and society. In the "New Freedom" he argued that the corporation had ceased to be a "private relationship." Rather, the time had come "when the systematic life of this country will be sustained, or at least supplemented, at every point by government activity."[43]

Nonetheless, political structures hindered political actors interested in reform. As David Robertson has shown, by setting "relatively autonomous political units in economic competition with each other," the federal structure made it extremely difficult to pass new legislation.[44] Despite nationalizing changes in both the economy and society, the states remained the building blocks of the political system, and political decentralization substantially augmented the political influence of business actors. Competitive industries operating in interstate markets were particularly adamant that social legislation would put state governments that were too aggressive at an economic disadvantage.[45] States that wished to attract or keep capital investment felt compelled to listen. In the industrialized Midwest and Northeast, states that should otherwise have been pioneers in the effort to build a welfare state lagged as governors who wanted to turn their jurisdictions into "laboratories of experimentation" found themselves pitted against other state governments and conservatives elites who warned constituents of the risk entailed by imposing new costs on mobile corporations.[46]

Simultaneously, federalism hurt reformers by raising the costs of successful collective action. With Congress hostile to nationalizing legislation, reformers had to mount campaigns in dozens of state legislatures or risk the backlash caused by uneven regulation. At the same time, federalism fragmented the movements for reform. Although national Progressive organizations tried to coordinate state-level reformers, activists still had to invest scarce political resources in building organizations and learning political lessons that had already been built and learned elsewhere.

The Progressives responded to the threat of interstate rivalry by trying to standardize reform, typically with model bills that could be adopted widely.[47] But reformers lobbying for uniform laws still had to assure business interests and conservatives in any given state legislature that reform would not put *that* state at even a temporary competitive disadvantage. On the assumption that business actors would be less likely to oppose programs that were based on their own voluntary experiences with "welfare capitalism" and self-regulation, reformers turned to business elites themselves for ideas on how to protect the local business climate. In this way, business-oriented ideas that limited employer obligations and worker benefits found their way into the formulation of Progressive policies.[48]

The structure of the electoral system raised other hurdles. The combination of single-member districts and winner-take-all elections encouraged a two-party system that by 1900 had become a bulwark against radical change. Despite periodic forays by oppositional political movements, including the launching of numerous radical third-party efforts (from the Greenback-Labor party in the 1870s to the Socialist party in 1900), the Democratic and Republican parties dominated American politics, killing off grass-roots, third-party challenges while simultaneously resisting calls for structural reform of the American political economy.

The Republicans brought together most finance and industrial capitalists, northeastern and midwestern farmers, and just enough industrial workers to forge a grand coalition that dominated party politics from the end of the Civil War through the Great Depression. The Democrats collected the remains, including southern loyalists, Catholic and new immigrant workers worried about Republican nativism, and those northern and western economic interests who, for one or another reason, were also uncomfortable in the Grand Old Party. Although largely shut out of the White House, the Democrats remained dominant in the South and in a handful of northern cities, giving them considerable clout in the state houses and in Congress. Together the two parties carved up the nation into a patchwork of regionally based, one-party fiefdoms.

At the same time, both parties proved flexible enough to absorb dissent. In 1896, the Democrats responded to the threat from the farmers' movement by nominating William Jennings Bryan, a faux radical just populist enough to divide the supporters of the People's party. Despite Bryan's ringing "cross of gold" rhetoric at the nominating convention, control of the party remained in the hands of a coalition of southern conservatives and northern and western capitalists. The Republicans absorbed their own "radicals"—the middle- and upper-class "mugwump" reformers who periodically challenged the patronage-based politics of the "Civil War" and "1896" party systems—at the congressional level. There, Progressive Republicans such as Albert Cummins of Iowa, Albert Beveridge of Indiana, and Robert LaFollette of Wisconsin (who would later bolt the party to lead another third-party assault in 1924) also fought to reform the internal procedures of the House and Senate so that government might finally respond to popular discontent. These intramural insurgencies kept the educated middle classes believing in the possibility of reform within the two-party system while voting for national candidates, from McKinley to Hoover, chosen by the party's plutocratic inner circle.

Winner-take-all elections reinforced the grip of the existing two parties by underrepresenting more radical movements and candidacies. In 1912, with 6% of the national vote, the Socialists won no representation in Congress (in contrast, approximately 7% of the vote in 1910 gave the British Labour party forty-two seats in parliament).[49] Moreover, both political parties responded to the decentralization of the state by creating decentralized organizational structures. Both operated as loose confederations of allied state entities, rather than centralized national organizations, reinforcing the tendency set in motion by the structure of the electoral system toward diffuse, coalitional politics, particularistic appeals, and centrist policies.[50]

In all these ways, the American party system—though both democratic in form and, in comparative perspective, relatively open to pressure from below—frustrated efforts to use the state to shield workers from the play of market forces. In contrast to European political systems, which often repressed or simply ignored worker demands, thereby forcing labor to build new political parties, the American political system seemed to welcome citizen participation, only to frustrate its independent political expression in ways that might have helped reformers build the electoral coalitions needed to overcome conservative opposition.

## Women and Children First

Class and state were not absolute barriers to expanding the American state in the early twentieth century: the Progressives overcame existing administrative infirmities, as well as middle- and upper-

class fears of patronage politics, in several policy areas, even when
corruption figured as one possible outcome. Progress was made in
banking regulation, transportation, public education, workmen's
compensation,[51] and mothers' aid.[52] Nor were the courts entirely im-
penetrable. Despite the attention paid to high profile decisions in
cases such as *Lochner v. New York,* and *Adair v. United States,*
striking down state laws protecting workers, the courts accepted
many regulatory and social reform initiatives—as long as organized
labor was not directly implicated.[53]

Nonetheless, the high barriers to reform erected by political
and institutional factors were real. When reformers tried to protect
full-time workers, and/or expand national state power, the coalitions in support of reform became thinner, the opposition more
broadly based, and the obstacles thrown up by state structures
harder to surmount. When the issue involved a significant extension
of the regulatory authority or fiscal capacity of the federal government and struck at the wage contract between capital and labor, opponents of reform almost always won. Equally important, maternalism was something nearly all reformers could agree on. Although it
did not strongly appeal to the left of the women's movement, leftwing women activists were willing to support it as a first wedge in
their campaign for more universal benefits.[54]

In contrast, redistributive programs—including laws that sheltered able-bodied male workers from the market, imposed substantial economic burdens on employers, or used public funds to supplement private incomes—had extremely rough sledding. Despite
Theodore Roosevelt's endorsement, and the AALL's public relations
campaign, contributory old-age pensions, health insurance, and
unemployment insurance failed even to make it onto the national
policy agenda. Apart from workmen's compensation reform, no
*state-level* social insurance proposal passed before 1929.[55] Only
Wisconsin succeeded in implementing unemployment compensation
before the congressional struggle over the Social Security Act (SSA)
in 1935. Even noncontributory pensions were rebuffed: by 1926,
only six states (Montana, Nevada, Pennsylvania, Wisconsin, Kentucky, and Maryland) had adopted them, and these programs were
minimal—small, means-tested benefits offered on a county-optional
basis. Nationwide, a mere thousand recipients received a total of
$200,000 in old-age assistance in 1929.[56]

Because they opened up the possibility that government would
force employers to increase workers' wages, minimum wages for
women also met substantial resistance from employers. Apart from
business interests that were either isolated from the competitive
pressures of the national market or employed few women, employers rejected the proposal. Reformers divided: the General Federa-

tion of Women's Clubs defected from the Women's Trade Union League's (WTUL) campaign, while organized labor finally came out in opposition, fearing that public minimums would become statutory maximums; even the state federations abandoned the WTUL on this issue. Reformers also worried about the very real possibility that, as eventually occurred in 1923, the Supreme Court would find minimum wage laws unconstitutional.[57] As a result, reformers succeeded in only fifteen (largely nonindustrialized) states and the District of Columbia. Among the industrial states of the Northeast and Midwest, only Massachusetts took this step, and business groups in that state succeeded in gutting enforcement provisions.[58]

Reformers did best when new legislation promised to lower business costs. With broad support, including that of business leaders seeking certainty and lower costs as well as middle-class professionals looking for "scientific" solutions to public policy problems, workmen's compensation was widely enacted, passing in thirty-eight states by 1918.[59] While business groups did not win every point, none of the state-level programs threatened their profitability.

Reforms that provided small benefits to "deserving" claimants without imposing substantial obligations on the public treasury or substantially raising business costs were also likely to succeed. In the case of mothers' pensions, government officials joined with women's clubs in the movement for universal, in-home support for widowed mothers with dependent children. Opposition existed: old-line charity organizations feared that mothers' pensions would transform charity into entitlement, diminishing their own role.[60] But, seeing no direct threat to their interests, employers were largely silent and the coalition in support of this reform triumphed easily.[61] Between 1911 and 1920, forty states adopted mothers' pensions that allowed local governments to pay indigent widowed mothers so that they might care for their children at home.[62] Progressives also had great success limiting women's work hours. In this case, the coalition was very broad, encompassing organized labor, women reformers, middle-class technocrats, and public officials.[63] In contrast, business opposition was mild. When the Supreme Court approved the principle in 1908 in *Muller v. Oregon,* a flurry of states either passed new laws or strengthened existing ones. By 1921, forty-one states had passed laws regulating the hours worked by women. Many states also passed prohibitions on night work or on women working in especially hazardous occupations and industries.[64]

The maternalist strategy also proved better suited to overcoming the obstacles created by America's fragmented political institutions. As Theda Skocpol has shown,[65] because it was spread throughout the country and locally organized, the women's movement was better situated than either the labor movement (which tended to be politically influential only in the most highly industrialized areas) or the AALL activists to influence Congress and the party system, which were equally decentralized.

The political rationality of maternalism had not been obvious at first. Theodore Roosevelt and the Progressive party endorsed AALL-style old-age pensions, health insurance, and unemployment insurance. Nor were advocates of European-style reform completely rebuffed. Although coverage and benefits were very restrictive, by 1923 most states had established state-level compulsory, contributory retirement pensions for *public* employees.[66] The left of the movement, including groups such as the National Consumers' League and the WTUL, and the settlement house workers, wanted a far more substantial role for government, including social insurance. But as conservative opposition to social insurance, the impact of state structures, and conflicts among the movements for reform did their work, reformers adapted to the reality. Progressives learned quickly that they fared better when it came to protecting women and children.

Maternalism was not always successful. The opposition to maternalism intensified when reformers proposed to use *national* power to aid the dependent. Legislation for women and children succeeded at the federal level only when it did not give government new regulatory power. Supporters of the Children's and Women's bureaus triumphed over conservative opposition because they were careful not to give these two new agencies the authority to compel anyone to do anything, instead limiting both agencies to research and investigation.[67] The national ban on child labor legislation that President Wilson had refused to support was undone by the Supreme Court in 1918, just as Wilson had predicted, although the law was supported by a broad coalition, including organized labor and a fair number of business actors.[68] Nonetheless, given the options, maternalism was likely the best the Progressives could have done.

## A Wrong Turn

In the end, the Progressives failed to establish what was, from a European perspective, the first principle of the modern welfare state: that male workers should be protected by social insurance. In America, advocates of a modern welfare state would have to wait another generation. Recently, some scholars have objected to any comparison of American social policy innovation in the early twentieth century with European initiatives that discounts what American reformers accomplished. Influenced by the feminist rethinking of social policy, they celebrate the struggle for maternalist social policies.

Skocpol goes further, arguing that "America came close to forging a maternalist welfare state, with female-dominated public agencies implementing regulations and benefits for the good of women and children."[69]

Maternalism's defenders have a case. The underlying assumptions of mothers' aid contradicted the laissez-faire and Social Darwinist assumptions that had guided American public policy for decades. And in working for public benefits for women and children, Progressive reformers did much to revalue and reward women's contribution to society at a time when that contribution was not respected. In establishing that widows deserved aid because they served the community as mothers, feminists challenged patriarchal ideas of what constituted service to the community, suggesting a new notion of citizenship that spoke more directly to women's lives. Nor were maternalists entirely unsuccessful in government: mother's pensions *were* the nation's first publicly funded social benefits. State and federal courts that had previously struck down protective laws for men as violating due process and freedom of contract accepted such laws when they were targeted more narrowly to protect the health requirements of women *as mothers*. In *Muller v. Oregon,* the Supreme Court validated the maternalist view of gender difference. By the early 1930s, mothers' pensions had swept the nation, adopted in forty-six of forty-eight states. And when the New Dealers took up the issue of aid to single mothers they built on this foundation, creating Aid to Dependent Children (which would become Aid to Families with Dependent Children [AFDC] in the 1950s) by adding federal funds to supplement existing state-level efforts.[70]

But this should not blind us to how little maternalist reformers accomplished, even on their own terms. Even if, as Skocpol argues, "social policies for women alone loomed much larger in early modern U.S. social provision than they did in the pioneering Western welfare states for workers,"[71] these targeted policies did not actually reach many women and children. True, mothers' pensions helped *some* poor widows.[72] But state-level legislation was uneven. In twenty-nine states, legislation only *permitted* but did not *require* local governments to give widows money. The majority of counties in the United States had no public aid programs *at all* before the creation of Aid to Families with Children. Many states restricted access with residency requirements and behavioral tests, including "suitable home" provisions that were used to discipline and exclude many poor mothers. Indeed, the agencies charged with implementing these new laws were often hostile to them. In many states, the same charity organizations that had opposed the program were given control of it. As a result, few women qualified, and those that

did received little: in the early 1930s, only 6.2% of the approximately 1.5 million female-headed families with children received
anything at all. As Linda Gordon notes, payments were "meager,"
never "intended to allow mothers to stay home with their children,"
and better understood as "a gesture rather than an achievement."[73]

The reach of the new wage and hour laws was similarly circumscribed. While three-quarters of the states had passed maximum-
hours laws by 1920, because of legislative exemptions that applied
to most employers only 12% of American workers were actually
protected.[74] In the end, neither mothers' pensions nor protective
regulation could match the scope of the already existing Civil War
pension system which, in 1912, covered two-thirds of non-southern,
native-born white men over age 65.[75]

The comparative record also casts doubt on celebratory accounts of maternalism. Everywhere in the industrial West, women
activists were less successful in protecting women and children
through maternalist policies than they were when allied with male
reformers and political actors seeking other goals, whether boost-
ing the birth rate or imposing public standards on corporations.[76]
As the fate of the Sheppard-Towner Infants and Maternity Protection Act of 1921 demonstrates, even when successful, maternalism
proved hard to sustain. Sheppard-Towner was the epitome of moderation, merely establishing clinics to educate expectant mothers
about personal hygiene and their children's health care. Yet even
this symbol of maternalist reform was easily killed by physician opposition in 1929. That physicians could stop a program that on its
face so clearly represented the best instincts of Progressivism suggests how poorly organized that impulse was.[77]

To make matters worse, maternalism may have actually helped
undermine efforts to establish a European-style welfare state in the
United States. While it may very well be the case that, as Skocpol
argues, "institutionalized social programs from the maternalist era
survived to become parts of America's new nationwide system of
public provision launched in the 1930s,"[78] it is not at all clear that
this was a good thing. By targeting benefits on the most vulnerable,
Progressive reformers helped establish the practice of dividing potential beneficiaries of government aid into different classes based
on their labor market participation. Though maternalism sought to
reward women who did not work in the paid labor market, the distinction between workers and mothers would later be used to stig-
matize beneficiaries and marginalize program advocates, as the history of the AFDC program makes clear.[79]

In important even if unintended ways, then, Progressive social
policies upheld rather than challenged the established order. Exploitative class, race, and gender structures remained in place while

government benefits were directed only to those who were not expected to adapt to them. Support was denied to working women
and blacks. Women "out of role" were disciplined by social policies
that rewarded the "respectable" and punished deviance. Able-bodied male workers were left entirely on their own to win whatever
terms they could from their employers. Left in place, these social
and economic structures, in particular, racial and gender structures,
continued to divide workers from each other.

As the next generation of reformers—feminist and nonfeminist
alike—would discover, it was exceedingly difficult to build on a maternalist foundation. As late as 1929, although it was the world's
leading economic power, the United States had failed to establish
even the beginnings of a national welfare state, and even state-level
social-welfare institutions remained rudimentary and uneven. As
Ronnie Steinberg has concluded, protective labor laws had to be
"completely severed from notions of the traditional distribution of
roles and responsibilities in the traditional family" before New Dealers could protect workers from exploitative market relationships.[80]
Gordon reaches a similar conclusion regarding mothers' aid:

> By the time of the Social Security Act, it was clear that these pro-
> grams had been outmoded from the beginning, not only in the in-
> adequate size of their stipends and the proportion of single moth-
> ers covered, but also in their fundamental design."[81]

In the crucible of the Great Depression, maternalism would be
dropped entirely and reformers would turn to a more European-
style effort to legitimate the idea of social insurance in class terms,
as protection for *workers*.[82]

# FOUR

# *The New Deal*

For a moment, the Great Depression lowered the barriers to building a European-style, welfare state in America. In a few short years, the relationship between the government and the economy changed dramatically: federal cash and work relief programs were established in 1933, social insurance in 1935, federal regulation of working conditions in 1938. Then, in 1946, with the memory of economic collapse still vivid, the Employment Act created policy-planning institutions to monitor and promote economic growth. By the start of the Korean War, the United States finally had a modern welfare state.

Nonetheless, even as it developed powerful new welfare-state institutions, the United States continued down a different path than most other rich capitalist democracies. In several ways, the American welfare state remained different—less national, less comprehensive, less capable of promoting employment security. When the political energy of the New Deal was finally spent in the late 1940s, America had created only a "semi" welfare state, as Michael Katz has put it.[1]

Proponents of a class-based approach to politics have suggested two different explanations for why the U.S. welfare state developed differently in the 1930s. The first argues that key capitalists supported Roosevelt and, in so doing, managed to turn reform to their own purposes, simultaneously lessening economic competition, dampening mass discontent, and warding off a more radical restructuring of the political economy. The second emphasizes the weakness of organized labor and the failure of workers and farmers to forge a cross-class, urban-rural alliance that might have supported social-democratic reforms.[2]

Class clearly mattered in the 1930s, but neither version of the class-based account is entirely successful. Business did not control the policy process during the New Deal, and while workers and farmers failed to forge a social-democratic alliance, that failure does not explain what *did* happen. To understand the New Deal's trajectory, we need to look more closely at the precise way in which po-

litical and institutional factors combined, the complex and contradictory admixture of constraint and opportunity that resulted, and
the responses of political leaders to both.

## A Second Window Opens

By calling the existing institutions into question and sending millions
of Americans looking for new solutions, economic collapse and political mobilization in the 1930s finally opened a more substantial
window for reform. By 1934, millions of voters had abandoned long-
standing partisan loyalties and established political elites, sending
shock waves through the political system. Most important, economic crisis caused workers and small farmers to abandon their
long-standing ethnocultural commitments to the parties in order to
search for leaders who would better represent their class interests.[3]
Though much of this was chaotic and unfocused, the potential for
mass mobilization and radicalization was real.

The depression also caused an unprecedented level of union
activity. Working-class movements, many quite militant, spread
quickly as dissatisfaction with the pace of change mounted. By
1934, direct action outside the American Federation of Labor (AFL)
was widespread. Steel and auto workers, migrant farm workers,
teamsters and longshoremen, electrical workers, and even newspa-
per reporters turned to unconventional forms of protest. Violent
strikes, many led by radicals and communists, were commonplace.
Some unions grew spectacularly: the United Mine Workers (UMW)
membership increased threefold in one year. By 1935, the Congress
of Industrial Organizations (CIO) secession movement was well un-
derway, providing the long-sought organizational vehicle through
which the interests of millions of industrial workers in public provision could finally be articulated.[4]

Not only workers protested. With the collapse of agriculture,
farmers once again became an active political force. As farm prices
and land values plummeted, farm strikes spread and new organizations, such as the Farm Holiday movement, arose to represent farmers' demands for economic relief. In 1933, careful observers feared
that a revolution would come not from the cities, but from a radicalized midwestern countryside. The aged also became a political
force, mobilized by the Townsend movement's demand for a publicly
financed, $200 monthly noncontributory pension for everyone over
sixty.[5]

As the depression deepened, mass politics also became more
class based and class conscious. Polarization was clear and consistent: blue-collar workers, low-income households, the unemployed,
and those on relief were far more likely to approve the New Deal

than were business people, white-collar workers, upper- and mid-
dle-income households, and professionals. Class-based voting also
increased steadily throughout the decade.[6]

In response, political leaders on the left and the right refash-
ioned their appeals, all making welfare, broadly defined, a central
demand. With welfare and relief as featured issues, the Communists made substantial organizing gains. Louisiana Senator Huey
Long's "Share Our Wealth" campaign called for a panoply of economic security measures, including public works, a minimum wage,
a shorter work week, redistributional taxes, a guaranteed family income, and universal pensions for everyone over sixty. Reverend
Charles Coughlin, the Michigan radio priest, argued for a public
works program that would guarantee a job and a minimum wage to
anyone who could not find work elsewhere. Economic crisis even
changed the AFL's mind about public provision, and the AFL's
national convention finally endorsed unemployment insurance in
1932.[7] The 1934 mid-term elections registered the shifting tide. The
congressional elections "almost erased the Republican party as a national force." After, the Democrats held sixty-nine Senate seats and
322 places in the House. State-level results were not much better: in
1935, Republicans held only seven governorships.[8]

The depression also changed the politics of business, causing serious divisions among firms and sectors about the role of government. As revisionist historians of the New Deal have been quick to
point out, some corporate elites embraced if not the principle, then
at least the practice of a welfare state. A number of prominent business leaders called for emergency national relief in the panicked
months of 1932.[9] There was also significant, if diffuse, support for
an unemployment insurance program that could regulate substan-
dard competition.[10] Five business leaders (Walter C. Teagle of Standard Oil, Gerard Swope of General Electric, Marion Folsom of
Kodak, Morris Leeds of Leeds and Northrup, and Sam Lewishohn
of Miami Copper) played particularly prominent roles, serving on
Roosevelt's Business Advisory Council and on the Presidential Advisory Council on Economic Security, a tripartite group of employers,
labor leaders, and independent experts created to help the Committee on Economic Security (CES) write the Social Security Act
(SSA). In that capacity, they supported a wide variety of Democratic
party policy initiatives, including the establishment of both old-age
pensions and unemployment insurance.[11]

Equally important, because the search for solutions to the economic crisis forced politics and policy making away from state governments and to Washington, business actors who did oppose the
New Deal could not as easily use the threat of capital mobility to
block reformers' initiatives.[12] Without the threat of disinvestment,

which had figured so prominently in debates in the 1910s over Progressive reforms, business leaders had to rely on direct lobbying—a less reliable method in a political climate in which both voters and politicians had become suspicious of business's motives.

The spread of working-class disaffection and the sudden decline in business influence did not, however, mean that American workers were either ready to mount a direct assault on the citadels of American capitalism or even well-positioned to force major concessions from the Democrats. While workers had finally made their presence known, the labor movement remained divided, disorganized, and unclear over how to use government, enormously complicating efforts to turn mass mobilization into a direct challenge to the status quo. As Linda Gordon has noted:

> Depression insurgency was remarkably restrained and limited, relative to the severity of the situation. Third-party efforts and extraparliamentary protests were mainly local and, despite their militancy, easily blocked and contained. Despite the widespread class-conflict rhetoric, even in Congress, no mass socialist orientation spread.[13]

Two kinds of problems handicapped organized labor. First, organizational differences rooted in economic conflicts made it hard for workers to speak with one voice. Indeed, the labor movement split decisively into two distinct tendencies. The CIO embraced social democracy, but the AFL had a hard time escaping its past commitments. Though it officially abandoned voluntarism in the early 1930s, the journey to state interventionism proceeded slowly and fitfully.[14] The Townsend movement, which put the issue of old-age pensions on the policy agenda, was led by a California doctor, not trade unionists. When the AFL finally took a position on social insurance, it supported the White House's proposal to create a self-insurance scheme and rejected the Lundeen bill, a social-democratic alternative to the Social Security Act that called for non–means-tested benefits, progressive financing, and payments to sick as well as striking workers.[15]

Racism also continued to confound efforts to build a left.[16] Labor's failures in this regard were long-standing. The nascent trade-union movement did little in the antebellum period to encourage abolition and it failed to champion the cause of freed slaves after the war. Some unions rose to the occasion. The Knights of Labor organized across racial lines in the South in the 1880s and 1890s. Alone among the AFL unions, the UMW not only organized black workers in the early twentieth century, but hired black officials, staff members, and organizers. But, as Michael Goldfield has shown, the independent railroad unions and "most craft unions

were openly racist, excluding Black members either formally or by
custom."[17] Even those unions that were led to cross the color line
because of the preponderance of African-American workers in the
targeted occupations and industries established separate, inferior
locals for them.

The Great Depression forced organized labor to rethink its position on race, but not, finally, to reverse course. The unions that
founded the CIO, including the UMW and the needle-trades unions
in New York, as well as many of the Communist party and socialist
organizers who helped build the new industrial labor movement, did
fight political campaigns against Jim Crow, working closely with civil
rights leaders, black churches, and black civic organizations in the
North and, immediately after World War II, in the South as well.
But many unions continued to refuse to accept black members or to
work with black political organizations. The practices of the craft
unions that remained in the AFL changed very little; they organized
black workers only where necessary, while continuing to give pref-
erential treatment to whites. But even those unions that were most
supportive of civil rights hesitated in the face of white resistance.
The Steelworkers and especially the Autoworkers publicly aligned
themselves with civil rights struggles, but they did little to mobilize
the white rank-and-file in support, encourage efforts by black workers to confront racist practices by employers, or even to discipline
locals that discriminated. Nor did the CIO directly challenge the
southern power structure that supported white supremacy. Afraid
of alienating southern supporters of the New Deal and too weak to
matter much in the region, the CIO mounted two short campaigns
against Jim Crow and withdrew.[18]

Nor did business suddenly reverse course and applaud reformers' efforts. To be sure, some capitalists worked with Roosevelt. Revisionists disagree among themselves about exactly which business
interests were drawn to the New Deal and why. One school of
thought argues that a group of free-trading "internationalists" lo-
cated in capital-intensive industries where the costs of labor and social reform were unlikely to matter greatly supported Roosevelt's
domestic policies in return for Roosevelt's effort to expand their
markets abroad.[19] Other revisionists suggest that the rigors of competition in an increasingly difficult economic environment drove
firms worried about cutthroat competition from low-wage, low-
benefit, non-union rivals to demand a publicly regulated social wage.
By working with Roosevelt, they hoped to influence government to
adopt pension and unemployment insurance programs that would
cap these labor-related costs and take them out of competition.[20]
Some revisionists suggest that firms and industries that had already
experimented with welfare capitalism in the 1920s and understood

the strategic value of reform were decisive, supplying both the ex-
pertise and the policy planners who would work with the CES to
draft the new legislation.[21]

Nonetheless, most business interests remained deeply suspicious of greater state intervention into labor markets, worried
about the impact of social welfare, and steadfastly opposed to the
higher taxes needed to pay for increased social spending. Support
for unemployment insurance, perhaps the most contentious issue,
was very uneven, and business interests were deeply divided among
themselves about how to proceed. Business interests also viewed relief with suspicion. Once the panic of 1932 receded, erstwhile business supporters of federal aid turned against relief, complaining
that federal grants raised local wages.[22] Few business actors lobbied
for old-age pensions.[23] Most employers, including both small businesses and large manufacturers, feared that social legislation would
undermine their control of labor costs and lead to profligate social
spending and tax increases.[24] Manufacturers' associations were particularly vocal about the importance of state control of social insurance in order to allow local programs to reflect local conditions.[25] Indeed, even the most reformist welfare capitalists worried about the
impact of federal intervention on already-established private programs.[26] In the end, most employers objected strongly to the SSA.
As Edwin Amenta, Sunita Parikh, and Theda Skocpol have argued,
Roosevelt's capitalists were a minority voice within their class.[27]

## The Southern Problem

Lobbying alone in the midst of the depression when capitalism
seemed to have lost much of its promise, business opposition to
state intervention did not figure as prominently in politicians' calculations as it once had: business leaders found it hard to argue that
they should be left to determine the fate of the nation when they
could not keep their own factories open. But racial politics strengthened business's hand and further complicated reformers' efforts.
Fearing the impact of nationalizing labor and social legislation on
their ability to control and exploit black labor, southern commercial
interests and their political representatives in Congress joined
forces with northern business leaders to defend the region against
what the federal government might do to upset the established
order. They, in turn, found additional support from commercial
farmers outside the South, who also feared the impact of New Deal
liberalism. Of course, many farmers supported reform. The poorer
among them, represented by the National Farmers Union, backed
the administration, while trying to push the New Deal to the left.
But the more affluent farmers suspected that by raising wages,

channeling aid to farm workers, and helping poor farmers compete for land and resources, federal legislation would upset the rural class system from which they profited. To make matters worse, their taxes would be raised to pay for new programs for the urban poor.[28] As the decade wore on, these alliances solidified, leading finally to the formation in Congress of the conservative coalition of southern Democrats and Republicans that ended the New Deal.

Southern commercial elites were particularly concerned about the direction of New Deal reform. As Ira Katznelson, Kim Geiger, and Daniel Kryder argue, they were not entirely at odds with Roosevelt. Rather, their interests were complex. On the one hand, commercial farmers wanted a powerful Democratic party because it gave them access to power. Southern elites also wanted a federal government that was strong enough to promote economic development in an area of the country that had historically lagged behind the rest of the nation: because it was relatively poor, the South stood to gain from new spending on relief or social insurance. As a result, except on civil rights and labor issues, in Congress "southern and nonsouthern Democratic voting behavior was virtually indistinguishable."[29]

But southern commercial elites were also apprehensive about the New Deal's impact on class and race relations in the South.[30] Large farmers were concerned that old-age and public assistance programs, as well as federal planning and employment policies, would diminish the supply of, and weaken elite control over, black labor. Southern bankers and industrialists were worried about the impact of New Deal labor and social policies on the region's low-wage, non-union environment, and on their plans to attract northern capital to the South on that basis. These economic and racial concerns dovetailed, leading southern elites to reject federal policies that might benefit poorer farmers generally or be used by African Americans to free themselves from the control of southern employers.[31]

This meant that the South had to have some sort of regional exemption from the New Deal. Southerners in Congress made it clear that they would support social welfare programs advocated by the labor wing of the Democratic party only if those programs applied *solely* to the industrial North.[32] Southern representatives demanded two things in particular: that black labor be excluded from New Deal protections and that new programs include decentralized administrative arrangements that would allow local elites to tailor their implementation to local labor-market conditions and employer demands. Of course, the southern elite did not entirely determine what southern legislators did. Representing a poor region with a history of populist resistance to big business and support for active government, southern politicians proved fairly reliable proponents of regulatory and class-redistributional measures. But southern

Democrats fought hard against efforts to interfere with southern race relations.[33]

In several respects, the structure of American federalism helped the South make its case against racial equality and for social policies tailored to elite interests. The southern political elite had already taken advantage of state-level control over voter registration to disenfranchise blacks and poor whites, constructing a one-party system that guaranteed their control of the region's politics.[34] Then, free from the rigors of partisan competition, southern Democrats had used seniority in Congress to dominate the national party. Though the Democrats' electoral success in the 1930s widened the party's coalition and forced southern elites to deal with new claimants, the New Deal realignment also gave southern Democrats control of many of the most important congressional committees and leadership positions on the Hill. Under these circumstances, it was extremely difficult for Roosevelt or the party to press its agenda without listening to southern legislators' demands for regional autonomy.[35]

Recently, there has been some controversy over exactly how political decentralization affected New Deal social policies. Theda Skocpol and John Ikenberry have suggested that Congress, because it was "composed of representatives from states and localities," defended not racial hierarchy per se, or the interests of southern employers, but the right of subnational communities to determine their own policies. This was a local, not a class or racial bias. Congress insisted that unemployment insurance be administered jointly by the federal and state governments, they argue, because several states (encouraged by the 1933 Wagner-Peyser Act), had already created their own programs and they did not want to see these preempted. Similarly, Congress wanted to leave mothers' pensions and old-age assistance to the states because both were already well established at the local level. Anticipating congressional opposition to nationalizing arrangements which threatened local prerogatives, the Roosevelt administration proposed joint federal-state arrangements instead. In contrast, because no state had adopted compulsory, contributory old-age insurance, that program was left entirely in federal hands.[36]

But support for and opposition to various New Deal proposals does not easily correlate with preexisting institutional arrangements, or the defense of purely local prerogatives. While southern representatives were ardent advocates of states' rights, they strongly supported nationalizing legislation that delivered benefits to the South as long as those benefits did not disrupt local labor markets or upset racial hierarchies.[37] Even the political struggle over the SSA does not conform to institutionalist expectations. In the case of unemployment insurance, only two states—New York and Wisconsin—had actually made much progress when the CES settled on the federal-state tax-offset plan. It is hard to imagine that the representatives and senators from forty-six other states would have given two states a veto over policy formulation on this highly salient issue.[38] In the case of public assistance, the preexisting mothers' pensions programs were small in number and reach (only 93,620 families were receiving benefits nationwide in 1931) and hardly worth defending against encroachment.[39] On its face, old-age assistance does meet the expectations of the state-centered hypothesis: twenty-three states had passed compulsory old-age assistance by the time that Roosevelt had appointed the CES to formulate the Social Security bill (five additional states had adopted county-optional plans).[40] But the congressional representatives of those states *with* programs did *not* object to transferring these costs to the federal government. Opposition to federal old-age assistance came entirely from southern states, none of which had an already established state presence in this area.[41] In short, the evidence suggests that state structures served specifically southern racial and class interests, forcing Congress to respect the South's regional interests as southern elites defined them.

## Building from the Center

The political and institutional conditions outlined earlier presented Roosevelt with both an unprecedented opportunity and a difficult choice. By temporarily silencing opposition and spurring mass discontent, economic collapse momentarily enlarged Roosevelt's options. But Roosevelt was not unconstrained: the vast majority of business elites could be expected to mobilize as soon as they believed their interests threatened, and the South was certain to demand a high price for its cooperation with the administration. As the Progressives had, New Deal policy planners also worried about what a still-conservative Supreme Court might say about social, economic, and labor legislation that shifted power to Washington.

Under these circumstances, Roosevelt had two options. On the one hand, he could construct a centrist coalition that would pay close attention to the needs of business and other conservative interests, respecting as much of the political and economic status quo as possible while still expanding government's ability to address the crisis. On the other hand, he could move to the left, and try to use public policy to cement a social-democratic coalition within the Democratic party, in effect replacing defecting conservative and, presumably, southern elites, with northern workers and blacks. Roosevelt's counselors gave him conflicting advice. Lewis Douglas, the budget director and a leader of the conservative faction within the administration, advised the president to leave the job of economic recovery to businessmen, doing only what was necessary to support their efforts. The liberals within the administration, including Rexford Tugwell, Harold Ickes, Harry Hopkins, and Eleanor Roosevelt (supported in Congress by urban liberals and progressive Republicans like Senators Robert Wagner, Robert LaFollette Jr., and George Norris), wanted Roosevelt to adopt policies in support of unions, government planning, deficit spending, and strict regulation of business. Their goal was not only economic recovery but a political realignment.[42] Eventually, Roosevelt would try both options. But in the early New Deal, he began with the first.

The "first New Deal" (1933–1934) was essentially corporatist. As William Leuchtenburg has put it, "Roosevelt presented himself not as the paladin of liberalism but as father to all the people."[43] The administration built out from the political center, proposing policies that encouraged business concentration and cooperation. The goal was "economic regulation through a concert of the major interests," not the redistribution of wealth or power.[44] Where necessary, special concessions were made to the right to placate opposition; the left received just enough to keep it from bolting. In fact, Roosevelt spent more time fighting inflationists and farm-state radicals than challenging conservatives. Even after his huge success in the 1934 congressional elections, Roosevelt worried more about reviving the economy through new business investment than social reform, and he adopted policies that might encourage business confidence—siding with employers in important labor disputes, agreeing to a purge of radicals in the Agricultural Adjustment Administration, and backing the private housing industry against Wagner's attempts to create a new public-housing program.[45]

Cooperation with business did not preclude structural reform of the economy, but the 1933–1934 program, including banking reform, the Agricultural Adjustment Act (AAA), the National Industrial Recovery Act (NIRA), and emergency relief was remarkably conservative. The administration's budget slashed veterans' payments and federal employees' pay and was far more deflationary than anything Hoover had attempted—closer to what the Democratic party's Wall Street faction wanted than even they might have hoped under the circumstances.[46] The banking bill, formulated even as the public was learning of widespread fraud and speculation in the runup to the crash of 1929, extended government assistance to bankers on their own terms. Calls from liberals in the administration and influential members of Congress to nationalize the system, or, at a minimum, impose strict regulations on it, were ignored. Agriculture and industry were treated similarly. Both the AAA and the NIRA allowed the best-organized interests to design and implement the new programs in their own interests. The AAA attempted to solve the farm crisis by restoring to health the large commercial farmers in the Midwest and South, while rebuffing pleas to come to the aid of the harder hit, smaller farmers. Demands to nationalize and plan the nation's railroads were rejected, leaving in place the existing system which allowed the industry to regulate itself under the auspices of the Interstate Commerce Commission.[47]

Even as he rushed to aid business, Roosevelt refused to commit the administration to fully funding relief and jobs programs, and stalled on labor-law reform. To be sure, given the scale of the crisis, spending on emergency relief exploded. But budgetary considerations still figured prominently in the administration's calculations. Costs led the administration to kill the Civil Works Administration (CWA) as soon as it had gotten the nation through the winter of 1933–1934, and led the White House to underbudget the Works Progress Administration (WPA) that replaced it. As a result, the WPA did not come close to providing enough jobs to meet the demand, serving perhaps three million of the ten million unemployed.[48] The White House also opposed Senator Hugo Black's 30-hours bill in spite of support from both the AFL and Secretary of Labor Frances Perkins. The administration did endorse the inclusion of Section 7(a) in the NIRA (recognizing labor's right to organize and bargain), but only after Senator Wagner and Secretary Perkins insisted. In 1934, when Senator Wagner introduced the Labor Disputes Act to strengthen further federal protections for workers, the administration pressured him to dilute the bill until it had become meaningless, sorely disappointing congressional liberals.[49]

The administration's decision making process during this period reflected its strategic vision. White House policy planners were careful to calculate "what representatives of industry would accept without protest."[50] Sympathetic economic elites and the middle-class experts employed by or associated with them were brought directly into the policy formulation process, while experts on the left were shut out. Consider the formulation of the SSA. Secretaries Perkins of Labor and Henry Wallace of Agriculture, and Harry Hopkins, director of the Federal Emergency Relief Administration, asked social scientists from the Wisconsin State Industrial Commission—known to favor the welfare capitalist model developed by employers in the 1920s—to staff the CES. Roosevelt personally sought the advice of Gerard Swope (president of General Electric) and encouraged Edwin Witte, the chair of the CES staff, to do the same. At the same time, every expert and leader of the movement for social insurance (including Isaac M. Rubinow, Abraham Epstein, and Paul Douglas) who was not in accord with the White House's plans was excluded from the deliberations, despite his or her long-standing involvement in the issue.[51]

Corporate elites did not *control* the process. The White House rebuffed several suggestions made by business advisors, including worker contributions to the unemployment trust fund, and a statutory exemption from the old-age insurance program for companies that had already established private, welfare-capitalist pension systems. However, the policy planning process was clearly designed to take big business's views into account. And since dissenting views were excluded, the business leaders who worked with Roosevelt had enormous influence over the parameters of the debate.[52] Welfare capitalists—those employers who had voluntarily experimented with private programs to promote worker well-being in the 1920s—wanted a social insurance system that mimicked market mechanisms as much as possible and, to a significant degree, the administration adopted that approach. Open-ended entitlements financed out of general revenues were rejected in favor of insurance funds and earnings-related benefits for unemployed and retired workers. In contrast to many European systems, where, by virtue of their status as citizens, workers were granted flat-rate benefits funded from Treasury revenues, American workers would have to "earn" benefits by working and/or paying insurance premiums. In response to the anticipated opposition of a coalition of medical providers, employers, hospitals, and insurers, national health insurance was also dropped from the SSA, despite a CES recommendation to include it.[53] At the same time, merit rating for unemployment insurance—another item on business' wish list—was included *despite* the CES's conclusion that it was impractical.[54]

Anticipating congressional resistance if they did otherwise, the SSA's architects also took southern employers' concerns into account: the White House proposed or accepted a series of restrictions on the scope of coverage that severely limited what the New Deal could accomplish. Not only would there be no effort to mobilize black voters or promote labor organization in the South, but the administration agreed to exclude from all labor and social legislation most southern black workers and to include decentralized administrative arrangements in the unemployment and public assistance programs that would allow the southern states to tailor new benefit programs to local conditions.[55]

By 1935, it was clear that corporatism had failed. The National Recovery Administration (NRA), created by the NIRA, was in ruins. The economy was in recession. Business criticism of Roosevelt was mounting. And popular discontent was rising. In response, Roosevelt shifted course, giving up on the idea that corporate capital and southern conservatives could provide the foundation for a centrist coalition and experimenting, instead, with a quasi–social-democratic strategy. To this end, the administration set about to build a more urban, labor-based coalition rooted in the northern working class and led by northern, urban liberals. New legislation was introduced to communicate the message, including a tough new labor-relations bill, and a "soak the rich" tax measure.

This more radical phase opened with the "Second Hundred Days," launched in June 1935 and carried through the 1936 election. The White House pushed five major pieces of legislation: the SSA; the National Labor Relations Act (NLRA); a second bank bill; the Public-Utilities Holding Company Act; and a revenue bill that increased inheritance and personal and corporate income taxes and created a new, undistributed corporate profits tax. The distinction between the "first" and "second" New Deals should not be exaggerated; nearly all of this legislation had been in the works since the beginning, but was held back while the White House sought to build bridges to business and the South. Nonetheless, the unveiling of new social and economic legislation in 1935 clearly marked a shift in emphasis. Roosevelt underscored the point during the 1936 electoral campaign, launching a direct assault on business, accusing "economic royalists" of trying to impose a "new industrial dictatorship" on the nation.[56]

But even as he moved toward the left, Roosevelt continued to worry about breaking too sharply with the right, and the administration's policy agenda showed it. In fiscal policy, the president remained committed to "sound finance," despite continued high unemployment. Indeed, Roosevelt continually sought to reassure business and banking interests of the soundness of his fiscal policies, rejecting the principle that government would have to run deficits deliberately if it wanted to stimulate the economy. Taxes were raised in 1935 and again in 1936 in a last-ditch attempt to balance the budget. The federal government was continually in deficit in the 1930s, not because Roosevelt became a Keynesian, but because tax revenues were simply too low, and relief and other spending too high, to balance the budget.[57]

Even Roosevelt's attack on big business in 1936 was more rhetoric than policy; no significant new social or economic legislation was forthcoming during the 1936 presidential campaign. Rather, the administration renewed its campaign to cut government spending. And despite Roosevelt's belated support of the NLRA, the administration's labor policies remained equivocal: though the president rejected conservative calls to quell the sitdown strikes of 1936–1937, he also refused to endorse labor's efforts to force employers to deal with them. The year 1937 seemed to promise a further turn to the left, with the president decrying a nation where "one third" were "ill-nourished, ill-clad, ill-housed." But that vision did not produce new social or economic legislation.[58]

No betrayal from business or the right was sufficient to cause Roosevelt to abandon his efforts to find a middle ground. Even after the forward momentum of reform had been stopped by conservative opposition, the White House remained cautious about confronting vested economic interests. Though Roosevelt publicly blamed big business for the recession of 1937–1938, and encouraged his trust-busters to investigate how monopolistic practices kept the economy from recovering, the White House continued to explore with business leaders the idea of reviving an NRA-like cartel approach to economic recovery.[59] The turn to fiscal policy in the late 1930s was also less radical than it might have seemed. As Herbert Stein has argued, in deciding in 1938 to commit government to economic stimulation through fiscal and monetary policy, Roosevelt made "essentially a conservative choice involving the least disruption of the existing economic system and the least political struggle."[60] The very idea of national economic planning was rejected. The pursuit of industrial and labor market policies—to the extent that any public agencies in America pursued them—was left in the hands of state and local governments.[61] Roosevelt also continued to court the South long after southern Democrats had abandoned his domestic agenda. Despite Eleanor Roosevelt's entreaties and to the great frustration of many of the administration's liberal supporters, the White House refused to publicly back any of the scores of civil rights bills introduced into Congress between 1937 and 1944, even distancing itself from its earlier support for a federal law abolishing the poll tax.[62]

## The Window Closes

It is clear, in retrospect, that with the signing of the NLRA in July 1935, and the SSA two months later, the New Deal reached its climax. Despite Roosevelt's best efforts to woo them, one by one the economic interests courted by the administration in the early New Deal abandoned the president. The 1935 concessions to labor and the administration's support for the Public-Utilities Company Holding Act signaled the beginning of the end.[63] The proposed Revenue Act's tax increases on large corporations, the rich, and inheritances, "greatly intensified" business opposition to Roosevelt's fiscal policies. The 1936 undistributed profits tax was the last straw.[64] In the end, even as Roosevelt tried to resurrect American capitalism, most business interests decided to fight social change, resisting the expansion of unions, lobbying against social spending, and fighting any turn to the left. Large farmers also turned against the expansion of federal power and joined business in a coalition against reform—once they had secured price supports and control over local agricultural arrangements through the AAA.[65] Rather than help the administration press the New Deal forward, commercial farmers worked against programs like the WPA and the Farm Security Administration (FSA) and opposed expansionary economic policies.

Changes in the preferences of economic elites were clearly reflected in Congress: despite Roosevelt's continued personal popularity and strong public support for the New Deal, congressional resistance to social reform stiffened even as the administration prospered at the polls. In 1936, Roosevelt's tax increases were rejected and the WPA cut back.[66] Nor could Roosevelt's landslide victory stop conservative opposition from congealing. Roosevelt's Court-packing plan, submitted to Congress in February 1937 with little consultation, only made matters worse, providing the administration's opponents with a clear and convincing argument against the president's leadership. In place of a social-democratic coalition for reform, a conservative coalition against change emerged, bringing together pro-business Republicans, southern Democrats, state and local leaders threatened by nationalizing reforms, and conservative Democrats in the East and Midwest who had survived the party's left turn. In the name of states' rights and fiscal responsibility, they began to check the New Deal.[67]

The New Deal revived briefly in 1938 but it was a false spring. As the economy plummeted for a second time, Roosevelt finally embraced the idea that government had to use fiscal and monetary policy to manage the economy, and congress agreed again to prime the pump.[68] For a moment, deficit appropriations revived the WPA, the PWA, and the FSA.[69] A second Agricultural Adjustment Administration again helped farmers with price supports and conservation payments in return for crop and acreage controls. Supported by business interests who wanted to standardize wages and hours, the Fair Labor Standards Act (FLSA) made permanent the NRA codes forbidding child labor and setting minimum wages and maximum hours.[70]

But the tide in Congress was clearly shifting rightward, and these victories proved partial and temporary. Congressional conservatives repealed the undistributed profits tax and reduced the capital gains tax. As the first had done, the second AAA helped the largest, most efficient growers at the expense of poorer farmers and farm workers. The FLSA excluded many of those most in need, including large numbers of workers in mining, agriculture, domestic service, and retail trade. Finally, with war in Europe looming, Roosevelt abandoned domestic reform entirely in 1939 to seek support for his foreign policies, much to the dismay of Eleanor Roosevelt and the liberals who had rallied around her.

With the onset of war, and then postwar reconstruction, congressional conservatives grew in strength. Southern Democrats, who had joined Republicans to defeat civil rights initiatives in the 1930s, began to work closely with them on labor issues as well.[71] Proposals to restructure or plan the economy were dismissed: both the FSA, which tried to represent poor farmers within the administration, and the National Resources Planning Board, which offered structural analyses of the business cycle and suggestions for planning the economy, were terminated.[72]

Perhaps most important, liberal efforts to add to the newly created welfare state a government-guaranteed right to a job were soundly rejected. In his January 1944 State of the Union address, Roosevelt had called for a far-reaching "Economic Bill of Rights" that would have deepened the New Deal's commitment to social justice and transformed the American welfare state. Although Roosevelt had not followed through on his address, congressional liberals, including urban liberals from the Northeast and some western progressives, did. Supported by a broad spectrum of liberal and labor groups, including the National Farmers Union, the AFL and the CIO, and the National Association for the Advancement of Colored Persons (NAACP), they introduced the Full Employment Act of 1945, which promised to "all Americans" who were "able to work and seeking work" the "right to useful, remunerative, regular, and full-time employment" and created a National Production and Employment Budget, under the control of the executive branch, to coordinate that effort.[73]

But most business elites, whose influence had grown as Roosevelt brought corporate leaders into government to plan and implement the war economy, opposed the measure and with the support of the commercial farm lobby, congressional Republicans, and southern Democrats, they fought to defeat this effort to extend the welfare state. With the conservative coalition intact, and organized labor divided and distracted by other issues, the bill was gutted.[74]

Once Republicans gained control of both chambers in 1947, liberalism's prospects only worsened. The antiunion Taft-Hartley Act was passed over Harry Truman's veto. A last-ditch effort by progressives within the Truman administration to restructure agricultural programs in the interest of poorer farmers collapsed.[75] Even after winning the White House and regaining Congress in 1948, the Democrats could not reverse the tide: the conservative coalition blocked every one of Truman's Fair Deal social initiatives, including national health care, public education, civil rights legislation, and the repeal of the Taft-Hartley Act. By the late 1940s, congressional conservatives had grown strong enough to stop in its tracks any effort to complete the New Deal, no matter which party controlled the government.

## The New Deal

While the New Deal changed fundamentally the state's relationship to the economy, both the structural obstacles and Roosevelt's decision in the early New Deal to accommodate business and the South limited what reform could accomplish. To be sure, much ground was gained. For the first time in American history, public relief and public employment were made readily available. The Federal Emergency Relief Act (FERA) and the CWA provided money and jobs to millions of the unemployed. In two years alone, FERA distributed more than $3 billion in direct emergency relief. At FERA's peak in April 1934, 4.5 million families and single persons were receiving aid. At its height in January 1934, the CWA employed over 4.2 million blue- and white-collar workers on public works projects. In 1936, the WPA—which had replaced the CWA—gave more than 3 million workers public sector jobs.[76] New regulatory institutions increased public supervision of banking and securities; stabilized agricultural commodity markets; and pledged to workers the right to join unions and to bargain collectively, free from employer harassment. The FLSA prohibited child labor and empowered the federal government to set national minimum wages and maximum work hour rules.

In social policy, the United States accomplished in one year what Europe had taken several decades to achieve: with the passage of the SSA, the New Deal committed government to providing a modicum of income security to working-class families and a minimal safety net for the urban and rural poor. The new unemployment insurance program created a joint, federal-state program that provided covered workers with cash benefits paid for by employers. The old-age pension program established a national trust fund, financed by payroll taxes on employers and employees, giving covered workers retirement benefits based on their work record. The new public-assistance program provided federal subsidies to states that offered cash benefits to the needy aged, the needy blind, and dependent children. In economic policy, the United States vaulted ahead of all of democratic Europe except Sweden, using fiscal policy in the late 1930s to steer the economy, and then formally embracing Keynesianism in the Employment Act of 1946.

But the cost of compromise is also striking. Roosevelt paid an especially high price for business and southern support in the early New Deal. Worried about alienating these two sectors and the impact that their opposition would have on Congress, New Dealers drew back from policies that would have substantially changed the distribution of public benefits and burdens among workers, farmers, and upper-income groups, or increased the state's influence over the economy as a whole. The result is evident across a wide range of policies. Consider FERA. The standard relief benefit provided recipient families with only one-fourth of a minimum subsistence income.[77] And because the program accommodated local interests, benefits varied widely from state to state, and "arbitrary and artificial" standards kept many needy people off the rolls.[78] Migrant agricultural workers proved particularly vulnerable. After 1935, the federal government returned the task of direct relief to the states and localities, despite the fact that many local officials still subscribed to the poor-law philosophy and worked hard to deny general relief to all but the most unemployable. In many jurisdictions, aging unskilled workers, women with dependent children, and the temporarily disabled were routinely denied benefits, notwithstanding the shortage of jobs for even the most eligible workers.[79]

The New Deal's effort to replace direct relief with jobs was equally problematic. Because the government would not spend enough, job seekers overwhelmed the agencies offering work. The WPA employed only a small portion of the unemployed (on average, the federal government managed to hire between 25% and 30% of the jobless between 1935 and 1940).[80] As the WPA's critics pointed out, the proffered jobs were usually less than satisfactory, often low-paid make-work. Legislative restrictions—Congress had forbidden the WPA to compete against private industry—and administrative problems, including a lack of skilled supervisory personnel, equipment shortages, and inadequate job training, eroded worker morale and public confidence in the program. The rule that only one family member could be enrolled discriminated against women and large families. At the end of 1936, intense opposition from the right, including Republicans and business leaders who opposed any federal presence in the job market, caused sharp cutbacks. WPA rolls were abruptly reduced. The agency's budget was cut in half in 1937 and then, after a temporary increase in spending during the depression of 1938, cut again in 1939, when Congress ordered the WPA to drop all workers who had been enrolled in the program for more than 18 months.[81]

In several respects, Roosevelt's decision to accommodate southern economic interests crippled the SSA. Roosevelt's initial vision of the program was inclusive: old-age insurance was to be a national program covering all workers. Though public assistance would be administered locally, federal guidelines would assure that states offered benefits broadly and without favor. But led by southern representatives, the House Ways and Means committee removed agricultural and domestic workers from coverage under both the old-age and unemployment insurance programs. Southerners on the Senate Finance committee modified Aid to Dependent Children to give the states greater discretion to discriminate against blacks.[82] States were neither required to offer categorical assistance nor held to a national standard; those states that chose to aid the poor were given enormous discretion in setting eligibility requirements and benefit levels.[83] A provision that would have forced states to establish minimum old-age assistance benefits sufficient to assure "a reasonable subsistence minimum compatible with decency and health," was removed after Virginia Senator Harry Byrd denounced it as an infringement on "state sovereignty."[84] Rejecting recommendations from Roosevelt's more liberal advisors to hold out for uniform national standards in social policy, the administration accepted these amendments.[85]

New Deal economic reforms were equally equivocal. In combination, the SSA's regressive payroll taxes, the repeal of the undistributed profits tax, and reductions in the capital gains tax undercut efforts to make the tax structure fairer. The Employment Act did even less for workers. The original bill would have established the sort of indicative planning that the French were to create in the 1950s by committing the federal government to increasing spending until the economy had achieved full employment, and established the administrative capacity to undertake that effort. In contrast, the bill that passed contained no specific commitments to do anything to promote employment and created little institutional capacity to plan public or coordinate private investment. In fact, Congress stripped both the "right" to a job and the goal of full employment from the bill. In the place of a government-guaranteed right to a job, Congress created the Council of Economic Advisors (CEA) to suggest to the president how the government might achieve "maximum employment, production, and purchasing power."[86]

These concessions to the right not only limited what liberals could accomplish, they complicated future efforts to build and sustain a reform coalition. As Theda Skocpol and Margaret Weir have correctly argued, the failure to construct "a permanent, nationally coordinated system of social spending" also made it impossible to institutionalize the kind of social-democratic coalition that emerged at this time in Sweden.[87] Rather, the Democrats' failure to cement a class alliance in support of progressive social and economic policies or to mobilize the poor in support of the welfare state undermined the very base needed to sustain the left. Ultimately, this would leave the party dependent on more conservative "swing voters" who would exercise enormous influence over the party's policies once the memory of the Great Depression had faded.[88]

The specific social policies adopted in the 1930s also harmed later efforts to make the welfare state more generous. By building on the two-track system of public benefits established in the Progressive period, the SSA made invidious distinctions between the worthy and unworthy poor that would come back to haunt liberalism. Poor women, especially poor black women, were left to depend on Aid to Dependent Children (shortly to be renamed Aid to Families with Dependent Children [AFDC]), the least generous, most stigmatizing program of all. In the 1950s and 1960s, when changes in labor markets and demography would expand and transform AFDC's clientele, the white working- and middle-classes would rebel against the program, eventually helping to sustain a backlash against the welfare state itself.[89] Finally, despite the obvious growth in public provision, the social policy framework constructed during the 1930s left Americans unusually dependent on market sources of income. The unions quickly recognized this and turned back to collective bargaining to promote workers' interests. Eventually, the middle classes would see this too, and look for nonstatist approaches to economic security.

## The Path Not Taken

Institutions clearly limited what the New Dealers could accomplish. The separation of powers and the decentralized party system empowered Southern elites who wanted federal social policy to sustain racial discrimination. The Supreme Court's ability to say no to nationalizing legislation, as it did in 1935 when it invalidated the Railroad Pension Act, the NIRA, and the AAA, haunted the administration. With four hard-line conservative justices, every attempt to expand the federal government's role hung in the balance.[90] Disorganization and division on the left also undercut state-building efforts, both limiting organized labor's ability to force concessions from Roosevelt and encouraging the administration in the belief that looking rightward would not lead the left to revolt. Those on the left who did look elsewhere were imprisoned by electoral structures that made third-party campaigns seem quixotic.

But as we have seen, Roosevelt's strategic decision to build from the center mattered too. Even as the New Deal built new public institutions, concessions made to powerful market actors limited what those institutions could do for Americans. By looking right for support in the early New Deal rather than trying to assemble a social-democratic coalition within the Democratic party, Roosevelt undercut efforts to construct a more comprehensive welfare-state and, ultimately, to turn the Democratic party into a more certain vehicle for reform. When Roosevelt finally turned left in 1935, he did so hesitantly, despite the fact that the window of opportunity had already begun to close and the administration's business supporters had abandoned it. Even in 1937, notwithstanding a huge electoral victory, the president wavered, finally proposing the Supreme Court

packing plan, rather than an agenda of new social and economic reform that might have galvanized his coalition.

Still, it is fair to ask whether Roosevelt really had other choices.
Roosevelt could not simply ignore business opposition, or the concerns of southern Democrats. Both remained important players in
government and the party system; as we have seen, the South was
especially well-positioned to stop reforms that it found objection-
able, particularly when it worked with midwestern commercial
farmers and business interests who also objected to social reforms
in the interests of workers, small farmers, and the urban poor. Nor
was it unreasonable to disregard the left, particularly at the outset.
While many observers took seriously the idea that the country was
on the verge of a social revolution, it was drifting, not rebelling.
True, there was serious unrest, including farm strikes, the bonus
march, and Communist-led demonstrations of the unemployed.
Protest movements like the Farm Holiday Association and the
Townsend movement were well-organized. But passivity was just as
common as protest. The 1932 election had *not* sent a clear message. Both the Communists and Socialists did relatively poorly; Progressive Senator Smith Brookhart and Progressive Governor Philip
LaFollette of Wisconsin were defeated. Voters seemed to be throwing out the party that had been in power when the economy collapsed, not choosing liberals or progressives.[91] Because the unions
were consumed by their own organizational conflicts and uncertain
about how to advance workers' interests in the depression, they
*could* be kept at arms length.

As the administration feared, the Supreme Court *was* a problem
for reformers. After blocking the New Deal in 1935, the Court
seemed to go out of its way in the spring of 1936 to find the Guffey
Coal Conservation Act unconstitutional.[92] Nor would it have been
easy to realign the Democratic party. When Roosevelt finally lis-
tened to his liberal advisors and tried to purge anti–New Deal
Democrats from the party in 1938, he was rebuffed. Despite personally campaigning against several southern conservatives in the
primaries, local loyalties trumped the president's efforts to restructure his party.[93]

Nonetheless, it is possible to imagine a different strategy that
would have taken better advantage of the economic and political crisis to build a more substantial welfare state. Certain conditions
were, in fact, highly favorable to the left. In 1933, business was both
desperate and divided; some bankers and industrialists supported
emergency relief, the nationalization of the banking system, and
even government wage and price controls. Those who did not found
their influence diminished—by the nationalization of politics, which
undermined their structural power, and by the realignment of

the party system, which in so damaging the Republican party, had also circumscribed business actors' principle means of influencing legislation.

For its part, Congress, including a newly constituted congressional left, was quite receptive to reform. That left, spanning urban liberals like Wagner, Progressive Republicans like LaFollette, and old-style southern populists like Black wanted the administration to do more on farm, labor, relief, and antitrust issues. Moreover, the House had been reorganized, giving Roosevelt greater influence than previous presidents had enjoyed over the course of legislation. Progressive Republicans were available in the Senate to decide the issue in the administration's favor in that chamber.[94] The press and the public were also strongly supportive of presidential initiatives.

Conditions only improved in 1935, after the midterm elections gave Roosevelt a massive majority for the New Deal, while nearly eliminating the threat of Republican opposition. The country, and with it, Congress, seemed finally to be moving left.[95] A number of Democrats were elected to Congress in 1934 on radical platforms that included public ownership and "production-for-use" provisions.[96] There was also organized pressure from workers and poor farmers as what had been inchoate in 1932 began to take shape in 1934. Public opinion was clearly on the side of reform: polls in 1935 indicated that 77% of respondents wanted the government to find jobs for everyone who wanted to work; 68% wanted government to levy taxes sufficient to pay for public works jobs; 74% wanted free medical care for the poor.[97] The electorate's overwhelmingly positive response to Roosevelt's 1936 campaign rhetoric confirmed that the nation was ready for more change. Not only did the administration win an unprecedented electoral victory, but the Democrats scored the most dramatic congressional victory of any party since 1800, winning 76 Senate seats, and 331 of 435 House seats in the 75th congress.[98]

There were also good reasons *at the time* to doubt that the centrist strategy would work. By the summer of 1934, Roosevelt's "coalition of all interests" had already begun to break up in response to the Securities Exchange Act (which imposed controls on the stock market), the Communications Act (which created the Federal Communication Commission to regulate broadcasters), the Railroad Retirement Act (which established pensions for railroad workers), and the mounting deficit. In August 1934, Director of the Budget Douglas—a fiscal conservative with close ties to the business community—resigned. That same month, anti–New Deal businessmen from both parties formed the Liberty League to lobby against "radical" reform.[99] Indeed, Roosevelt's commitment to this strategy often left his progressive supporters confused and dismayed.[100]

What would have happened if Roosevelt had tried to marshal support from labor, the poor, small farmers, and the middle classes to pass more effective regulatory and more generous social-spending policies? It is possible that such a program would have had a galvanizing effect on Roosevelt's natural base and a salutary effect on the balance of power within his party. Several legislative options were available. Roosevelt could have attempted to nationalize the banking system in 1933; there was considerable support for it, even among some bankers (though not the big bankers that Roosevelt called to Washington to consult on the banking bill).[101] He could have supported stronger labor legislation earlier (including Senator Blacks' 30-hours bill, and the original version of Senator Wagner's Labor Disputes Act in 1934). The Agricultural Adjustment Act could have provided more aid for small farmers. A larger public works program financed by a progressive income tax (this is what the left in Congress wanted) would have provided jobs, incomes, and economic stimulation.[102] The administration could have also sent a clearer message about race relations by endorsing civil rights initiatives. A more redistributional social security system, relying less heavily on employee contributions, introduced and implemented as soon as possible (the original program was not scheduled to begin paying benefits until 1942), might have fixed popular support for public provision and encouraged demands for even more.

There is, of course, no guarantee that Roosevelt could have traveled this path successfully. Policies such as these would have provoked even greater opposition from business and the South. That opposition, as the administration feared, might have killed the forward momentum of reform. But these policies might also have provoked the political realignment that would have opened further (and kept open) the window of opportunity created by economic collapse.

Why did Roosevelt refuse to consider this alternative in the early New Deal? In part, the answer is that he miscalculated the depth and duration of business antagonism to reform. Until the very end, Roosevelt imagined that business would come to understand the administration's procapitalist orientation, and validate his centrist strategy. The very fact that at least some prominent business leaders supported federal old-age pensions and unemployment insurance reassured him. How could a welfare state be anathema to capitalism, as many businesses complained, if some of the largest firms and most influential business spokesmen, like Swope of GE and Folsom of Kodak, supported it? Support from these elites likely encouraged Roosevelt in the belief that business opposition to the New Deal was more shallow and less extreme than the more vocal trade associations made it seem, and would give way to grudging support once it had become apparent that Roosevelt was on their side.[103]

But more than miscalculation was at work. In the end, ideology took its toll—not the public's commitment to Lockean liberalism, as some would have it, but Roosevelt's own beliefs and values about capitalism and government. While Roosevelt was far more comfortable using government as a positive force than his predecessors had been, he had, as Kenneth Davis has written, an "unexamined basic commitment to Capitalism-as-Democracy" and an "intuitive recognition of, (and) instinctive aversion to any suggestion of fundamental change in the economic structure whereby power-and-property would be transferred from have to have-nots."[104] It was Roosevelt who insisted that, contrary to European practices, the new old-age pension system not draw any funding from general revenues. Though he would later explain this decision in political terms—a system based on contributory financing would be impossible to undo—Roosevelt's choice was entirely in keeping with his larger political project and his distaste for frankly redistributional policies.[105]

Roosevelt believed that the purpose of reform was, as he put it, "to save our system, the capitalistic system."[106] He liked, respected, and *wanted* to work with businessmen.[107] And since he intended to save capitalism, he thought that capitalists would want to work with him. Once rebuffed, he did become disillusioned with business leaders (particularly bankers), and this disappointment led him to attack "economic royalists" in the 1936 campaign.[108] But to the very end, Roosevelt's commitment to the capitalist system remained intact. This is not to say that Roosevelt was indifferent to social injustice. But he was a moralist interested in humane reforms rather than a radical social reformer.[109] His vision of reform was hierarchical: his role was to develop social legislation for workers rather than empower workers (and especially unions) to govern themselves.[110]

Roosevelt's centrist strategy also fit perfectly with his view of the left: those who claimed to represent workers and the poor threatened to take the nation away from its economic foundations. The president's role was to resist radical reform, pulling the country back from the precipice. Davis's characterization of what Roosevelt thought of the Hundred Days, and of the 1934 midterm elections, makes the point best: "The main purpose, and indeed, achievement of all the tremendous flurry of the Hundred Days had thus been preventive, defensive, diffusive of radical energies. And this remained his own essential purpose."[111] Roosevelt thought that the 1934 midterm elections were a vindication of his efforts to fight off the radicals. His role was to continue to brake the speed of reform so that the nation might not travel too far to the left. On that assumption, he rejected the left's calls for radical action and continued instead with plans for work relief and for social insurance, hoping that these more modest reforms would satisfy the public's demand for change. But in limiting reform in this way, Roosevelt may have also helped bring the New Deal to a premature end.

# FIVE

# *The Great Society*

Changes in the political and institutional environment opened a third window in the 1960s, and liberals responded. The results were dramatic: a War on Poverty, the extension of medical care to the aged and the poor, the liberalization of public assistance, the expansion of social security. But rather than narrow the differentiation between the U.S. and European welfare states the gap widened: instead of building institutions that might support a commitment to full employment or developing social policies to help working families, the United States embraced a conservative version of Keynesianism that privileged tax cuts for business and the affluent and adopted a limited set of income-maintenance and social-service programs narrowly targeted on the very poor.

Proponents of the state-centered account have suggested that the Great Society was undone by the legacy of the New Deal. When presidents John Kennedy and Lyndon Johnson looked in the 1960s for new approaches to economic insecurity, they found ample precedent for expanding income-maintenance programs and using fiscal policy to promote economic growth, but little experience with or institutional support for creating the kinds of labor-market policies (including education, training, and relocation services for displaced and unemployed workers) popular in Europe.[1] Moreover, building on the two-track system introduced by the Progressives and deepened by the New Deal's bifurcation of social security and public assistance programs, reformers were led to adopt a targeted approach to poverty rather than rely on more universal economic or social policies.

But the New Deal's legacy was ambiguous: reformers could have also decided to expand the universalistic unemployment-insurance and old-age-pension programs established by the Social Security Act (SSA). Nor was administrative underdevelopment determinative; the decision to expand social services to fight poverty also meant that new institutions would have to be built. To understand the trajectory taken by the Great Society we need to look not only at the institutional inheritance, but at the continuing impact of class and

79

race on American politics, and efforts by Kennedy and Johnson to extend liberalism in the face of them.

## A Third Window Opens

Whereas economic crisis had precipitated reform in the 1930s, the Great Society was made possible by a very different set of circumstances. Rather than an economic collapse, followed by working-class mobilization, liberalism was renewed in the 1960s by both newly found affluence and the demands of African Americans, who had been left out, for a place at the table. Institutional changes, including the changing role of southern legislators and the growth of presidential power, also helped facilitate reform.

It is worth pointing out that economic growth was not nearly as robust as retrospective accounts of the "golden age" of American capitalism have suggested. Two recessions in the 1950s took their toll. By international standards, the American economy grew slowly and unemployment remained high (among the major industrial powers, only Italy's jobless rate was higher).[2] Nonetheless, between the end of World War II and the mid-1960s, average hourly earnings and median family incomes had grown steadily (up by 58% and 75%, respectively, between 1947 and 1967), and income inequality had declined significantly. All the while, corporate profits remained healthy.[3]

Rising standards of living and robust profit rates prepared the ground for reformers in several ways. Economic success softened business's attitude about the state; knee-jerk opposition to government and reform was replaced by a more pragmatic attitude about the state and capitalism. Business moderation can clearly be seen in the decline in the attractiveness of radical rightwing ideas among business actors. The appeal of organizations like the Liberty League, founded in the 1930s to oppose the New Deal, waned considerably. By the 1960s, few CEOs were interested in fighting the principle of government intervention into the economy, or even the idea of a welfare state.

In fact, there was good reason for corporate leaders to think that government might have had something to do with capitalism's success. Social and defense spending played an important part in the postwar boom. Many firms and industries had actually done quite well working with the same government regulatory agencies that conservative intellectuals attacked; the Cold War search for new, high-tech weapons was particularly rewarding for defense contractors. Even labor policy had helped: firms that were highly unionized benefited when the federal government established social standards that forced nonunion competitors to pay the same benefits that the unions had forced on them through collective bargaining. Many business elites also saw political advantage in supporting moderate reform. Business strategists clearly understood that their close ties to the Republican party and, by association, with unemployment and recession, were a liability that could best be addressed by embracing at least some version of progressive change.[4]

Incentives for business to cooperate with government only increased in the 1960s. For individual firms with multiracial work forces, civil rights laws promised to ease workplace tensions and shift the responsibility for managing racial conflict and making concessions to black workers from employers to government agencies. Public subsidies for urban redevelopment created new markets and enhanced existing real estate values.[5] Public programs that supplemented workers' private benefits transferred some of these costs to taxpayers.[6]

Prodded by the Committee on Economic Development (CED), many corporate executives realized that business generally prospered when Keynesian economic management stimulated consumer demand. Though American firms continued to experiment with welfare capitalism in the 1950s, they no longer saw it as an alternative to public provision. Indeed, many corporations came to prefer the contributory, employment-based social-insurance system controlled from Washington to state-level old-age public assistance programs that allowed for discretionary spending from general revenues. These firms could be relied on to support changes in the pension system, including increases in coverage, the tax rate, and the wage base. Even business groups such as the Chamber of Commerce and the National Association of Manufacturers, which traditionally represented smaller, more labor-intensive firms who were more likely to oppose social reform, gave up trying to repeal social security. In turn, congressional conservatives gave up their efforts to roll back the New Deal protections, despite Republican control of the White House.[7]

By the early 1960s, the CEOs of America's largest corporations had begun to rethink their position on economic policy as well, including the federal budget. Traditionally, even those business leaders most sympathetic to labor's demands worried about the political and economic implications of government social spending. They worried that liberals would use social-welfare dollars to buy workers' votes, that increased budgets would lead to larger federal deficits, and that deficits would lead to new taxes on the affluent and corporations. But under the tutelage of the CED, business elites warmed to the conservative version of Keynesianism proposed by the CED in which government stimulated demand by cutting taxes on business and upper-income groups rather than increasing redistributional social spending or public works.[8] By the time the Kennedy tax-cut proposal had made its way to Congress, even the Chamber of Commerce, the National Association of Manufacturers, the American Bankers Association, and the New York Stock Exchange had acceded.[9]

Although unsettled by Kennedy's public confrontation with United States Steel CEO Roger Blough over price increases, business's rapprochement with liberalism proceeded apace in the mid-1960s.[10] Barry Goldwater's nomination and his radical attacks on the foundations of the postwar political-economic order deepened the bond, and an unprecedented number of the nation's top CEOs supported Johnson in 1964.[11] And after having supported the president, big business leaders worked closely with the White House. With the economy booming, firms enjoying the fruits of the Kennedy-Johnson tax cut, and the administration backing social policies that neither limited corporate autonomy nor empowered anticorporate constituencies, conservatives found it hard to mobilize business opposition to the War on Poverty or the early Great Society.[12] Indeed, business groups helped formulate, implement, and lobby for many of the Great Society programs. The Poverty Advisory Council, for example, worked with the Johnson administration to plan antipoverty policies. The National Association of Home Builders and the National Association of Mutual Savings Banks lobbied Congress in support of the administration's proposal to create the Department of Housing and Urban Development (HUD).[13] As protest movements mounted in the mid-1960s, business's willingness to work with liberal reformers who did not want to revolutionize the system only increased. In the face of a rising tide of anticorporate sentiment, well-known business leaders, including the heads of Xerox, Ford, and Chase Manhattan encouraged their colleagues to take more seriously business's social responsibility to consumers and workers.[14]

Economic growth also made it easier for organized labor to get its views taken seriously by political elites. Having eschewed radical reform for liberalism, the labor movement could credibly claim to have helped make the system work. At the same time, the institutional stability that came with economic growth had helped the unions build a sophisticated electoral and lobbying apparatus to push for policies of interest to their members. Working with northern Democrats, organized labor kept the party's attention focused on health care, housing, education, the minimum wage, and public assistance. Indeed, the AFL-CIO single-handedly jump-started the "gray lobby" to push for benefits for the aged, creating and funding the National Council of Senior Citizens and other grass-roots organizations to lobby for Medicare in the early 1960s.[15] And having

helped elect Democratic majorities in Congress and having sent
Kennedy and Johnson to the White House, the labor movement
enjoyed unparalleled access to both institutions. Not surprisingly,
many of labor's demands—notably Medicare and social security reform—found their way onto the legislative agenda.

In this political context, the political mobilization of African
Americans against racial discrimination in the South had a galvanizing effect on public opinion in general and liberalism in particular.
Especially in the late 1950s and early 1960s, before civil unrest in
the nation's cities alienated many whites, civil rights demonstrations
generated enormous sympathy among northern voters and elites
and focused attention on unmet social problems. And while the civil
rights movement did not ask for an expansion of the welfare state,
by calling for an end to social inequality and the expansion of economic opportunity it helped prepare the ground for it. The movement's demand that the federal government end segregation also
helped legitimate the idea that national authorities had an obligation
to intervene in social problems where other actors, including states
and localities, would not.

The 1964 elections registered these changes as Lyndon Johnson
overwhelmed Barry Goldwater and voters elected the most liberal
Congress since 1936.[16] Even the early civil disorders reinforced the
sense that government had to do something to address America's
racial problems, pressuring the Democratic party to demonstrate its
commitment to reform and helping liberals in Congress make the
case for expanding social spending, if only to calm the nation's
cities.[17]

Changing conditions in the South and in government and party
institutions reinforced these tendencies. Like business, the South
had learned to live with a more powerful Washington. The region
had clearly benefited from federal programs such as the Tennessee Valley Authority, as well as from Cold War defense spending.
Changes in the southern economy and society had also lowered elite
resistance to federal laws ending Jim Crow. The mechanization of
agriculture and the shift into less labor-intensive crops reduced
southern commercial farmers' interest in maintaining the paternal-
istic system of labor control that they had devised after the Civil
War to maintain control over the black labor force. Because southern elites no longer were as eager to protect the low-wage rural
economy from reform, they cared less about whether southern legislators opposed social policies that might undermine that system.
Simultaneously, the industrialization of the South had created commercial and manufacturing interests who looked to the North for
skilled white-collar workers and capital investment. Seeking to market the region to the rest of the nation, these "new" southerners

worried about the South's political isolation. Both trends softened
elite opposition to the expansion of federal power.[18]

The civil rights movement also forced changes in the Democratic party. With expectations rising that government could and
should solve social problems, and congressional liberals waiting to
act on their long-delayed agenda of leftover New Deal-Fair Deal reforms, northern Democrats redoubled their efforts to break the
South's control over the party. In truth, the South's power had already diminished, as had southern influence in Congress. Not only
had the erosion of the solid South, begun in the late 1940s when
southern Democrats had split with the national party over President
Harry Truman's civil-rights policies, loosened the southern Democrats' influence over the party, northern Democrats (interested in
securing the urban black vote and the organizational support of the
industrial unions, whose black membership was growing) had become increasingly amenable to challenging southern Democrats on
civil rights. Changes in internal rules and procedures increased
their chances of success by further curtailing Southern committee
chairs' ability to block liberal legislation.[19]

### Complicating Factors

Reformers were not, however, entirely free to act as they wished.
Even as the barriers to reform lowered, a variety of complicating
factors remained. For one, while organized labor had finally come of
age, its position was not as secure as it, or its political allies, believed. Ironically, the moderation that had gained the unions access
to government had also undercut their influence. Acting as one
among many interest groups rather than as a class-conscious political movement, labor had given up its claim to speak for workers as
a whole. Some industrial unions, such as the United Auto Workers
(UAW), remained committed, in principle, to the social-democratic
vision of the welfare state articulated by the CIO in the 1930s and
1940s, including national economic planning, industrial democracy,
and sharply progressive income taxes. But the goals of the mainstream of organized labor were far tamer and less inclusive than
the rhetoric suggested. Indeed, throughout the postwar period, the
unions remained ambivalent about which strategy to pursue. On the
one hand, they could try to increase pressure on government and
employers by raising the level of industrial and political conflict. On
the other hand, they could work within the parameters established
by the "postwar accord," bargaining for higher wages and expanded
private benefits while lobbying for public policies such as fiscal
stimulation, public-sector spending, and stricter labor laws that
could supplement those efforts. For the most part, the labor move-

ment split the difference, pursuing the "mixed-benefit" strategy developed in the late 1940s while focusing on collective bargaining.[20]

Even the former CIO unions, the champions of political action, focused on organizational-maintenance issues and the collective bargaining process. Although the CIO had committed itself wholeheartedly to the fight for control of Congress in the 1940s, the industrial unions continued to emphasize wage and benefit negotiations rather than public provision. After World War II, the best organized industrial workers all but gave up on the struggle for universal public provision to wrestle with employers over private benefits, including health insurance, which had been dropped from the Social Security Act (SSA).[21]

As a result, despite their regular participation in liberal political coalitions, the unions' support was rock solid only when proposed reforms were both of immediate economic interest to organized workers and politically feasible in the short term. Equally important, organized labor's determined pursuit of the mixed-benefit strategy made it almost impossible to mount an effort to win universal public benefits or redistributional taxes. The resources spent by American unions to wrest benefits from employers for already-organized workers were resources not spent on lobbying for a different welfare state. Success in pressuring employers to establish internal labor markets that benefited existing workers and to expand private benefits removed practical incentives for unions to pressure government to expand the welfare state for everyone.[22]

In fact, although not immediately apparent at the time, the unions' organizational clout was already in decline. Membership had peaked, and the unions' ability to organize new workers had deteriorated precipitously in the decade between the merger of the AFL and CIO and Johnson's election in 1964.[23] Nor was the labor movement doing much to reverse the tide. Despite declining membership, the AFL-CIO did little to organize new workers or to address the needs of a rapidly changing workforce in which service-sector jobs were replacing manufacturing jobs, and women and black workers were growing in numbers and importance. Instead, the AFL-CIO leadership remained committed to the established strategy: influence government by gaining access to established elites while quietly lobbying the major executive and legislative players.

Nowhere were the limits of this strategy more obvious than in the failed struggle in 1965 to repeal Section 14(b) of the Taft-Hartley Act. In this case, labor went toe to toe with business and lost decisively. Although both the unions and the White House—sympathetic to organized labor's demands—sought partners in this struggle, neither could muster the votes to break a Senate filibuster over the opposition of a coalition of southern Democrats and Republicans.[24]

Organized labor's ability to support a liberal agenda was also undermined by racial divisions within the working class. Conflicts over race made it harder for the unions to expand their base and simultaneously tempered many union members' (and leaders') enthusiasm for social reform. The labor movement was an early proponent of civil rights, of course, supporting the desegregation of public accommodations in the 1950s and helping Johnson pass landmark civil-rights legislation (including Title VII of the 1964 Civil Rights Act, which prohibited discrimination in union constitutions and practices). But in the 1960s, the unions were not eager to accept black workers. The AFL had discriminated against African Americans from its founding, and most member unions had either excluded blacks from membership entirely or organized them into separate unions under the supervision of white workers. Well into the 1960s, even while labor leaders were endorsing civil-rights legislation, many unions continued to discriminate against black workers by prohibiting black membership, creating and maintaining segregated locals, and denying black aspirants access to well-paying "ladder" jobs.[25]

When union practices finally came under scrutiny in the late 1950s and early 1960s, most unions reacted defensively, as Jill Quadagno has documented. Only the UAW supported a campaign by the NAACP and black unionists to bring the issue of racial discrimination to the federation's 1959 convention. To the contrary, the AFL-CIO censured A. Philip Randolph, the head of the Sleeping Car Porters and the only African American in a top leadership position, for publicly criticizing the unions' racial policies. When civil rights activists picketed union construction sites in the early 1960s, the trade unions resisted internal reform. Organized labor did take token steps to refurbish its liberal image, publicly pledging to end discrimination. But the unions fought hard to control membership rolls, job referrals, apprenticeship programs, and job training—the very mechanisms that favored white workers. The building-trades unions were particularly recalcitrant, arguing that government job-training programs for minorities would weaken union-controlled apprenticeship programs.[26]

In the mid-1960s, even as they supported the War on Poverty, George Meany and the leaders of the building trades openly opposed job-training programs sponsored by the Office of Economic Opportunity (OEO) because these programs limited the unions' ability to discriminate in favor of existing members and their children.[27] As a result, black employment "remained minuscule" in the craft and construction unions, with little improvement into the early 1970s. The industrial unions did better, but still disappointed civil-rights activists. Union seniority and transfer rights made it especially hard for blacks to find high-paying and prestigious skilled jobs in many industries.[28] Even after the AFL-CIO agreed to work with the federal government to desegregate, little happened. The AFL-CIO's Outreach program reached few workers. The affirmative-action program adopted by the building trades accomplished little.[29] Even labor's political alliance with the civil rights movement was thinner than appeared: while the UAW contributed to Martin Luther King Jr., it did little to publicize the cause of civil rights or educate its own members.[30]

Having failed to do more to confront racism themselves, the unions were poorly positioned to keep their white members loyal to liberalism as racial conflicts exploded. Though many factors were at play in the revolt of the working-class ethnics, including rising crime rates and student protests, opposition in the white, ethnic enclaves of the North to "enforced" integration, including open housing and school desegregation, fed the blue-collar revolt. As Congress stepped up enforcement of civil-rights laws outside of the South, northern opinion turned against liberalism. Working-class support for Democratic candidates in the big northern cities sagged, and white enthusiasm for civil rights declined.[31]

Urban riots reinforced this retreat, feeding public demands for law and order and public disaffection with the party of liberalism. Republicans quickly learned how to exploit these fissures and resentments, turning white resistance to enforced integration, opposition to student protests and the counterculture, and fear of crime into opposition to the same federal government that had so recently been seen to champion working-class interests. Conservative candidates who were out of step with the electorate on most other issues benefited, pulling just enough white voters who otherwise supported populist economic programs away from northern liberal Democrats to undermine the Democratic party's ability to sustain the Great Society.

Organized labor's ambivalence about the poor further tempered its enthusiasm for a more comprehensive welfare state. The unions did push to improve public assistance, lobbying to liberalize eligibility and increase payments, and to add auxiliary benefits, including food stamps and public housing, to the mix. Organized labor served on the OEO Labor Advisory Board, and established the AFL-CIO Anti-Poverty Office to work with local organizations of the poor. But organized labor also saw the poor as an economic threat, worrying that large-scale, government-run manpower-training programs would undermine union control of apprenticeship training, that "dumping" millions of newly trained workers on the labor market would drive down the wages and benefits of already-employed workers, and that government wage subsidies to private employers to hire marginal workers—or a "guaranteed income"—would cause employers to lower their own wage offers, making workers even more dependent on government benefits.[32]

As a result, the unions were less than enthusiastic about efforts to end poverty as such, preferring instead to attack the problem conventionally by stimulating the economy, raising the minimum wage, and improving social security. When it became clear that a concerted attack on poverty would be launched, labor insisted that the new programs be as narrowly targeted as possible—focusing on the most marginal workers—and that job creation programs be confined to the public sector. Only in this way, they believed, could the disruptive impact of antipoverty programs on private labor markets and organized workers' wages be contained.[33]

Despite business support for state intervention in the postwar period and changes in the southern political economy, reformers also continued to face problems from the right. Business support for reform, even for policies designed to appease business interests, was uncertain. American capitalists remained suspicious of social spending and labor-market programs that threatened to boost wages, raise taxes, or limit managerial prerogatives. If most large American corporations no longer fought tooth-and-nail against the growth of social benefits and coverage, they still did not want to see a major expansion of either. If public benefits were to increase, business wanted workers to pay for them, preferably through payroll taxes.[34] Most business leaders also wanted balanced budgets, preferring "sound" fiscal policies even as they accepted the turn to Keynesianism. Business tolerance of the Great Society's social initiatives depended on exactly what was being proposed. Policies that interfered with corporate profits and labor discipline were highly unpopular: the Johnson administration's efforts to reform the unemployment system in 1965 and 1966 by imposing federal standards on state programs (including uniform duration and benefit levels and extended benefits) were killed by a broad coalition of business interests.[35] The Medicare proposal drew fierce resistance from the insurance industry, which joined the American Medical Association to wage what was likely the most expensive lobbying campaign in American history against the bill.[36]

American business leaders also wanted government to let private, profit-making entities play as large a role as possible in producing and distributing whatever new public benefits and social services were created. The National Alliance of Businessmen made its support for new job-training programs for the hard-core urban unemployed contingent on the creation of a mixed public-private effort, rejecting both expanded public works and public service employment.[37] Health insurers agreed to support Medicare as long as government health insurance for the aged did not limit insurers' au-

tonomy or profits. Business elites demanded that federal labor market policies be confined to the fringe of the labor market where they
would interfere as little as possible with employer autonomy.

Although corporate elites maintained good relations with Johnson in the first years of his administration, they also worried that
liberals would hijack the Democratic party and that social spending
would soar. When budget deficits did increase under the combined
pressure of military and social spending, key business leaders lobbied the administration to cut expenditures, demanding cuts in social programs in return for their support for the tax surcharge
needed to help pay for the war.

Nor had the southern political economy changed enough to free
liberals from the fear of southern opposition in Congress. While the
South could no longer veto any and all civil rights legislation, the
racial caste system continued to exert a powerful influence on southern politics, and southern legislators continued to wield enough influence to complicate northern Democratic efforts to press a liberal
agenda. Those southern employers who relied on low-wage labor still
scrutinized new social policies and labor legislation; for them, even
modest improvements in welfare payments (such as increasing welfare benefits to levels that would have done little to disrupt northern
labor markets) would have provided black workers with a way to escape the harshest exploitation.[38] And while southern industrialists
wanted to refurbish the South's image, they did not want federal legislation that would either weaken their competitive advantage over
northern industry or help southern workers organize.[39] Finally, many
working and middle southern whites still opposed reforms that would
dismantle Jim Crow and the racial privileges that they enjoyed.[40]

In response, southern representatives fought federal programs
once they moved from symbolic affirmations of equality to actually
challenging segregation in housing, jobs, and education. Well into
the 1960s, the South's commitment to racial inequality remained an
obstacle to extending the welfare state's reach: southern representatives required constant attention from the party's leadership to
prevent them from joining with Republicans to block the northern
Democrats' legislative agenda, as they had done in the 1930s. And
once again, southern resistance to reform proved especially effective where opposition to racial liberalism dovetailed with big business's concerns about the growth of government. The shift in northern white opinion in the mid-1960s further complicated matters.

## The Flood Tide of Liberalism

As they had in the 1930s, political and institutional factors presented reformers with both an opportunity and a difficult choice in
the 1960s. American politics was again moving left. In 1964, voters

sent the most liberal Congress to Washington since 1936. But even as liberalism surged, the conservative coalition that had dominated congressional politics remained in the wings, to be reconstituted if voters turned against reform, or if enough business interests went into opposition. Johnson himself was acutely aware of the problem, warning his advisers that the window of opportunity would close quickly. In the end, Kennedy and Johnson in the 1960s faced the same choice that Franklin Roosevelt had faced thirty years earlier: whether to build from the political center and accommodate those economic interests that might fight reform or to move decisively to the left, attempting both to mobilize the Democratic party's mass base and, if possible, realign the party system.

## Kennedy

Kennedy responded cautiously. Though he adopted the congressional Democrats' domestic policy agenda as his own, he refused to take on the hardest fights, including civil rights, until the last possible moment.

Kennedy's approach to the economy was extremely conciliatory: the administration went to great lengths to assure corporate leaders who were worried about a Democratic administration after the pro-business Eisenhower years that the Democrats were equally concerned about corporate profits and the incomes of the rich. Two early missteps—the highly publicized confrontation between commerce Secretary Luther Hodges and the Business Advisory Council, and the president's fight with U.S. Steel over price guidelines—initially soured relations with business leaders, but Kennedy redoubled his efforts to demonstrate his administration's faith in business. Plans to increase social spending and reform the tax code were dropped in 1962, and, to the great relief of the business community, the idea that the United States should try to match the European record on employment was officially abandoned.[41] The White House also embraced the conservative reinterpretation of Keynesianism: tax cuts, not social spending or labor market interventions, to stimulate consumer spending and business investment.[42] In rapid succession, the administration endorsed an accelerated depreciation schedule to reduce the taxes of large, capital-intensive corporations, an investment tax credit for all companies, and a proposal, sent to Congress in January 1963, to reform the tax code and cut taxes across the board, with substantial benefits for corporations and upper-income earners.[43] As if this were not enough, the White House agreed to drop tax reform entirely in response to intense business lobbying and asked Congress only for tax cuts.[44]

Liberals and organized labor were not ignored; the administration was concerned about maintaining its links to the party's mass base and northern supporters. The administration adopted the congressional Democrats' already-established domestic policy agenda largely as was, committing the White House to backing moderate increases in social spending for urban renewal, manpower training, aid to education, health care for the aged and the poor, and the redevelopment of depressed areas. But Kennedy was personally uninterested in domestic policy and put off by the need to court congressional leaders in order to pass domestic legislation. When conservatives blocked the administration's major social programs, Kennedy turned his attention elsewhere.[45]

Kennedy equivocated on civil rights, hoping to maintain close ties to the South and avoid an intraparty struggle. The administration's early record was not entirely without merit. It created the Committee on Equal Employment Opportunities in 1961 to investigate discriminatory hiring practices. It increased the number of blacks employed by the federal government. Five African Americans, including future Supreme Court Justice Thurgood Marshall, were nominated to the federal judiciary. The Interstate Commerce Commission (ICC) was pressured to ban segregated facilities in interstate travel. The Justice Department was involved in voting-rights complaints against southern officials. But just as often, the administration stalled or rejected requests for help, claiming that federalism denied the national government the police power to intervene when local officials declined, even if it left civil rights activists vulnerable to repression. Indeed, the White House left decisions about how best to protect freedom riders and sit-in protesters to the Federal Bureau of Investigation (FBI), despite the director's antipathy to Dr. King and other civil rights activists. Kennedy also resisted calls for new civil rights legislation. Action on a campaign promise to eliminate discrimination in public housing was deferred until after the 1962 congressional elections. Two early executive orders issued by the White House to deal with discrimination by unions and contractors on federal projects proved toothless.[46]

Widely publicized police violence against civil rights marchers in Birmingham, Alabama finally forced the administration's hand in May 1963, leading Kennedy to propose long-delayed civil rights legislation, including provisions covering voting rights, public accommodations, and public education. But even that legislation was "crafted cautiously" with an eye to congressional moderates: before the Department of Justice could sue in support of nondiscriminatory public accommodations, individuals had to initiate suits on their own. The section on schools dealt only with de jure discrimination. Police brutality and employment discrimination were left unaddressed.[47]

Fatefully, prodded by advisers who feared that the rightward tilt in economic policy would make the administration seem indifferent to the poor, the White House decided to balance tax cuts with a new, federal antipoverty policy.[48] The federal government was already involved in welfare, of course: Aid to Dependent Children, renamed Aid to Families with Dependent Children (AFDC), had grown dramatically in the 1950s. In 1961, with White House support, Congress had created AFDC-UP (for "unemployed parent"), which allowed states to offer welfare payments to two-parent families in which the principal breadwinner was unemployed and had exhausted unemployment benefits. But liberals wanted more, and a Health, Education, and Welfare Department (HEW) task force, led by Wilbur Cohen, a long-time advocate of expanding public provision, endorsed their demands, recommending federal support for general assistance, higher welfare payments, and the equalization of benefits across states. The task force presented Kennedy with a dilemma: to satisfy liberals, the administration had to make good on at least some of these recommendations, but any effort to nationalize social policy or to increase the welfare rolls was guaranteed to spark controversy, and encourage southern Democrats to resist the administration's domestic agenda.[49] Once again, Kennedy sought the middle ground. The Public Welfare Amendments (PWA) of 1962 gave something to both northern and southern Democrats. Liberals secured a five-year extension of the AFDC-UP program and a small pot of new money for targeted, rehabilitative services for the poor. Southern Democrats were given a provision that allowed the states considerable flexibility in the implementation of these new welfare services. The PWA also required the stricter enforcement of existing restrictions on benefits and eligibility.

More important, however, in a key decision in late 1962, the administration decided to explore the possibility of building on this base by developing a more far-reaching antipoverty initiative. The Council of Economic Advisors' (CEA) staff was assigned the task of developing a proposal for the 1964 legislative program, and three days before his death Kennedy committed the administration to act on the issue as part of the 1964 legislative agenda.[50] Still, political considerations sharply limited what the White House was willing to propose. Despite the CEA's conclusion that direct transfers could remove all the poor from poverty for $11 billion a year and that the fiscal surplus that would follow from the implementation of the tax cut would support this new level of social expenditure, White House advisors rejected cash assistance of this magnitude as "a political and budgetary impossibility."[51] To the end, the political constraints on Kennedy remained an important part of the administration's policy planning.

## *Johnson*

From one perspective, it appears that Johnson simply followed Kennedy's lead, adopting the tax cut, the omnibus civil rights bill and the antipoverty initiative as his own. A case could be made that all that separated the two presidents were opportunity (because of Kennedy's assassination, Johnson could ask Congress for more), interest (unlike Kennedy, Johnson was not bored by domestic policy), and skill (a master politician, Johnson was better at manipulating Congress). Indeed, Johnson took great pains to link his 1964 domestic-policy agenda to Kennedy's unfinished New Frontier. But on closer examination, Johnson's vision of government was substantially different. Much more was involved than simply breathing life into stalled legislation. Johnson constantly raised the stakes, setting more ambitious goals and arguing for a far more active role for the federal government. Where Kennedy had been content to carry legislation developed by congressional liberals in the 1950s, Johnson wanted to push beyond the New Deal to tackle new problems with new solutions, from air and water quality to occupational safety and health regulation.

Not every subject was new, but Johnson's more ambitious vision was reflected even in the administration's approach to agenda items inherited from the Kennedy administration. Kennedy's tentative foray into welfare reform became a War on Poverty, including an Office of Economic Opportunity to pull together existing low-income programs into a single, tightly focused effort. A wide variety of new programs targeted on the most disadvantaged was instituted, including VISTA, the Job Corps, Upward Bound, the Neighborhood Youth Corps, Head Start, Operation Mainstream, and Community Action. The administration also returned to and redefined the public housing program begun during the New Deal, winning congressional approval for a new Department of Housing and Urban Development in 1965, and in 1968, authorization to build 600,000 federally subsidized housing units per year for a decade.[52] The Food Stamp Act turned the existing food program, largely an outlet for farmers' surplus commodities, into a supplementary income-maintenance program to expand the purchasing power of the poor. Medicaid, passed in 1965, created a means-tested entitlement to health care. Kennedy's carefully calibrated civil rights bill became a major assault on discrimination.

Indeed, civil rights became Johnson's top legislative priority and, after winning legislative approval in June 1964, the administration set out to enforce it. The Justice Department became more aggressive in filing suits, and HEW began issuing far more stringent guidelines and timetables for school desegregation. Executive Order

11246, issued in 1965, prohibited discrimination in employment by firms doing business with the federal government, requiring them to take "affirmative action" to remedy past discrimination. In 1966, Johnson lent his support to fair housing legislation designed to deal with the roots of both school desegregation and urban poverty.[53]

But like Roosevelt, Johnson was also convinced that only a broad centrist coalition could sustain reform over the long term, and he sought to incorporate as many interests as possible into a cross-class, "big tent" coalition. Wherever possible, Johnson maintained close relationships with the Republican leadership in Congress and even wooed southern Democratic support as he pushed hard on civil rights.[54]

Predictably, this strategy took its toll on domestic policy (as it had in the 1930s). Unwilling to ask Congress to raise taxes on the upper and middle classes to fund new domestic spending, the Great Society was chronically underfunded. In his June 1965 speech at Howard University, Johnson declared that liberalism had to push beyond equality of opportunity to "equality as a fact and equality as a result." But to his aides, Johnson made clear that he would not raise taxes to finance the effort. Robert Lampman, a University of Wisconsin economist who worked with the CEA in the spring and summer of 1963 to gauge the size of the poverty population, had estimated that it would take $11 billion a year to lift the poor out of poverty. For its "unconditional" war, the administration proposed asking Congress for $1.5 billion, and later reduced that request to $962.5 million (and only $500 million of that was actually new money).[55] In fact, acutely aware of corporate concerns about increased social spending, Johnson promised to pare total expenditures to *below* Kennedy administration projections; business leaders were assured that defense cutbacks and administrative reforms would provide whatever new funds were needed to pay for social policy initiatives.[56]

In place of new social spending or income redistribution, the administration chose to rely instead on a combination of civil rights enforcement, fiscal stimulation, and social services, including psychological services, job training, and remedial education. The tight labor markets that everyone assumed would follow from Keynesian growth policies would provide all the jobs needed, and civil rights laws and antidiscrimination policies would open doors to those jobs for the poor and African Americans. Services would restore the discouraged's desire to work; job training would provide the newly motivated with the skills that employers wanted. Even after the Watts riots, when Johnson shifted the focus of the War on Poverty from community action to jobs, the administration eschewed job *creation* in favor of job *training*. The condition of the job seeker remained the focus of social policy, with government promoting on-the-job experience and classroom training to prepare the jobless poor—the workers at the end of the job queue—for work.[57]

In fact, the administration rebuffed calls for labor-market policies to deal with low wages, unemployment, and underemployment. Secretary of Labor Willard Wirtz's proposal to create jobs in place of transfer payments was ignored.[58] Proposals to do more to develop economically depressed areas were tabled. The supply of jobs, the quality of the jobs on offer, the availability of ladder jobs in inner cities—all were treated by the administration as secondary issues. As Henry Aaron would later comment,

> Perhaps the most striking characteristic of this view of the poverty cycle is the absence of any mention of the economic system in which it operates. Apart from the problem of high unemployment that the individual is powerless to solve, the poor person was viewed as poor because of shortcomings of his own that may be traceable to his own or his parents' poverty.[59]

The White House also made sure that the Great Society created opportunities for vested economic interests to make money. Sargent Shriver, the director of the antipoverty effort, assured the Business Council that, wherever possible, job training would be subcontracted to private firms, and companies that contributed to the antipoverty effort would be given generous tax deductions.[60] Employers were told that the small number of public-sector jobs to be created would be only a temporary step before moving onto permanent, private-sector, job ladders.[61] Medicare was designed to take the economic and professional interests of doctors, insurers, and hospitals into account, essentially providing third-party payments for fees determined by private entities, giving administration of the program to private carriers. In effect, the administration offered an open-ended public subsidy to the existing medical-care industry without imposing (indeed perhaps precluding) effective regulation.[62]

Finally, Johnson proved unwilling to give up his pursuit of military victory in Vietnam despite its impact on his domestic policy agenda. At first, Johnson delayed escalating the war in part to protect the Great Society from its repercussions. Even after he had decided in late 1964 to expand American involvement, he tried to do it "in a calibrated and incremental way" so as not to jeopardize the passage of his domestic legislation.[63] When the administration's intentions became apparent, Johnson resorted to hiding the war's costs, ordering Secretary of Defense Robert McNamara to falsify and hide the budget numbers, even from the Council of Economic Advisers and the Treasury. Nonetheless, the war's costs quickly mounted and took their toll on domestic reform. Whereas McNamara had predicted an increase of between $3 billion and $5 billion, the defense budget rose by $12.8 billion in 1965. The federal fiscal year (FY) 1966 deficit jumped to $9 billion, not the $1.8 billion the administration had forecast.[64]

Johnson publicly denied that there was any necessary trade-off between the war and domestic programs. In his 1966 State of the Union address, the president insisted that the nation could do both, and he proposed another round of social reforms to cement the Great Society, even while escalating the war: "This Nation is mighty enough, its society is healthy enough, its people are strong enough," he said, "to pursue our goals in the rest of the world while still building a Great Society here at home." Economic growth would allow government to pay for both, according to Johnson. Committed to the idea that the war would be costless, Johnson rejected the idea that taxes should be immediately raised to cover the likely shortfall. In the end, however, fiscal reality took hold: escalating costs made a mockery of the administration's economic planning and emboldened conservatives in Congress to demand cuts in social welfare programs to fund the war.

## The Window Closes

Discussing the prospects for Medicare legislation after his decisive victory in 1964, Johnson warned his aides that the window of opportunity that had just widened would close more quickly than they imagined. As he understood Franklin Roosevelt's experience, the most important lesson was the inevitability of opposition: "Every day while I'm in office, I'm going to lose votes. I'm going to alienate somebody," he told them; time was of the essence.[65] Johnson was right. In the end, he had twenty months, from the beginning of the second session of the 88th Congress in 1964 when he took over from Kennedy, to the end of the first session of the 89th in late 1965.

By 1966, changes on two fronts had combined to limit his opportunities severely. With new defense spending flowing into an economy already near full employment, prices and wages began to spike upward, alienating the financial and industrial interests who were so important to Johnson's big-tent coalition strategy. Business leaders drew the line in 1966, making their support for the Great Society contingent on capping the federal budget at $100 billion—a level already achieved under Kennedy. Pressure from the Business Council increased steadily from that point on, as corporate leaders worried about the budgetary and tax implications of mounting federal spending. With the costs of the war rising and inflation emerging, business stepped up pressure on Johnson to make domestic

cuts. In 1968, the Business Council insisted that Johnson reduce social spending by $6 billion if he wanted their support for a tax sur-
charge to finance the war.[66]

Racial conflict also tore at the big-tent coalition. Johnson had
counted on southern defections and, as he had anticipated, southern
whites showed their displeasure in 1964. The majority of white votes
in the deep South went to Goldwater, costing Johnson the states of
Mississippi, Alabama, South Carolina, Louisiana, and Georgia. But
northern whites also joined the retreat from liberalism. White resistance to enforced integration combined with white antipathy to
urban rioters and black militants to send blue-collar ethnics in search
of alternatives to the New Deal coalition. Intense opposition to open
housing led Congress to kill new omnibus civil rights legislation even
before the midterm election.[67]

The 1966 election returns pushed Congress further to the right.
In the House, the number of northern Democrats shrunk from 194
to 158, while Republicans gained forty-seven seats. Seven southern
Democrats who had supported the Great Society were defeated.
Democrats who won reelection, particularly moderates from northern, blue-collar districts, found themselves pressured to reign in the
party's racial liberalism. Equally important, unlike their predecessors, the new Republicans were more likely to be racial conservatives.[68] To be sure, the Democratic party still had a healthy majority
in both chambers, but in just two short years congressional conservatism had been revived. The leadership of the 90th Congress made
clear to the White House that it was not interested in and could not
sell new legislation or new social spending.[69]

Johnson was not easily deterred. Even after Congress had
turned against him in 1966, he continued to push for urban reform,
securing $5.3 billion over three years in federal subsidies for low-
cost housing, federal matching grants for education, health care,
crime prevention, and recreation services. The administration even
managed to secure new open housing legislation in 1968.[70] But increasingly the right found it could block or trim administration initiatives, particularly those that touched on race. An administration
effort to improve AFDC benefits in 1967 was met with fierce opposition from conservatives on the House Ways and Means and Senate
Finance committees, opposition widely perceived to be an effort to
punish black militants for urban unrest. Led by Wilbur Mills, the
Ways and Means committee completely rewrote the law, cutting
benefits, freezing program expansion, and requiring that recipients
work (and place their children in day care centers). These provision
were ultimately modified in the Senate, but the handwriting was on
the wall. A House bill to spend federal money to fight rat infesta-
tions in slums was roundly defeated. Even though it had become

painfully obvious that the War on Poverty would not solve the problem of inner-city joblessness and that private sector initiatives were
not going to provide the needed jobs, Congress simply lost interest
in black poverty.[71]

In turn, the growing backlash against liberalism left fiscal conservatives in a better position to force the administration to choose
between war and social reform. Mills' response to Johnson's pledge
to both prosecute the war and extend the Great Society made that
very clear: "The administration," he said, "simply must choose between guns and butter."[72] After wavering, Johnson finally agreed in
his 1967 State of the Union address for a two-year, 6% surcharge
on corporate and personal income taxes to finance the war. Conservative Democrats and Republicans responded by demanding cuts in
the Great Society. At a June 1967 meeting, Johnson accepted the
principle. After another year of negotiations and Johnson's decision
not to run again, a final agreement was reached: taxes were increased by $10 billion and spending cut by $6 billion.

## The Great Society

As the New Deal had done, the Great Society changed the state's
relationship to the economy significantly. But as had also happened
in the 1930s, political and institutional constraints—and presidential
responses to them—had taken their toll. It is important not to un-
derestimate what was accomplished. New entitlements to food and
health care were established. Federal spending on nutrition soared:
food stamp spending alone increased from $36 million in 1965 to
$1.9 billion in 1972, while federal spending on other food programs,
including school lunches and dietary supplements for women and
young children, more than doubled (from $870 million to over $1.8
billion).[73] Congressional action, court decisions, and civil unrest
helped extend AFDC to constituencies that had been left unpro-
tected in the 1930s. Political education by welfare rights organizations, including agencies funded by the government, led more people to assert these rights.[74] The "takeup" rate increased sharply and
by the end of the 1960s nearly 90% of the poor who qualified were
receiving AFDC.[75] The War on Poverty's focus on opportunity, even
if it overemphasized behavior, broke new ground by attempting to
explain poverty rather than simply blame and punish the poor. With
spending on both the poor and the aged increasing sharply, total social spending leaped upward, more than doubling as a percentage of
gross national product (GNP) between the early 1960s and the mid-
1970s.[76]

Contrary to the often-repeated claim that the War on Poverty
failed, a good deal was actually accomplished. Medicaid and Medi-

care brought first-time medical care to a substantial number of the nation's poor. Medicaid led to a dramatic increase in the number of prenatal medical visits by poor women. By lowering legal barriers to eligibility and increasing the value of welfare benefits, the poor were more likely to seek and get financial assistance from the government. Black poverty rates declined from 39.3% in 1967 to 31.4% in 1973;[77] poverty among children declined from 16.3% to 14.4% during the same period.[78] Though new government programs were not the only factors at work, a substantial amount of the reduction in the poverty rate at this time *was* the direct result of increased transfers: government programs were five times more effective in reducing poverty rates than was economic growth.[79] Infant mortality rates dropped significantly, particularly among blacks and the poor; life expectancy increased; and the gap between black and white life expectancy narrowed.[80] The 1966 amendments to the Fair Labor Standards Act (FLSA) extended coverage to low-wage workers in hospitals and nursing homes, schools, hotels and restaurants, food processing companies, and big farms. The 1967 amendments to the Social Security Act increased old-age benefits and by raising the wage base, made the system more progressive.

But as in the New Deal, the limits of reform are also striking. Antipoverty programs were never well-funded. OEO's initial budget was very modest, and most of it went to administrative costs and providers' fees, not to the poor.[81] And while these programs grew rapidly in size, they never constituted a significant part of government spending: in 1972, all OEO and *related* special antipoverty programs, from Legal Services to Model Cities, cost $4.7 billion— only 2.5% of all social welfare spending.[82] Nor were AFDC, food stamps, or Medicaid generously funded. In the end, old-age assistance took the lion's share of new spending. Even after eligibility for public assistance was liberalized and benefits increased, huge holes remained in the safety net. In 1972, means-tested public assistance lifted only 12% of poor, female-headed households with children out of poverty.[83] Most poor families remained below, often substantially below, what the government admitted was a subsistence standard of living.

Nor was much done to build coherent, national policy-making institutions that could address the problem of employment security, despite all the talk of getting the poor to work. To the contrary, the Great Society moved in the opposite direction, divorcing the issue of poverty from the organization of the national economy. Even the relationship between industrial structure and inner-city unemployment, presumably the principal target of the War on Poverty, was obscured. Instead, the cities were left to decay, encouraging those who could do so to flee to the suburbs and start over in white en-

claves. The Great Society also failed to reach beyond the poor to
provide working families with social policies that might help them
adjust to a changing economy. Millions continued to hover near
poverty, highly vulnerable to changes in labor markets and the business cycle, but without access to programs that might help them improve their lot.[84]

Finally, in cutting nominal tax rates for individuals and corporations (the highest individual rate went from 91% to 70%, the lowest
from 20% to 14%; the corporate rate dropped from 52% to 48%),
but not reforming the tax code, the Kennedy-Johnson tax cut had a
profoundly negative impact on both the government's fiscal capacity
and fiscal politics. Not only were revenues that might have been
spent on social purposes lost, but the White House unleashed the
conservative "fiscal policy genie" (as John Kenneth Galbraith would
put it) that would haunt it and future administrations: when in
doubt, cut taxes.[85] Once committed to this conservative interpretation of Keynesianism, Johnson was trapped by it, loathe to consider
raising revenues to pay for the war in Vietnam or to expand the
War on Poverty—even though it quickly became apparent that existing spending was insufficient to pay for either.

### The Path Not Taken

As in the 1910s and 1930s, political and institutional factors clearly
limited what reform could accomplish in the 1960s. Bankers' fears
of inflation, business anxiety about higher taxes, employers' appre-
hension about the labor-market effects of public provision—in combination, these put tremendous pressure on liberals to moderate
their ambitions. After first spurring reformers' efforts, racial politics
also cut against liberalism by causing deep divisions within the coalition that might otherwise have supported an expanded welfare
state. State structures in turn continued to favor the right generally,
and racial conservatives in particular, who used the separation of
powers against a White House intent on change.

But, as we have seen, political actors' choices mattered too.
Both Kennedy and Johnson self-consciously pursued strategies that
built from the political center, even as they pursued new social policies. Kennedy was more conservative than Johnson, and he went to
great lengths to please business executives and racial conservatives.
His welfare-state agenda was limited to the parameters set by Cold-
War liberalism as it had been defined by congressional Democrats
in the 1950s: a modest program that did not entail redistributional
reform. The look and feel were new, but the substance was not. The
result was predictable: a small increase in the minimum wage (from
$1.15 to $1.25 an hour), a modest program for manpower training,

and limited aid to depressed areas. In contrast, Johnson was much more ambitious, proposing to expand the government's role over a wide range of areas, and much more successful. But Johnson pursued the same centrist strategy, tailoring his initiatives to the concerns of fiscal conservatives and business elites even as he tried to build a bigger welfare state. Johnson embraced this strategy in 1963–1964, when, lacking the legitimacy of an elected president, he sought to build a broad, nonpartisan coalition to carry him through the November election. But even after his crushing victory, Johnson continued to court a broad array of interests, including moderate Republicans, southern Democrats, and corporate executives, hoping to keep the big tent intact.

I suggested in the previous chapter that Roosevelt might have chosen differently in 1933, moving left rather than right; that strategy might have widened his room to maneuver. Did Kennedy or Johnson have similar alternatives? Could they too have acted differently?

Apart from civil rights, it is hard to see what Kennedy could have done differently, and even there, he was deeply constrained by political realities. Kennedy had narrowly beaten Richard Nixon in 1960, and while the Democrats retained control of Congress, they had actually lost twenty seats in the House. Conservative Democrats continued to chair the major committees and worked with Republicans in the early 1960s to block liberal initiatives as they had done since the late 1930s. After a decade of turmoil over race relations, southern Democrats were ready to use their remaining institutional leverage to block social reforms that might challenge Jim Crow. Big business also remained suspicious of what the Democrats, finally back in the White House after eight years, might do. With the conservative coalition intact, the fate of Kennedy's program depended on moderate Republicans, and they were not particularly eager to see a major expansion of the federal government's role. In the end, Congress blocked *all* of the New Frontier's major social programs, including health insurance for the elderly, the creation of a new urban affairs department, and federal aid to education, leaving the White House with few options but tax-cut Keynesianism. Even Kennedy's moderate civil rights legislation had been stalled by southern Democrats at the time of his death. Kennedy could have used his executive power to better protect civil rights demonstrators from violent reaction, but his leverage over Congress was limited. To do more than he did, Kennedy would have had to construct a coalition that simultaneously stimulated the economy and satisfied liberals without alienating moderate Republicans, big business, or the South. It is hard to imagine how this could have been done.

Because Johnson had considerably more room to maneuver, his

choices mattered more. Moreover, as we saw, the limits of the centrist strategy soon became obvious. What had seemed possible in 1963–1965 became unworkable by 1966. Once the conservative coalition regrouped, the administration was stopped in its tracks. Centrism no longer made sense even as a practical matter. Increasingly, Johnson came to rely on narrowly partisan congressional majorities built around northern Democratic votes. Medicare and Medicaid, two programs with wide popular appeal, passed in just this way. Of course the war in Asia made things much worse. As its costs increased so did fiscal pressure, and conservative leverage in Congress. Ultimately Johnson was forced to sacrifice his plans to expand the War on Poverty to secure business support for the war.

What then might Johnson have done differently? For one, a more clearly social-democratic domestic agenda might have attracted more popular support. This would have meant pushing the Great Society even further in 1965–1967 (and perhaps into a second term) by refocusing it on class issues (as both Martin Luther King and Robert Kennedy urged in 1967–1968). Concretely, the administration would have had to accept the need to spend more money on Great Society programs. The combination of overpromising and underfunding was a disaster because it set up programs to fail and encouraged opponents and erstwhile supporters to see in those failures the limits of government itself. Johnson would have also had to care less about accommodating business interests. The public, already in an anticorporate mood, was seemingly ready for this, as support for the public-interest movement's consumer, environmental, and workplace protection proposals indicates. Johnson might also have revisited the issue of tax reform, dropped by Kennedy in 1963 after concentrated business lobbying, and proposed to raise taxes on upper-income groups. Finally, the administration might have pursued Labor Secretary Wirtz's proposal to build new labor-market institutions to take care of displaced workers generally. In foreign policy, the alternative was obvious: negotiate a peaceful end to the war.

This is of course hindsight, and since we cannot run history over again, it is impossible to know if decisions of this sort would actually have changed the outcome. If popular support for a more social-democratic program did not emerge or if conservatives were able to block these initiatives, the administration might have been stymied anyway. Nonetheless, it is worth asking why Johnson failed to change course.

Ideology does not appear to have been the decisive factor. Although Johnson obviously took for granted liberal-capitalist institutions, there is no evidence that he shared Roosevelt's view that the president was supposed to guard the system against radical reform.

To the contrary, Johnson appears to have been far more liberal than Roosevelt (and certainly Kennedy) and far more willing to entertain policies that changed social structures. Johnson clearly understood that equality of condition required, as he put it, "equality as a fact and equality as a result," and that meant a more substantial role for government in the economy.

But Johnson was also convinced that he could not move ahead without substantial support from the political center, including moderate conservatives, and they would not support the kind of taxing and spending programs needed to implement the Great Society. Indeed, as a former congressional leader, Johnson was acutely attuned to the problem of building majorities in both chambers and the obstacles to liberal reform imposed by the conservative coalition. As president, he believed he needed to win the votes of both Republican moderates and southern Democrats.[86]

Congressional resistance to reform after 1964 confirmed this view. In fact, the 89th Congress was nowhere near as liberal as is sometimes imagined; the Democratic party's huge margin of victory was to a significant degree a result of the public's repudiation of Goldwater. Sixty-one Democratic House seats had been won with less than 55% of the vote; thirty seven with less than 53%. Many Democrats were elected in formerly Republican districts that could have easily reverted to the Republicans in 1966.[87] The administration's political vulnerability was apparent in Congress's change of mood *before* the 1966 election. Johnson was also convinced that the public's support for social reform was limited by its unwillingness to pay for it, particularly if the majority thought that the money raised by new taxes would be spent on poor blacks who had taken to rioting.[88]

For Johnson to have done more he would have had to directly confront public perceptions and the power of private interests. To do that, he would have had to use public policy aggressively to build a biracial class coalition in support of reform. That, in turn, would have meant spending money on programs of general interest to the working and middle classes. In doing so, he might have been able to isolate racial reactionaries and temper racial resentments about targeted programs.

This, of course, bring us directly to Johnson's decision to escalate the war. Absent the war, Johnson would have had more money for domestic programs. The blue-collar backlash against liberalism might also have had less bite if liberals did not have to deal with the class and generational polarization caused by student opposition to the war effort and the blue-collar working class's defense of it. And without the economic pressures caused by military spending, business complaints about the budget and inflation would have mattered less. In truth, Johnson suspected as much and worried that his war policies would undo his domestic agenda. In June 1965, he spoke to several advisors about the effect of World War I on Woodrow Wilson's New Freedom and of World War II on the New Deal. "I don't want that to happen to the Great Society," he told them. "I don't want to get involved in a war."[89] Fearful of congressional opposition to any effort to do both, Johnson put off escalation and then tried to hide from Congress the extent of American involvement. "I knew from the start," he said later,

> that I was bound to be crucified either way I moved. If I left the woman I really loved—the Great Society—in order to get involved with that bitch of a war on the other side of the world, then I would lose everything at home. All my programs. All my hopes to feed the hungry and feed the homeless. All my dreams.[90]

Johnson would have still faced enormous obstacles to extending the Great Society. Structures and institutions still mattered greatly in the 1960s, as we have seen. Johnson's own sure political instincts told him that he was operating at the margin of the politically feasible in 1964–1965. But it is also true that in pursuing the war, Johnson threw away what was likely the last real opportunity in the twentieth century to push the American welfare state in a different direction.

# SIX

# *Backlash*

Just as they have constrained reformers who have wanted to build a more generous welfare state, class, state, and race have shaped efforts to roll back what liberals accomplished in the 1930s and 1960s. To date, conservatives have launched three major campaigns to cut public provision: the first was led by President Richard Nixon in the late 1960s and early 1970s, the second by President Ronald Reagan in the early 1980s, and the third by Speaker of the House Newt Gingrich after the 1994 midterm elections. In each case, the same political and institutional factors that determined the trajectory taken by reform influenced the politics of retrenchment.

As of this writing, the conservative assault on the welfare state has had mixed results. Advocates of retrenchment have been unable to stop social spending from increasing, let alone restructure old-age pensions and Medicare, the largest entitlement programs. But the right has made important inroads. Though not stopped or reversed, the rate of growth in social spending has slowed—a not inconsiderable feat given both the growing demands for public aid caused by uneven economic performance and the presumption, built into so many entitlement programs, that government would respond to distress. Indeed, as I noted in chapter 1, the United States is one of only three countries where weak spending growth in the 1970s was followed by further restraint in the 1980s (Britain and the Netherlands are the other two), and the only one of these three to retrench again in the 1990s. And the social spending growth rate declined more precipitously here than in those two countries—despite the fact that the United States spent a smaller share of its GDP on social purposes to begin with.[1]

Moreover, some programs have suffered significant spending cuts, sometimes because Congress has restructured eligibility criteria and benefit schedules, but more often because government has simply failed to act in the face of greater need. Over the long run, small changes brought about by the 1983 amendments to the Social Security Act (SSA) will have large effects, raising the retirement age and significantly lowering replacement rates (the percentage of preretirement income replaced by pension benefits) for retirees.[2] The unemployment-insurance and social-service programs have been especially hard hit, despite a significant run-up in poverty rates in the 1980s. In 1996, conservatives finally succeeded in killing Aid to Families with Dependent Children (AFDC), devolving control to the states while imposing time limits on cash aid and imposing a strict work requirement. Of the various public assistance programs targeted on the poor, only Medicaid has grown dramatically, not due to expanded coverage or improvements in the quality of service to the poor, but to medical cost inflation.[3] The Reagan administration was also able to make, or at least cause, significant changes in the political and institutional rules governing decision making over social policy, and these changes have limited, and are likely to continue to limit, what reformers can do about public provision well into the twenty-first century. In this chapter, I shift ground and turn to these efforts to undo liberalism.

## Right Turn

As class-based accounts would predict, changes in the balance of class power since the 1960s have transformed the politics of social policy. Such changes have undermined support for liberal politicians who have sought to protect the welfare state from retrenchment, and they have undone the modus vivendi between business and labor that supported government intervention into the economy in the postwar period. These changes have registered both in specific program cuts and, in the 1980s, in the Reagan administration's ability to restructure the underlying financial and budgetary relationships that supported public provision in the United States.

### *The Resurgence of American Business*

The political mobilization of the business community beginning in the 1970s and its effort to restrain social spending and cut taxes have both helped revitalize conservative resistance to the welfare state and hurt liberal efforts to defend it. Corporate support for social reform in the 1960s was based on a variety of calculations. Some firms—those with large investments in urban real estate, for example—profited directly from the reconstruction of the cities. Others—large, unionized employers in particular—gained when the government took over responsibility for benefit programs that would otherwise have been funded by the employers themselves. Some business interests, such as hospitals and medical suppliers, sold services to the government or sold to markets enlarged by government benefit programs.

By the mid-1970s, however, the economic situation of corporate America had changed substantially. Even with a relatively high corporate income tax, after-tax corporate profit rates had averaged 7% between 1948 and 1973, peaking at near 10% in 1965. Profit margins plummeted in the recession of 1973–1975, and then stagnated, averaging less than 6% between 1973 and the end of the 1980s.[4] The economic situation of organized labor changed, too: heightened capital mobility in an integrated world economy, in combination with slack labor markets, forced unions onto the defensive. As unions became weaker, firms had less reason to worry about their support. These changes freed American business to renegotiate its relationship with organized labor and with the regulatory and welfare-state institutions that had organized relations between the business community and the wider society for decades.

American business moved against liberalism on several fronts. At work, employers froze and cut wages and benefits, increased their use of contingent labor, established two-tiered pay systems, streamlined work rules, expanded production in nonunion sites, exported jobs, and battled unions.[5] At the same time, corporate interests lobbied government for a wide variety of pro-business policies, including a renewed commitment to defense spending, tax cuts, and economic and social deregulation. The business offensive was not driven by worries about out-of-control social spending; regulatory costs and labor policies were more important considerations. But social-welfare programs quickly came under attack.

First, generous public benefit programs made it harder for employers to cut labor costs because they cushioned workers from the shock of unemployment. In fact, public benefits had become quite important to worker well-being as the growth in social-welfare spending outstripped the growth in real wages in the postwar period. By 1977, as Bowles and Gintis report, each week a single worker (i.e., a production and non-supervisory employee) with three dependents received social benefits from the government worth approximately 75% of his or her take-home pay.[6] And, from the employer's perspective, the problem was getting worse. While spendable earnings increased negligibly between 1965 and 1977 (3% in 12 years), social welfare expenditures more than doubled.[7] By 1977, social welfare expenditures accounted for more than one-quarter of total workers' consumption in the United States.[8]

The corporate political offensive began in the early 1970s and by mid-decade a broad front had formed to lobby against government regulation, labor-law reform, and social spending, and for tax cuts targeted on business. A large number of firms and a cross-section of American industries participated, including traditional business lobbying groups—such as the National Association of Manufacturers (NAM), the Chamber of Commerce, and the National Federation of Independent Businesses (NFIB)—a growing army of trade-association lobbyists, and the Business Roundtable (formed in 1972 to give voice to the CEOs of the nation's top 200 firms). These lobbying efforts were reinforced by the activities of corporate political-action committees with a shared interest in retrenchment.[9]

Business groups that had been defeated in the 1960s by the public-interest movement found themselves winning battles across a wide range of issues, including taxation, social spending, economic and environmental regulation, and inflation. The impact of the corporate mobilization was clearly felt in the mid-decade battle over the Humphrey-Hawkins bill. In its original form, Humphrey-Hawkins created a legally enforceable right to a job; it would have obligated the federal government to become the employer of last resort whenever the unemployment rate rose above 3%. The first serious attempt by the Democrats to enact full-employment legislation since the struggle over the Employment Act in the Truman administration, the bill had stalled in Congress during the Ford administration. But even when the White House changed hands, liberals were unable to overcome business resistance and business efforts to turn Democratic votes. When the Democratic Congress finally passed a bill in 1978, the legislation had been eviscerated.[10] Business lobbyists handed organized labor a second defeat when President Jimmy Carter and the Democratic congressional leadership let a Republican-led filibuster kill a labor-law reform bill that would have made it easier for workers to join unions and harder for employers to resist. Liberals lost on long-delayed tax reform as well, as the Democrats passed a bill that was sharply tilted toward corporate interests and upper-income groups.[11]

Typically, corporate lobbyists were less directly involved in the formulation or passage of new social policy initiatives. But corporate interests did help fund a variety of conservative public-interest think tanks, including the American Enterprise Institute, the Hoover Institution, the CATO Foundation, the Heritage Foundation, and the Manhattan Institute to develop a conservative social policy agenda. These efforts, in turn, were reinforced by corporate lobbying to restrain social spending generally and to cut back the various entitlement programs that drove it. Corporate PACs were particularly successful in the late 1970s in pressuring Democrats, particularly Democrats elected from suburban districts, to abandon the liberal-labor agenda for something more cost conscious and business oriented.[12]

## The Decline of Organized Labor

Business's change of heart about the postwar accord would probably have been less consequential had organized labor been better able to defend the principle of public provision as European unions did. But as business's political power grew, organized labor's already limited influence receded, and with it critical organizational support for liberalism.

Labor's political power ebbed for two reasons. Most obviously, union membership declined. This was an internationally unique phenomenon. Union density had been declining since the mid-1950s, but the subsequent drop-off was precipitous as the most unionized sectors, including historic union strongholds in mining, construction, trucking, autos, and steel were hit especially hard by recession, the declining competitiveness of American manufactured goods on world markets, antiunion public policies, and the economic and organizational restructuring imposed by management.[13] By 1994, less than 15% of the civilian labor force was unionized, compared with nearly 35% just forty years earlier.[14]

For a time, the decline in private-sector density was masked by large gains in public sector organizing (union density in the state sector rose from 13% to over 50% between 1956 and 1980).[15] But once public-sector unionization tailed off in the late 1970s, the trend was apparent. Indeed, for the first time since the 1930s, the overall number of workers in unions actually began to fall: from 22.4 million in 1979–1980 to 17 million in 1987–1988.[16] The unions' membership losses could not help but reduce their political power. Already a regional phenomenon, the unions saw their strength in former union citadels, including big cities and the manufacturing districts of the industrial Northeast and Midwest, decline with their numbers. The damage to traditional union sectors was especially dramatic after 1980.[17]

Organized labor compounded its problems by failing to forge alliances with the new reformist forces that were transforming liberalism and the Democratic party. By the late 1960s, the trade-union leadership's political integration within the Cold War consensus and the Democratic party establishment had led to organized labor's alienation from nearly every major social and protest movement on the left, including the civil-rights, antiwar, feminist, and environmental movements; the fight over Hubert Humphrey's nomination in 1968 made this quite clear. The battle between the AFL-CIO leadership and Democratic party reformers over the party's presidential nominating system in the early 1970s, and the party's nomination in 1972 of George McGovern, deepened the rift. Eventually, nearly every liberal and left organization, including traditional labor allies such as the Americans for Democratic Action, the National Committee for an Effective Congress, the NAACP, the Democratic Study Group, Public Citizen, the ACLU, and the Urban League found themselves at odds with the unions on one or another issue, leaving labor dangerously isolated as the business offensive mounted.[18]

The union leadership adopted new political tactics after 1980 in an effort to regain their lost leverage. Organized labor once again became a full participant in the Democratic party's nominating process, committing itself to Walter Mondale in the 1984 election even before the caucus and primary season had begun. Labor did more to influence election campaigns at the grass-roots level and to mobilize workers to lobby legislators; and it learned to better target money in close legislative elections, stepping up financial support for the Democratic National Committee and pro-labor Democratic candidates.[19] But none of this addressed the problems created by declining numbers and too-fragile political alliances. For the most part, American unions remained locked into the collective bargaining model of the New Deal long after many corporate leaders had abandoned it, leaving them unprepared to respond effectively to the management offensive. By the 1990s, declining membership and the impact of a decade of corporate and government hostility had so eroded the position of organized labor that tactical changes no longer made any difference.

Labor's decline had far-ranging effects on the Democratic party, liberals, and liberalism. The impact in Congress was immediate. In the nine states where the unions' decline was most precipitous (California, Colorado, Idaho, Nevada, Oregon, South Carolina, Texas, Utah, and Virginia) the Democratic party's share of Senate representation fell from 10 to 4 members between 1970 and 1983.[20] Traditional liberals proved particularly vulnerable when union supporters, such as the auto and steel workers, lost hundreds of thousands of members. The unions suffered a net loss of sixteen pro-labor senators in just four years (between 1978 and 1982); the 1980 Senate elections were particularly traumatic, eviscerating labor's power in Congress.[21]

Equally important, as the unions lost influence, moderates in swing districts who might have otherwise felt pressured to vote with organized labor found that they could defy the unions with impunity. The reformist "Watergate" Democrats were particularly independent. Unconcerned about alienating union voters, they eagerly tapped into the flood of corporate giving, showing little interest in liberalism's traditional social and economic agenda, preferring, instead, to work with business interests on their economic issues.[22] The results were apparent in the Carter administration when congressional Democrats distanced themselves from the unions, allowing common situs picketing, labor-law reform, and tax reform to be defeated by massive corporate lobbying campaigns. Knowing that the unions had nowhere else to go, the party's national leadership became openly dismissive of labor's defense of New Deal liberalism in the early Reagan years.

At the same time, however, organizational decline also undercut labor's willingness and ability to defend the welfare state. Many unions responded to the corporate assault defensively, using whatever clout they still enjoyed to lobby for measures of immediate concern to organized workers and union leaders. Domestic content legislation, quotas on foreign steel, and the defense of the Davis-Bacon Act (requiring all federal contractors to pay union wages) moved to the top of the autoworkers', steelworkers', and construction trades' respective legislative agendas. While still sympathetic to social policy issues, the unions were no longer available to lead the mobilization against cutbacks in welfare-state programs. Nowhere was this felt more keenly than in the ineffective defense of the unemployment insurance program, which withered in the face of the Reagan administration's hostility.[23]

Other interested parties did come to the defense of the welfare state. Provider and public-interest groups responded to threatened cutbacks, as did organizations of the aged and other program participants. State and local officials who feared that cutbacks at the federal level would increase their financial obligations lobbied for federal funding. The feminist movement also turned its attention to social policy, discovering the "feminization of poverty" and the particular stake that women and children had in public provision. In some cases, these groups were able to mount effective campaigns to block retrenchment. The American Association of Retired Persons (AARP) proved particularly adept at defending social security and Medicare. The intergovernmental lobby fought off Reagan's effort to end the federal government's responsibility for AFDC and food stamps. But these efforts proved to be rearguard actions, and many programs were left without defenders. Indeed, organized labor's decline and its estrangement from the left made it nearly impossible to mount the class-wide defense of public provision that many on the left anticipated.

## Race and the New Deal Coalition

Racial divisions also hampered efforts by liberals to defend social programs. Public disaffection with liberal social policy was not driven *only* by a white backlash against a welfare state perceived to be biased toward blacks. Since the 1960s, many other factors had driven a wedge between liberals and working- and middle-class white voters, including crime, rising taxes, and a general sense that liberals had been on the wrong side of a cultural divide between a hard-working, church-going, "middle America" and a growing number of ungrateful, disgruntled, "oppressed" minorities.

But race played a critical role in tying all of these complaints together and turning them against liberalism. As a rule, white and black Americans came to see American politics differently, as Jennifer Hochschild has reported. On the one hand, white voters believed that the civil rights legislation of the 1960s was successful, that blacks now had as many if not more opportunities than whites, and that the African Americans who remained poor, unemployed, or trapped in inner-city ghettos were there largely because of their own actions and attitudes. On the other hand, the majority of blacks were convinced that racial discrimination was alive and well (indeed, middle-class blacks were even more certain of this than poor blacks), and that white America had given up on its commitment to equality of oppor- tunity.[24] Great Society social policies played an important part in shaping both perceptions. For whites, as William Julius Wilson points out, it was a very short step from the War on Poverty's focus on dysfunctional behavior to an antireform agenda emphasizing the personal irresponsibility of inner-city single mothers and unemployed teenagers.[25] Believing that the Great Society had "thrown" billions of dollars down that "sinkhole," it is not surprising that many concluded that more spending was unjustified.

Civil rights legislation and antipoverty programs were particu- larly important to white southern voters who abandoned liberalism. Not that the South resisted all reform: by the 1970s, a majority of southern whites had accepted the *principle* of racial equality; these attitudes have held steady since.[26] But a significant minority of southern white voters, principally the less educated, who might have supported economic populism, did not change their racial views.[27] They remained hostile to the idea of black equality after the civil rights revolution had come and gone, and they blamed liberals for the change. Over time, this minority was joined by white south- ern suburbanites who, while not opposed to the idea of racial equality, resented federal taxing, spending, and affirmative action policies that were perceived to help inner-city blacks at their ex- pense.

Though the economic modernization of the South played a part in the revival of the Republican party, white hostility to racial liber- alism finally made the party a viable political alternative in the re- gion. The defection of the South from the Democratic party had been a real possibility since the 1930s. Southern political leaders were among the first to abandon the Roosevelt coalition once it turned to the left in 1935. Party leaders in the region strongly re- sented the national leadership's elimination of the two-thirds rule in 1936 that had given the South a veto over presidential nominations. For their part, southern economic elites suspected that Roosevelt had encouraged CIO organizing activities among southern industrial workers during World War II. Relations between the party's northern and southern wings only worsened after the war. The 1946 midterm elections that gave Republicans control of both houses of Congress also showed that the GOP could make inroads in the South, as ten Republicans replaced Democrats in the border states. President Harry Truman's support for civil rights, however halting, accelerated the trend, leading to the Dixiecrat rebellion, the independent candidacy of Strom Thurmond in 1948, and southern support for Eisenhower in 1952.[28]

The 1964 campaign brought this ground shift to a head, showing that a Republican presidential candidate running on a strong states-rights campaign could attract white southern working-class voters who were ordinarily quite hostile to the business-oriented GOP.[29] Although Goldwater lost badly in 1964, he carried Mississippi, Alabama, South Carolina, Louisiana, and Georgia—five Deep South states that the Republicans had failed to win since Reconstruction. The political opportunity caused by white southern opposition to racial change was not lost on the Republican party, and party leaders quickly adopted a political strategy to court the region's racially disaffected white voters. The "southern strategy" did what anticommunism had failed to do in the late 1940s and 1950s, allowing the Republican party to extend its reach beyond the "New South" business and white-collar elite to the southern working class.

Race also helped alienate northern blue-collar workers who had traditionally supported New Deal social policies. Though they were quicker to endorse the principle of civil rights than southern whites, many northerners had deep reservations about its implementation, and the spread of the civil rights movement northward in the mid-1960s caused a second wave of white reaction. The March on Washington, school boycotts, open housing campaigns, the forced integration of trade-union apprenticeship programs, community action, urban riots—all strained northern white, working-class voters' political loyalties. George Wallace's ability to do well as an avowedly segregationist candidate in three northern and border-state primaries in 1964 revealed the growing fissure in the Democratic party. By 1966 it was clear that working-class support for Democrats was eroding not only in the South, but also in big cities in the North, including the Democratic strongholds of New York, Chicago, Boston, and Detroit.

For a brief moment, it appeared that racial conservatives would remake the Democratic party too. Other Democratic politicians followed Wallace's lead, appealing to working-class voters by simultaneously endorsing traditional social-welfare policies and attacking forced integration and racial liberalism. Disaffected blue-collar workers in northern cities sent hard-line, conservative Democrats like Frank Rizzo in Philadelphia, Sam Yorty in Los Angeles, and

Louise Day Hicks in Boston to city halls and state legislatures. In the
end, however, it was the Republicans who established themselves as
the unalloyed party of racial conservatism and, in doing so, reaped
the rewards. Nixon received nearly 80% of Wallace's 1968 vote,
capturing the support of enough discontented Democrats to create
a "middle-American" Republican majority. The Republican's new-
found advantage proved decisive in 1972, when Nixon beat George
McGovern handily in a two-way race.[30]

More than racial animus drove opposition to welfare spending,
of course. Long-standing concerns about the deservedness of welfare recipients, particularly in programs that appeared to reward
nonwork, also mattered.[31] But race affected perceptions of welfare,
how people assigned blame for poverty, and public support for programs like AFDC. Images of black welfare mothers came to dominate white perceptions of the program, feeding on white prejudices
and stereotypes of African Americans.[32] Two decades after the civil
rights movement, a majority of whites still believed that blacks had
worse jobs, income, and housing because they did not have "the mo-
tivation or willpower to pull themselves out of poverty," and that
African Americans were "less intelligent, lazier, and . . . more in-
clined to stay on welfare than whites. . . . ."[33] Having never accepted the idea that government owed special economic assistance
to racial minorities, whites were far less likely than blacks to support policies perceived to favor minorities, whether affirmative action programs or AFDC.[34]

By the early 1970s, most whites had simply stopped worrying
about the condition of blacks and started thinking about the impact
of compulsory, compensatory policies on themselves.[35] Americans
came to see welfare recipients not as equal citizens with justifiable
needs, but as the undeserving poor, and welfare not as deserved
support for the needy, but as handouts for shirkers. Support for income maintenance and other social-welfare programs targeted on
the poor and minorities dropped significantly in the late 1970s and,
despite public resistance to sharp cuts, never recovered.[36] In that
context, race began to work against public provision, hardening
white opposition to social policies, such as food stamps and AFDC,
thought to differentially benefit minorities.[37]

Race also played a critical "bridge" role in discrediting liberal reform. By focusing on how social policy encouraged family break-
down, teenage pregnancy, welfare dependency, and the growth of a
black underclass, conservatives were able not only to raise questions about welfare, but to influence mass perceptions of liberalism
itself. Initially, the battle to extend the welfare state in the 1960s reinforced mass perceptions that government was a positive force and
that Democrats and liberals were interested in the economic well-

being of wage earners generally. But after capturing the Republican party and turning it against racial liberalism, conservatives were able to alter these perceptions. Increasingly, in the public's mind, social-welfare spending was associated with racial indemnification; this made it far harder for Democrats to appeal to white, working-class voters by promising to expand public provision. Indeed, Democratic efforts to expand social welfare programs raised questions in many white voters' minds about the party's racial loyalties. In 1991, according to a New York Times/CBS poll, 56% of Americans agreed that the Democratic party "cares more about the needs and problems of blacks" than Republicans do—a politically devastating finding given the widespread public perception that programs in aid of minorities did not work and actually discriminated against whites.[38] In this way, working-class and middle-class voters, both southern whites and northern blue-collar ethnics, were brought into a coalition with business interests who opposed social reform generally and liberalism in particular for very different reasons.

## The Antinomies of State Power

For the most part, political fragmentation continued to favor efforts to defend the status quo after the 1960s, but because the status quo now included a far more active government than had previously been the case, fragmentation also helped liberals stop conservative efforts to reverse that trend. Whereas conservatives in Congress had once used their institutional leverage to frustrate reform, after 1968 (and until 1994), Democratic congressional majorities were able to use the separation of powers to resist retrenchment efforts by Republican presidents. Nixon found it nearly impossible to make promised legislative changes. Reagan had greater success in 1981 because Republicans had taken control of the Senate and "boll weevil" southern Democrats joined Republicans in the House to cut taxes and spending. But Democratic gains in the 1982 midterm election stiffened congressional resistance and ended the Reagan revolution.[39] Federalism also helped liberals resist retrenchment when state and local authorities mobilized in opposition to efforts to shift welfare costs to the states in the 1980s.[40]

But liberals were not always able to count on political institutions to defend their accomplishments. Even while state and local officials were lobbying to maintain federal commitments, federalism allowed conservatives to erode national commitments at the local level, particularly in programs that were jointly administered. In New York City in the mid-1970s, bankers won major cuts in social spending when the city turned to them for help with its bills. Budget cutting quickly spread, with many governors and state legislators seeking to limit welfare rolls and financial obligations. The Reagan administration tried hard to use federalism against established programs by shifting burdens to the states, hoping that competitive federalism would take its toll, in effect shrinking the welfare state without ever bringing the issue to a vote on Capitol Hill.

Welfare-state institutions themselves also affected the struggle over public provision. In certain respects, existing program commitments helped liberals by creating organized constituencies that supported social spending. To a significant extent, the people who rallied to defend social security, Medicare, Medicaid, and AFDC had been brought together by the programs themselves, which established ongoing relationships that clients and providers thought worth defending. Social security is the most famous example, of course: by unifying an otherwise diverse group of people over sixty-five into a single constituency of social security beneficiaries, the program all but guaranteed the creation of a huge lobby in support of itself. That lobby proved remarkably effective at defending the program against efforts to retrench. But other programs had similar, if less spectacular, effects. Social-services providers whose livelihood depends on the welfare state often rallied in support of agency budgets. Private providers with an economic interest in ongoing programs did the same. Grocery stores, for example, were a reliable ally in the struggle to defend food stamps, which has accounted for a significant proportion of their revenues. At times, welfare-rights activists were able to organize clients at the local level to demonstrate against proposed cutbacks.

But in certain respects, the structure of the welfare state also made it harder for liberals to defend public provision. By targeting benefits on the very poor while failing to deal adequately with the employment and income problems of average working families, the social policies of the Great Society heightened the potential for distributional conflict between these two constituencies. Then, by assigning to government the responsibility for tasks that it was institutionally unprepared to undertake, the expansion of the welfare state encouraged the working and middle classes to believe that government was *inherently* incompetent. In this way, the structure of the welfare state itself both divided potential supporters and encouraged people who might be expected to benefit from public provision to ally themselves with the same corporate elites and upper- and upper-middle class voters who had traditionally opposed economic liberalism.

New budget rules, developed by Congress in response to the fiscal effects of the Reagan revolution, created additional obstacles to expanding public provision. In the 1980s, the combination of supply-side tax cuts and sharp increases in military spending drove the federal budget seriously out of balance. Pressured by business and fiscal conservatives to do something about these record budgetary shortfalls, Congress changed the rules of the budget process itself. In 1985, the Balanced Budget and Deficit Reduction Act (known as the Gramm-Rudman-Hollings Act, or GRH), imposed five yearly, sequential, across-the-board reductions in federal spending (unless Congress acted). Though GRH lacked teeth (48% of government programs were exempt, including most entitlements and interest on the national debt), GRH's deficit-reduction targets became a central feature of the budget process from 1986 to 1990.

In 1990, the Budget Enforcement Act further tightened the noose on social spending, establishing maximum limits on "controllables" (and giving the Office of Management and Budget, or OMB, sequestration authority if Congress exceeded these caps) and requiring that changes in entitlement programs or taxes be "deficit neutral." "Pay-as-you-go" (or "paygo") restrictions were not new, but the Budget Enforcement Act made paygo central to the budgetary process, creating a zero-sum fiscal environment that gave opponents of social spending new credibility when they demanded that liberals find some way to pay for their programs, either by cutting other programs or by raising taxes. Though not inviolate—Congress and the White House could ignore the rules in an emergency—paygo succeeded in shifting the burden of proof to proponents of new spending, and forced liberals to make difficult and often impossible political choices between cutting social spending, raising taxes, or attacking other politically popular programs.[41]

Finally, proponents of expanded public provision were handicapped by two fundamental changes in the political process itself. First, there was a steady and disproportionate decline in the political participation of those groups (notably lower-income Americans) with an interest in public provision and in the success of liberalism. Second, campaigning changed dramatically, becoming more candidate centered and capital intensive. Where candidates once relied on party organizations to mobilize voters and communicate issues, they now ran semi-independent, media-oriented campaigns that depended heavily on private funding. In response, most candidates (and both political parties) turned to relatively well-off constituents, typically business interests, the upper-middle class, and the rich for contributions. The problem for liberals was that these constituencies typically wanted to limit government, if only to limit their taxes and regulations on their behavior. The precipitous decline of the labor movement and the mobilization of corporate interests against government in the 1970s and 1980s made the problem acute, sharply skewing the balance of available campaign resources against reformers precisely when so many other political and institutional forces were working against them.[42]

## The Conservative Revolution in Social Policy

The political forces just outlined—the race-based backlash against the Great Society, the revitalization of the business lobby, the decline of organized labor, the transformation of the political process—created an unparalleled opportunity for the right to challenge the welfare state. Conservatives took advantage of the opportunity, escalating their attack as the movement built and liberalism faltered until, in 1995, the right challenged the very idea of public provision. As of this writing, apart from welfare reform, the right's most ambitious goals remain unachieved. But each assault made important inroads, causing significant changes in key policy areas, from old-age pensions to public assistance, and, perhaps most important, causing much of the electorate to question the liberal social-policy agenda that had dominated social-policy politics since the New Deal.

### Nixon

Richard Nixon challenged the racial loyalties of the Great Society reformers, not the idea that government had a role to play in promoting economic security. To the contrary, Nixon believed in activist government and understood the political uses of the welfare state. His interest in domestic policy appears to have been entirely strategic; he proved more than willing to use federal spending to promote his own political fortunes, overseeing an *expansion* of the welfare state in the competition for working-class votes. Nonetheless, Nixon clearly saw how a "southern strategy" that used race to move poor southern whites from New Deal liberalism to Republican conservatism might help him win and hold the White House, and Nixon worked very hard to make clear just how conservative the Republican party could be on race. Though he never rejected the *principle* of civil rights, he made clear that his administration would not use federal power to force compliance with it. The idea of states' rights figured prominently in the administration's campaign rhetoric, with Nixon taking very visible positions opposing court-ordered busing for school integration and open housing. Courting racial conservatives, Nixon promised to appoint "strict constructionists" to the Supreme Court and refused to publicly endorse the Civil Rights Act.[43]

Having not yet built the cross-class electoral coalition that they sought, Republicans could not really deliver on their promises in the late 1960s and early 1970s. In office, Nixon faced a Democratic

Congress intent on protecting the Great Society, improving social security, and defending the gains of the civil rights movement. Nonetheless, even as it compromised, the Nixon administration was able to signal to both its supporters and its critics the future of the Republican party.

The administration's racial policies were clearly designed to reward its white southern supporters, and where it could act alone, the administration acted decisively. Nixon nominated two southern racial conservatives to the Supreme Court and appointed individuals in tune with the administration's racial philosophy to key positions in the executive branch. The impact on policy was immediate: the Department of Health, Education, and Welfare (HEW) and the Justice Department dropped strict compliance timetables for school integration and, for the first time since the start of the civil rights revolution, the Department of Justice went to court on the side of white southern defendants seeking to delay desegregation orders. The administration also applied the southern strategy to social policy, targeting social programs that were popularly perceived to aid blacks. The Office of Economic Opportunity was restructured and the stand-alone War on Poverty programs were devolved to Cabinet-level departments where they could be more firmly controlled by presidential appointees. The Job Corps was reorganized and sent to the Department of Labor. Head Start was moved to HEW. Spending on the Job Corps and the rural loan program was cut.[44]

Nonetheless, the lion's share of the welfare state was spared, and indeed grew, during Nixon's years. No effort was made to cut the rate of growth of social spending or even the poverty programs. Instead, Nixon supported congressional efforts to amend the Social Security Act (SSA), increasing and indexing pension benefits, and adding a new benefit program for the disabled. Antipoverty funding was increased as Nixon signed nearly every welfare-state measure passed by the Democratic majority in Congress, including expanded funding for the War on Poverty, AFDC, and food stamps. As a result, spending on *every* major category of social policy, including means-tested transfers, social insurance, and targeted education and training, increased significantly, both absolutely and as a percentage of GNP, between 1970 and 1975 (the fiscal years for which the Nixon administration was directly responsible). Indeed, had Nixon's Family Assistance Plan passed Congress, it would have created a European-style family allowance, albeit with a modest work requirement.[45]

## Reagan

Ronald Reagan took the conservative revolution considerably further than Nixon, but also stopped short of challenging the foundations of liberal social policy. Though clearly more of an economic conservative than Nixon, Reagan was neither opposed to the New Deal nor particularly interested in slashing social spending. But unlike Nixon, Reagan did want to roll back the Great Society, in particular the social-service programs created in the 1960s. It was, he said, "LBJ's war on poverty that led us to our present mess."[46]

The attack on the Great Society was broadly conceived, and proceeded on four fronts. The first involved immediate and direct benefit cuts in means-tested cash, in-kind, and social service programs. These were contained in the 1981 and 1982 Omnibus Budget Reconciliation Acts (OBRA). The administration proposed to reduce antipoverty spending both by lowering benefits and tightening eligibility. If these changes had been adopted fully, they would have led to the first nominal cuts in welfare benefits since the program was established in the 1930s, and reduced public benefits available to mother-only families with children absolutely. Total spending on the Special Supplemental Food Program for Women, Infants, and Children (WIC), food stamps, AFDC, public housing, and Medicaid would also have been reduced substantially. The White House also proposed to reduce radically (and in some cases eliminate) the employment and social-services programs established during the 1960s and early 1970s. Congress was asked to end Community Services Block Grants and the Work Incentive program (WIN) and to slash outlays on compensatory education, general employment and training, the Job Corps, social-services block grants, vocational education, and guaranteed student loans. Simultaneously, the administration tried to strengthen work requirements for welfare clients who remained on the welfare rolls, proposing that states *require* AFDC mothers to work for their relief checks in community work-experience programs. Finally, the White House proposed eliminating benefits for the *working* poor. Beginning in the early 1960s, Congress had amended AFDC to make it easier for low-income wage earners to mix work and welfare: low-wage workers had been allowed to deduct some work-related expenses, including transportation and child care costs, from their income when AFDC eligibility was calculated. By the late 1970s, a significant number of AFDC clients had taken advantage of these changes. By tightening eligibility, Reagan intended to force the working poor to choose between welfare and the labor market. The administration also initiated a review of disability claims that resulted in the removal from the rolls of nearly 500,000 participants.[47]

Second, the administration tried to devolve authority over AFDC and food stamps to the states in return for the federal assumption of the costs of Medicaid. From the administration's perspective, decentralization would have served several purposes. Presumably, economic competition between states would have made it harder for any state to adopt redistributive policies. In addition, since interest groups that defended the welfare state were less powerful outside Washington, devolution would have weakened their ability to defend existing programs. Finally, decentralization would have allowed the White House to shift blame for cutbacks to the state and local officials who had been forced by devolution to make them.[48]

Third, the White House sought to lock-in these cuts by restructuring the tax system to reduce the federal government's revenue-raising capacity—by purposefully running budget deficits and then securing a legislative mandate to balance the budget. The administration believed that these changes would create tremendous pressure over the long run to restrain social spending. Indeed, tax reduction was Reagan's first piece of domestic legislation (the Kemp-Roth bill), including a regressive 30% cut in personal income tax rates, indexed tax brackets, and substantial tax breaks to business. Though supply-side economists touted the Kemp-Roth bill because it promised to stimulate the economy, conservatives also knew that it would eliminate much of the fiscal overhead that could otherwise have been used by Democrats to restore program cuts, or even increase social spending, if the White House or Congress should change hands.

Fourth, Reagan reaffirmed the Republican party's racial loyalties. Reagan had had a long and successful association with racial conservatism, opposing fair-housing legislation in California, the federal Civil Rights Act of 1964, the Voting Rights Act of 1965, and legislation to create a national holiday to honor Martin Luther King, Jr. As a presidential candidate, he had promised to end "special privileges"; after the election the Justice Department declared its official opposition to goals, timetables, and quotas in affirmative action. The budgets of the Equal Employment Opportunity Commission (EEOC) and the Office of Federal Contract Compliance were sharply cut. The White House publicly condemned legislative efforts to strengthen the Voting Rights Act. The Department of Education cut back on efforts to enforce civil rights regulations. And the administration's largest social-spending cuts were reserved for the means-tested programs that served a disproportionate number of black clients and that were, in many cases, staffed by a disproportionately black civil service.

Because Reagan's electoral victory was more decisive than Nixon's and more easily interpreted by Democrats as a defeat for liberalism, his administration had more room to maneuver. With Republicans in control of the Senate, the corporate mobilization cresting, and many congressional Democrats, particularly southern Democrats, eager to distance themselves from the Great Society, the administration won watershed votes on taxing and spending. The early cuts were deep. Changes in AFDC eligibility rules forced as many as 500,000 working-poor families off the rolls, and 400,000 individuals lost food stamp benefits. The school lunch program lost a third of its budget. Housing appropriations were cut by a third in 1981 and cut again in 1982. The Comprehensive Employment and Training Act (CETA) was eliminated, replaced by the Job Training Partnership Act, and funding for direct job creation was eliminated. OBRA made it harder to extend the unemployment insurance extended-benefit program, forcing state governments with troubled trust funds to reduce unemployment benefits and coverage.[49]

But neither the 1980 nor the 1984 elections produced the conservative realignment that the right had hoped for, and strong Republican gains at the presidential level were not matched by a strong showing in either Congress or the states. As it once had protected conservatives from liberal initiatives, decentralization in Congress in the early 1980s provided liberal committee chairs in the House with the institutional leverage to veto conservative cutbacks. The 1981 tax and budget bills proved to be the high-water mark of the Reagan-era retrenchment. The effort to devolve authority for AFDC and food stamps to the states died. Except for CETA, *no* means-tested program was eliminated. Congress also rebuffed White House efforts to require that states impose *mandatory* workfare on clients. Efforts to trim social security ran into immediate trouble.

The fight over proposed social security cuts was the turning point. Though the bipartisan commission that Reagan turned to for pension reform would eventually recommend significant, though incremental, changes in the system (which Congress would adopt), Reagan's effort to touch this "third rail" of American politics broke the spell, and after 1982 the administration turned away from social policy. Reagan put welfare reform back on the political agenda in his 1986 and 1987 State of the Union addresses, but the White House no longer controlled the social policy debate. Conservatives who wanted to turn AFDC into workfare were forced to accept liberal demands that any new work requirement be combined with an expansion of the AFDC-UP program nationwide and increased "transitional" aid to make clients "job ready," including basic literacy, remedial, and English-language educational programs, and job skills, job readiness, and job search training. To encourage participants to leave the welfare rolls and stay in jobs, clients were also offered Medicaid and child care benefits for one year after leaving welfare.

Liberals also managed to exclude most single mothers with small children from the requirements of the Family Support Act (FSA). As conservatives complained, this new legislation actually forced very few people to work. Mothers with children under three were exempt from the work requirements. Although states could, at their own discretion, lower the cutoff age of a child to one, a welfare mother with a child under three could not be obligated to work more than half-time. Even after her child had reached three years of age, a welfare mother could be excused from the program if she had another child. Taken together, these provisions effectively excluded 50% of the current caseload from the Act's provisions. Nor were all states required to enroll all suitable mothers in the Job Opportunities and Basic Skills (JOBS) program offering education, training, and work activities; only 20% of the non-exempt caseload had to be enrolled by fiscal year (FY) 1995. Finally, welfare clients could meet their JOBS obligation by taking part in education and training programs rather than in work itself.[50]

But while Reagan failed to roll back the Great Society, conservatives won what may have been the more important welfare-state battle. By driving deficits to record heights, the combination of income-tax cuts, increases in military spending, and the indexation of tax brackets both eliminated the resources that would otherwise have been used to fund increased social outlays and focused attention on deficit spending. With the total national debt doubling in just four years, the percentage of the budget spent on debt service jumped dramatically (from approximately 9% to nearly 14% during Reagan's first term). The result was disastrous for advocates of public provision, who were forced to make their case for social programs against escalating pressure to bring the federal deficit (which jumped from less than $80 billion in FY 1981 to more than $200 billion in FY 1985) under control without raising taxes. Moderates in both parties joined the right in demanding a balanced budget, forcing the deficit issue to the top of the national policy agenda while crowding out calls for more government spending on growing social needs.[51]

## Gingrich

The rightwing effort to cut back the welfare state intensified in the mid-1990s, as a new generation of more ideologically conservative activists (who were deeply disappointed by the Reagan Revolution) came to power, first in the states and then in Washington. Far more committed to deficit and tax reduction, and more visibly upset about the growth of government than the party's elder statesmen, they were far less willing to work within the system. This was more than renovated Reaganism: supported by well-organized and well-funded antigovernment, antitax lobbying groups and coordinated by the national Republican leadership, these conservative activists targeted not only the Great Society but the New Deal as well; the goal was not only to roll back the War on Poverty, but to challenge the very idea of federal entitlements.

These efforts were reinforced by the political mobilization of religious conservatives. Coordinated by the Christian Coalition, founded by TV evangelist Pat Robertson and directed by Ralph Reed, the Christian right sought to mobilize the 50 million evangelical Protestants (and as many other orthodox Christians as possible) behind like-minded politicians who supported a legislative agenda designed to limit "secular humanism" and promote "traditional" values. Composed of groups and movements with distinct if overlapping agendas, the Christian right lobbied for and against a wide variety of issues, including abortion rights (against), homosexual rights (against), home schooling (for), prayer in school (for), and the censorship of sexually explicit books, music, and films (for). But welfare played a particularly salient role in the political iconography of the movement. Programs like AFDC, they argued, undermine the moral fiber of the nation by encouraging illegitimacy and validating irresponsible behavior. The solution, according to many conservative religious activists, was to privatize, letting church-based charities take care of the poor.[52]

Led in Congress by political leaders from the newly Republican South—most notably Newt Gingrich of Georgia, who lent his name to this third wave of opposition to the welfare state—these conservatives proposed even steeper tax cuts and deeper cutbacks in social spending than anything attempted by Nixon or Reagan. Their targets included the elimination of the federal entitlement to public assistance, Medicaid, and food stamps, and the partial privatization of Medicare and social security.

The 104th Congress took up a wide variety of these measures. Based in part on the Contract with America, a 1994 Republican campaign document that sketched what a conservative policy revolution might look like, Congress moved on three issues directly bearing on the welfare state: attaining a balanced budget in seven years (to be accomplished either through a constitutional amendment or the normal budget process), cuts in Medicare, and welfare reform. The cuts outlined in the FY 1996 budget bill, which would have brought the federal budget into balance by 2002, were truly draconian—twice the magnitude of those contained in Reagan's first budget package. In addition to reducing the rate of growth in Medicare expenditures (below projected needs), the Medicare reforms would have created a second, privatized track with vouchers and medical savings accounts, encouraging the elderly to opt out of the system. The welfare provisions—designed to satisfy governors who wanted more control over the program, and social and religious conservatives who wanted government to take a stand against moral decay—proposed to end entitlements to public assistance, Medicaid, and food stamps altogether, while imposing new rules on the personal conduct of welfare recipients.[53]

As it had in the early 1980s, the right was forced to settle for far less than it wanted. After a prolonged battle with President Bill Clinton in 1995, congressional Republicans were forced to give ground on nearly all the right's budgetary goals, including sharp cuts in social programs. The struggle over the budget was fought on three different terrains: the FY 1995 recessions bill, the Balanced Budget Amendment, and the FY 1996 budget bill. In each case, the Republicans presented proposals that would have deeply cut Medicare, Medicaid, the Earned Income Tax Credit (EITC), and public assistance. In each instance, the White House and the Democratic minority in Congress forced the majority to moderate its demands.

Conservatives were particularly disappointed by the defeat of the Balanced Budget Amendment, which would have forced huge cuts in Medicare as well as programs for the poor: the Congressional Budget Office (CBO) estimated that in order for the Republicans to both balance the budget by 2002 (fulfilling their seven-year goal) and cut taxes (as they had promised), Congress would have to reduce projected spending by $1.2 trillion. Since the Republicans had pledged not to slash social security or defense and could do nothing about interest on the debt, the pressure to cut health care costs and antipoverty programs would have been intense.

Gingrich's effort to use a government shutdown to force Clinton to adopt a FY 1996 budget bill with similar cutbacks was also defeated. Designed to lead to a balanced budget by FY 2002, whether or not the Balanced Budget Amendment passed, the Republican FY 1996 Reconciliation Bill cut spending by approximately $900 billion over seven years by abandoning the principle that federal programs should be funded at levels that corresponded to need (i.e., that kept up with price inflation and increases in the number of program beneficiaries), and by devolving programs serving the poor to the states, including Medicaid, food stamps, and AFDC. The poor would have been particularly hard hit; nearly half the savings were in targeted entitlement programs despite the fact that these accounted for only 25% of entitlement spending. The Republicans also proposed to deny legal immigrants Medicaid, food stamps, and other assistance, to cut the EITC, which served the working poor, by 18% at the end of the seven year period, and to cut Medicare spending by $270 billion.[54] But when two government shutdowns caused the public to turn on congressional Republicans, Gingrich backed off, agreeing to a series of temporary spending measures that allowed the party to retreat from what the public perceived to be an irresponsible extremism.

Still, despite these defeats, this third assault on the welfare state did far more damage than was apparent at first sight. Most important, the Gingrich Republicans had changed fundamentally the terms of the public-policy debate. Nixon and Reagan had raised doubts about liberalism, but had not been able to put conservative ideas at top of the social-policy agenda. Though it included a workfare component, the Family Support Act reflected liberal thinking about poverty and welfare. In contrast, in the mid-1990s, Washington was debating rightwing ideas, including balanced budgets, private charity, personal behavior, and the virtues of laissez-faire. For the right, this was a substantial and necessary victory: it all but assured that when the core entitlement programs were revisited, it would be on terms more congenial to the right.

Indeed, Clinton won the budget fight not by fighting on principle (the word "entitlement" dropped from his public vocabulary), but by focusing the attention of affected groups on exactly how the Republican cuts would hurt them. And by fighting over the details rather than the public philosophy behind the Contract with America, Clinton fought on ground defined by the right. In fact, despite his public denunciation of Republicans' "heartlessness," Clinton won this struggle only by moving substantially in their direction. In the end, Clinton accepted the two most important Republican demands: that the budget would be balanced in seven years and that the rate of growth in Medicare would be cut to pay for that. Clinton won this battle not because he defended the welfare state, but because the Republicans misjudged Clinton's political skills and overestimated the public's taste for brinksmanship. The right's success in redefining the social-policy agenda became clear in 1996 when congressional Republicans forced Clinton to accept a radical restructuring of public assistance that incorporated many of the conservatives' ideas about the poor and public policy.

Although Congress would not admit it in 1988, the success of the Family Support Act's JOBS program depended on the willingness and ability of the states to fully fund it. But when the economy went into recession in the early 1990s, most governors and state legislatures lost interest in spending money on the poor—even for programs that promised to end welfare dependency—and looked instead for ways to cut costs. Since the FSA did not require them to provide the most important skill-building services, the states chose less expensive alternatives, such as job-search classes, basic education, and simple workfare.[55] In the end, because no one would commit sufficient resources to it, the FSA accomplished little. In Arkansas, touted as one of the more successful state programs, job-search activities reduced welfare rolls by just 18% after three years. In San Diego's SWIM (Saturation Work Initiative Model) program— considered the single *most* successful workfare program in the na- tion—a full-scale effort to get the entire AFDC caseload to train, work, or search for work lowered the rolls by 9% after the first year; 13% after the second. Nationwide, by 1994, only 7% of the 4.4 million adults on AFDC had actually enrolled in a JOBS-related program. Between 1991 and 1993, only 24% of teen mothers—the FSA's target population—had participated in any JOBS component.[56]

Pressured by both fiscal and social conservatives, the Republi- can leadership turned to welfare reform after Clinton's election, an- ticipating that the administration would offer its own bill to, as it had promised, "end welfare as we know it." Three conservative ap- proaches were on the table. The first focused on work: in return for a substantial increase in federal funding for child care, training, and supervision, welfare clients would be required to take jobs after two years and eventually give up public aid altogether. At bottom, this was a conservative version of the "transitional support" plan that everyone expected the Clinton administration to propose. The second approach, associated with Jack Kemp, former secretary of Housing and Urban Development under Reagan, and Senator Robert Dole's vice-presidential candidate in 1996, proposed to launch "a conservative war on poverty" with empowerment zones, vouchers, subsidies to tenants to buy public housing, and looser rules governing the accumulation of assets by welfare recipients. The third approach focused on the behavior of the poor. Social conservatives, including Christian conservatives and conservative intellectuals such as Charles Murray, Marvin Olasky (Gingrich's preferred social-policy analyst), James Q. Wilson, and former Sec- retary of Education William Bennett, argued that AFDC caused women to have children out of wedlock and families to break up. Faced with the failure of the FSA, some state governments had al- ready experimented with policies intended to change welfare moth- ers' behavior.[57]

The Contract with America compromised between the work- oriented and behavior-modification views, proposing to enroll 1.5 million recipients in work programs by the year 2000 while also al- lowing states to abolish benefits to mothers under twenty-one if they wished. But after meeting with the Republican Governors Associa- tion immediately after the 1994 election, the Republican leadership changed direction, deciding instead to turn AFDC and other public assistance programs into block grants, letting the states decide what to do with the money. This was far more radical than anything the Contract with America had proposed: by "block granting" a pro- gram, Congress ended the entitlement to it. States would spend only what they had budgeted for the program; when that money ran out, potential recipients, even if they qualified by virtue of need, could be denied benefits. Pressure from religious and social conservatives led the Republican leadership to add several provisions designed to change the behavior of the poor. The final Republican bill, passed overwhelmingly by Congress in late 1995, included a two-year work requirement on the receipt of cash assistance, a five-year lifetime benefit limit, and a "family cap" denying benefits to women who had additional children while on welfare (although states were allowed to opt out of that provision if they chose).

Clinton's preferred approach was not unlike the one taken in the FSA: government should force welfare clients to work, but also provide them with social services, financial support, and, if necessary, public-sector jobs. Indeed, the administration had developed a bill along these lines, but the health-care struggle and bitter fights within the administration between liberals and "New Democrats" over time limits, the extent to which mothers with young children could be exempted from work requirements, and just how much money would be spent on transitional support had delayed its introduction.

The 1994 elections made the White House's proposal irrelevant. After having made welfare reform a central issue in his 1992 campaign, Clinton found himself shut out of the policy-formulation process. Forced again to react to initiatives from conservatives, Clinton shifted ground several times, first criticizing House Republicans, then praising the Senate's effort to moderate the House's work, then vetoing the conference committee bill after it restored the family cap.[58] But eight months later, in the midst of the 1996 presidential campaign, Clinton finally signed the Republicans' welfare bill. The changes were historic. AFDC was converted to a block grant, ending its entitlement status. A tough work requirement was imposed: the law required states to place at least 25% of cash welfare recipients into jobs or work programs by 1997, and 50% by 2002. Adults who failed to find work within two years were to be denied all federal funds. No one could receive federal cash assistance for more than five years. States could deny welfare benefits to women who had additional children while on welfare, and to unmarried persons under eighteen. Federal funds were denied to unmarried parents under eighteen who did not live with an adult and attend school. Legal immigrants' access to any form of public assistance was radically limited. In one fell swoop, the nation had given up its commitment to income maintenance as a "right."

## The Liberal Defense of the Welfare State

Clinton's capitulation to congressional conservatives first on budgetary principles and then on welfare reform were major defeats for liberalism. Though Clinton had taken great pains to distance himself from the liberal label, he had assured the party's left that his plan to "reinvent" government would protect liberalism's basic commitments to social investment, a safety net for the poor, and economic security for the working- and middle-classes. Yet by 1996, Clinton had backtracked on each of these promises, leaving reformers in his own party without effective political representation. But, in truth, the Democratic party's shift to the right had begun two decades earlier in the second half of the Carter administration. Indeed, Reagan's tax and spending cuts would not have passed without the cooperation of a significant number of Democrats, including the House leadership, in 1981–1982. Clinton's capitulation to Gingrich in 1995–1996 simply underscored the point: liberals were no longer able to defend the core principles of the welfare state. Nonetheless, it is worth asking a fourth time whether reformers could have done anything differently—in this case whether different political choices by liberals might have avoided this debacle?

Once again, it is hard to ignore how many problems were caused by larger forces. Long-standing racial divisions clearly played a large part in undoing liberalism: reformers were never able to recover fully from the public's perception that the welfare state gave benefits to racial minorities. That perception was distorted to be sure—little of the Great Society was racially targeted; even the War on Poverty's effort to help the urban poor was not restricted by race, and affirmative action was soon broadened to include women and other minorities—but the War on Poverty *had* served blacks disproportionately.[59] The problem was that it had become linked to race for good reasons. Blacks *were* disproportionately poor, concentrated in economically depressed urban areas, and in need of assistance.[60] African Americans received a disproportionate share of new means-tested social spending and job training funds because they were more likely to qualify for them, not because the poverty warriors wanted only blacks to receive aid.

Changes in the tax system further complicated liberals' efforts. Since the 1960s, political pressure from business lobbyists had led Republicans and Democrats alike to lower taxes on corporations and the rich, while raising payroll, property, and sales taxes—typically the most regressive levies.[61] And the growing tax burden gave the working and middle classes even more reason to resent the welfare state. But liberals had resisted the downward shift of the tax burden only to be defeated by moderate and conservative Democrats, who had joined with Republicans to lower taxes on corporations, investors, and upper-income earners.

Social-democratic critics have suggested that liberals might have adopted a different approach to social policy, relying more on universal entitlement and social-services policies while paying more attention to job security for the working and middle classes.[62] But liberals tried much of this and failed because political realities in the 1970s and 1980s made these sorts of adjustments in social and economic policy all but impossible. Liberals made jobs an issue in the early 1970s as soon as the economy went sour, supporting the Emergency Employment Act of 1971 and, in 1973, the Comprehensive Employment and Training Act (CETA), which consolidated existing training and public employment programs into a full-fledged, countercyclical, public-employment program. Even after the recession of 1974–1975 had ended, liberals continued to argue for an aggressive, expansionary, macroeconomic policy to assure employment opportunities for the able-bodied. Contrary to the social-democratic critique, liberals pushed for universal policies too, including public employment, wage supplements, and education and skills training programs to increase opportunity for unemployed youth, regardless of race.[63]

But liberals could not, on their own, overcome the political and institutional obstacles facing this agenda. The decline of organized labor was one major factor. Liberals should probably have addressed this issue more expeditiously by pushing harder for labor-law reform, but the growth of public-sector unionism in the 1960s had masked the extent of the problem, as did the ability of many industrial unions to protect their members' jobs and incomes through the 1970s.[64] By the time organized labor's problems became clear, liberals who were sympathetic to labor had themselves become isolated within the Democratic party as the party moved away from labor liberalism to more business-oriented economic policies that appealed to suburbanites and (some) independent voters, as well as to those corporate interests who become increasingly important to the party's fundraising efforts. As we saw, in the late 1980s and 1990s new institutional routines, including the reformed budget process, as well as the rise of candidate-centered, capital-intensive campaigns made matters even worse.

For the most part, Clinton's reform efforts were undone by these political and institutional circumstances. Elected with only 43% of the popular vote, constrained by a dismal fiscal environment and new budgetary rules, facing a panoply of corporate interests and a well-organized revolt against "big" government, Clinton had very little room to maneuver. His decision to construct a centrist coalition that was friendly to business but that could also support modest reforms was a shrewd (if disheartening to liberals) reading of the possibilities and limits inherent in that environment. It is worth remembering that Clinton began not by proposing to cut taxes, deregulate the economy and the environment, or spend less on social purposes, but by arguing for "social investments" in education and job training supported by tax credits and subsidies. That even this incremental, market-oriented reform strategy failed so completely indicates the depth of the problem.

The defeat of Clinton's health care proposal in 1994 is instructive in this regard. Introduced with great fanfare in 1993 after a prolonged policy-planning process, the Health Security Act (HSA) proposed exactly the kind of universal entitlement to health care that social-democrats wanted while recognizing the political hazards facing the administration. The HSA proposed to provide all Americans with guaranteed health insurance and control health costs by combining "managed competition" with direct cost controls. Employers would be required to purchase health coverage for their employees (paying 80% of the costs of a standard benefit plan). All but the largest employers would be required to purchase coverage through "health purchasing alliances" that would sponsor all the health insurance plans that could be offered for sale in a given state or region; through these alliances, the government would set minimum benefit standards and, if necessary, impose premium caps (i.e., price controls) on insurers.

The plan's design was driven by real need (approximately 38 million Americans lacked health insurance for all or part of the year in 1992), economic urgency (medical costs as a percentage of GDP had risen from 11.5% to 13.9% in just the four years of the Bush administration), and careful political calculation. Designed to demonstrate both Clinton's commitment to active government and his New Democrat sensitivities, the administration's bill proposed a public-private partnership rather than a government takeover of health care, all the while extending coverage and controlling costs. The uninsured would be covered, either by employers (nearly 86% of Americans without health insurance worked or were dependents of workers), or, as a last resort, by government.[65] Inflation in health care costs would be brought under control by competition among insurers for employers' business; by the presumed (because it would be cost-efficient for employers) channeling of workers into managed care systems; and, if necessary, by backup price controls. Because coverage would be universal rather than targeted, it was expected to appeal broadly to the working and middle classes. Indeed, had the plan been adopted, it would probably have led to the elimination of Medicaid as the poor were brought under the protection of the new system. In contrast to a Canadian-style, single-player plan, supported by the congressional left and by the labor, consumer, and elderly lobbies, or to proposals before Congress to expand Medicare to include the uninsured, the Clinton plan required no new taxes.[66]

The HSA was also designed to appease big business and the largest insurers by building on, rather than supplanting, existing private-sector efforts.[67] Rather than impose substantial new burdens on insurers or eliminate them entirely as the single-payer plan would have done, the HSA would have opened up new markets for them, including the opportunity to administer the managed-care networks that would have been the building blocks of the new system. At the same time, cost controls would have equalized costs both for American firms that are at a competitive disadvantage with foreign competitors who pay far less for their workers' health care, and for domestic firms that compete with employers who do not offer health benefits at all.

Manufacturing industries such as auto and steel, with unionized work forces and/or substantial health care commitments to early retirees, signaled their support precisely for these reasons. The HSA also promised public subsidies to compensate small businesses which would have incurred substantial costs to comply with the employer mandate. To compensate for increased regulation, medical-care providers, including doctors, drug companies, and hospitals, were offered new market opportunities to serve the newly insured and to help administer managed care. Finally, state governments were given a large role to play in the implementation of the plan, as well as the opportunity to control Medicaid costs by enrolling the poor in managed-care plans.

Yet, despite initial polling that indicated widespread support for the idea, including many of the specific provisions,[68] by mid-1994 a broad coalition had formed against the HSA. Instead of the hoped-for cross-class coalition of large employers, labor unions, hospitals, nurses, the elderly, the uninsured, and progressive doctors in support of the bill, the administration faced a massive mobilization against it, including small business, midsize insurance companies, the pharmaceutical industry, and social conservatives and antitax lobbying groups that wanted to stop any effort to expand governmental authority over health care. Led by the National Federation of Independent Businesses (NFIB) and the Health Insurance Association of America (HIAA) (representing small- and medium-sized insurers who believed that mandatory health alliances would benefit only the largest insurance companies), opponents poured vast sums into an unprecedented lobbying campaign to defeat the HSA—by one estimate, between $100 million and $300 million was spent in the struggle, the lion's share by opponents.[69] Members of Congress from districts with large concentrations of small employers were targeted. Even the corporate leaders on whom the administration had counted joined the effort. In the end, all three major employer groups—the Business Roundtable, the Chamber of Commerce, and the National Association of Manufacturers—opposed the HSA.[70]

Refracted through Congress, this tidal wave of lobbying created insuperable obstacles for the administration. At the same time, institutional fragmentation made it all but impossible for supporters of health care reform to coordinate the mammoth undertaking.[71] Paygo budgeting rules made matters worse. The Congressional Budget Office's estimates of the costs of the original proposal and various modifications to it continually frustrated the administration's effort to convince the undecided that the program could be financed without raising taxes or cutting spending elsewhere.[72]

Fearing that Clinton would reap enormous political benefits from the passage of health-insurance reform, and that universal health insurance might help liberal reform efforts generally, the Republican leadership also committed itself to defeating the bill. The leadership's decision was particularly important because it provided political coordination for the campaign against reform and short-circuited efforts by moderate Republicans to develop a compromise bill. Once the issue became, as Gingrich argued, the defeat of Clinton in 1996 (and perhaps even a Republican takeover of Congress in 1994), legislative compromise was impossible.[73] Republicans used the separation of powers and the decentralization of power within Congress to stop reform.

Once it became clear that the administration did not have the votes to pass its plan, a variety of substitutes was considered, each designed to appeal to moderate and conservative Democrats, many from southern and border states with large numbers of small businesses, and to the handful of moderate Republicans who seemed willing to buck their party. But in the end, the Republican leadership's intransigence and the administration's refusal to abandon the principles of universal coverage and cost control killed the bill.

Perhaps, as the left argues, a simpler, single-payer bill would have been easier to sell to the public. Undoubtedly, the specter of managed care and the loss of physician choice scared many voters. But just as likely, because it would have eliminated private insurers entirely, single-payer would have led to an even more vociferous campaign against reform, a campaign that would have easily taken advantage of the multiple veto points created by the fragmented state structure to kill reform. New budget rules would also have required the administration to make explicit how it proposed to pay for this universal entitlement, forcing a debate over payroll and/or income tax increases.

This is not to deny that a more forthright economic populism might have helped protect the welfare state from the right in the mid-1990s. The Clinton administration's capitulation to the bond market in early 1993 when it moved deficit reduction to the top of its agenda, and its embrace of both the North American Free Trade Agreement (NAFTA) and the General Agreement on Tariffs and

Trade (GATT), clearly undermined the Democrats' ability to serve the constituents who had looked to the party for relief from the regressive tax and economic policies of the Reagan-Bush years. Undoubtedly, the welfare state would have been better defended by mobilizing poor, working, and middle-class voters with policies that spoke directly to *their* economic interests. Conceivably, a more principled defense of the welfare state might have won the Democratic party as much support as Clinton's policy of "triangulation," which required that he distance himself from both Republican conservatives and Democratic liberals. But the defeat of Clinton's health insurance initiative, the success of the Republican's draconian welfare-reform bill, and the White House's shift to the right on budgetary issues all reflected just how politically isolated liberals had become, and how powerful conservative political forces had grown since the 1960s.

# SEVEN

# *The Future of Reform*

To this point, I have considered the political and institutional constraints on welfare-state development in the United States and reformers' responses to these. I have argued that the structure of American politics, the balance of power between business and labor, and racial divisions have discouraged all but the most modest reforms—even in crisis situations. The result is the market-oriented welfare state described in chapter 1, a welfare state that provides fewer public benefits and, as the rightwing's recent success in reforming welfare and restraining the growth of social spending has revealed, is more vulnerable to efforts to retrench than most other welfare states. I do not think that the decisions taken by reformers in the four periods under discussion were the only possible ones. Indeed, I have argued that both Roosevelt and Johnson might have profitably chosen differently. But I have suggested that the long-term trajectory of liberal reform has, to a significant extent, been determined by the rational adaptation by reformers to the political environment in which they have acted.

In this chapter I want to consider what this analysis suggests about the future of reform in the United States. With the recent collapse of liberalism, reformers have begun to take stock of their situation and consider alternatives. Do any recently developed proposals address the problems I have outlined?

## Building from the Left?

Reformers to the left of New Deal and Great Society liberalism imagine two scenarios, both resting on the assumption that, in some way, a changing economy will teach the working and middle classes that market-oriented social policies do not serve their interests, and that a new, more radical politics of social reform will emerge from that experience.

In the first scenario, European-style social democrats assume that economic stagnation (and perhaps crisis), combined with growing class inequality and declining American competitiveness on world markets, will lead salaried professionals, managers, and technicians worried about the threat of job loss, overwork, and a deteriorating quality of life to abandon their employers to make common cause with other workers in class conscious political struggle. Progressive political elites will also see the threat to national well-being from these new circumstances. A cross-class coalition to rebuild the American economy will emerge, and this coalition will rebuild the social-safety net.

There are several problems with this scenario. For one, public opinion appears to be becoming more, not less, disordered, making difficult the party-based assertion of public control over the economy that social democrats imagine. Increasingly, Americans do not seem able to sort out the causes of or remedies for the economic troubles experienced by the bottom 80% of the population. For their part, the two major political parties are less and less prepared to represent working- and middle-class demands for economic-structural reform. Nor does the rush simultaneously to deregulate the economy and cut back the federal government inspire confidence that established elites will act to prevent public institutions from deteriorating further, if only because heightened capital mobility in an increasingly international market makes it risky for government to impose controls and costs on firms who might exit their national economies if regulatory and tax burdens grow.

Social democracy has also historically depended on unions, and American unions are weak and declining. Although the labor movement now appears to recognize the gravity of its situation, and new leadership is emerging, it remains unlikely that union decline will be reversed easily. Indeed, changes in the social structures of the advanced capitalist societies may be making traditional social democracy obsolete *everywhere*. Throughout the West, the traditional industrial working class is shrinking and labor organization is faltering. Changes in the division of labor are undermining solidarity among wage earners, exacerbating conflicts between workers in secondary and primary labor markets, between the unemployed and underemployed and the employed, between public-sector employees and private-sector workers.[1] Not everyone is doing poorly; many American firms are highly competitive on world markets, and while their success has not "trickled down" to most workers—indeed many have lost their jobs in the recent restructuring that has helped to sustain profit rates—some employees have done reasonably well.

In fact, intraclass inequality is likely to increase in a global economy which best serves asset holders and highly skilled workers. As income distributions diverge even more widely throughout the rich capitalist democracies, divisions among the potential supporters of the welfare state are likely to deepen and solidarity become even more difficult to sustain. Faced with higher tax burdens to pay for universal benefits, the better-paid white-collar employees may want to be allowed to purchase privately the pensions and other services that welfare states once supplied publicly. Such decisions by the more affluent middle classes to choose private market solutions over public goods and universal access to state-run programs will reduce the incentives for the kind of cross-class coalitions that elected social-democratic governments in the first place.

In this environment, the various constituencies with an interest in public provision are likely to compete with each other for benefits (and to avoid tax burdens) rather than coalesce. Racial divisions are also likely to continue to fracture future efforts to unite individuals and groups with an economic interest in maintaining or expanding the welfare state. If anything, the current divide between black and white Americans' perceptions both of the present situation and the value of positive government will continue to widen, making cross-race movements for reform even less likely in the future.[2]

Social democracy also presupposes a different sort of state structure than exists in the United States—one that makes it less difficult to plan social and economic policies, to translate majority sentiment into public policy, and to coordinate bargaining among sectors and groups. Even if a general consensus were to develop that the American government had to actively intervene in the economic interests of the less well-off, the extreme fragmentation of the American state would continue to make political coordination around social reconstruction difficult and costly for all parties involved. Instead of a redistributive politics of social citizenship, interest-group politics in the United States could easily result in a "beggar thy neighbor" defense of existing distributive shares.

Social democrats argue that these conditions can potentially be changed through decisive political action. That is undoubtedly true, but everything would have to be done at once and under extremely adverse circumstances. Moreover, even if a coalition capable of doing so were to suddenly materialize, the public policies needed to build and sustain it might not favor the disadvantaged. Because political support for social democracy typically rests on both a union movement and political alliances between organized labor and the white-collar middle class, social-democratic welfare-state policies have been biased toward those constituencies. Indeed, social-democratic welfare states are *more* likely than liberal welfare states to spend money on relatively well-off constituencies. Social-democratic economic and labor policies also benefit the best-organized workers. And because they are better educated, less intimidated by professionals, feel more efficacious, and act more "appropriately," the middle classes tend to be far more successful in gaining access to and utilizing public benefits.[3]

These problems will continue to trouble the United States, where poverty is so intractable. It is quite likely that social policies to lift the poor would require more targeting here than in, for example, the Scandinavian social democracies. And full employment policies might easily fail those workers who are at the bottom, deeply alienated from the labor force.[4] The suggestion that American social democrats "target within universalism" by providing both universal entitlements and resources targeted on particularly unyielding problems—including manpower training and education programs for those with the least training, skills, and education—makes political and policy sense as long as the costs are ignored.[5] But with relatively large numbers of poor people and a large economic, social, and cultural gap between the very poor and the rest of the society, universal policies that simultaneously benefited the working and middle classes and addressed poverty would be very expensive.

Postindustrialists suggests a different route to reform.[6] They readily acknowledge that changes in the economy and society make European-style social democracy unlikely. But all is not lost: social and economic changes make possible a new scenario of progressive reform, building on the emancipatory aspects of European socialism while jettisoning its archaic dependence on centralized state structures and bureaucratic trade unions.

To postindustrialists, both the information revolution and the development of "flexible production" have rendered older forms of capitalism and public policy obsolete. New information processing capacities have put a premium on knowledge and skill and on a social organization that promotes and takes advantage of them. Flexible production—both flexible specialization by firms (turning out a variety of products in small batches geared to rapidly changing markets) and new forms of worker cooperation (working in teams to identify and solve problems)—will soon displace the high-volume, standardized mass production assembly lines that were once the envy of the world. Though unemployment will follow in their wake, postindustrialists welcome these changes because they promise an escape from the rigid, hierarchical division of labor and, simultaneously, they vastly increase labor productivity. If America embraces these changes, they argue, Americans will work less, better enjoy the work that they do, and still prosper. Americans will also have the opportunity to rethink the economic incentive systems that have traditionally motivated them, even delinking work and wages, creating a "more collaborative, participatory, and egalitarian" society.[7]

According to postindustrialists, these changes will have radical implications for social policy as the welfare state adapts to them. New economic and social relations will upset traditional lifestyles and career patterns. Individual lives will become more chaotic. Unconventional jobs and careers will proliferate. Education and life-long learning will become more important as technologies change. In the face of these developments, welfare states that assume an industrial capitalist model of work and career will become obsolete. All people, not just the poor or the unemployed, will need continuous help from government if they are to adapt easily and willingly to this new world of work and technology. Societies that wish to compete and prosper will have to make enormous investments in human capital. Government services, from education and training, to preventative health care, to social programs that rehabilitate and motivate individuals to accept change, will become an essential component of that commitment. Government will also have to encourage labor market flexibility, intervening on both the supply and demand sides of labor markets as well as promoting new work relations that facilitate the adoption of new technologies and the utilization of employee problem-solving capacities. In short, government will have to help everyone lead more adaptable lives.

Governments that take on this challenge will have to change their welfare state *structures* as well. Social policy institutions will need to deliver benefits that are as deeply individuated, highly specific, and flexible as the postindustrial environment in which government intervenes. The industrial welfare state organized public provision around, and restricted benefits to, broad categories based on income loss due to catastrophic risks, such as old age, accidents, or unemployment. These programs developed along separate lines, each dealing with clearly identifiable categories of need. Eligibility and benefits were linked to employment and performance since individuals who had jobs presumably did not need help.

In a postindustrial world, highly centralized, heavily bureaucratized state institutions and generic programs of public provision tied to labor-market status would be abandoned. In their place, more decentralized institutions would emerge that could target interventions more carefully and tailor public aid to individual cases, recognizing the interdependence of different categories of need among individuals, and the inevitability of rapidly changing life circumstances.[8] In this new world, governments would presumably have more resources and new ways to address poverty. The rigid separation between the employed and the unemployed could be overcome as people moved in and out of jobs and careers. Universally available education and training would benefit all sectors of society. A guaranteed income would seem far less threatening in a world of widely shared affluence, where the standard work week had shrunk and jobs had become far more rewarding. In effect, postindustrial-ism would end the need to compel labor and thus would undermine the ideological separation between the deserving and the undeserv-ing poor.

But while obviously appealing, the postindustrial scenario makes too many heroic assumptions about the capacities of the political and economic systems to realize the liberating potential of new technologies. For one, postindustrialism would require new state in-stitutions. A more active government, including greater public con-trol over investment, would be necessary to deliver the benefits of new technologies to workers and consumers rather than stockhold-ers and managers, and to unleash postindustrialism's participatory potential. This means that the American government would have to do far more than it has ever done, or shown the capacity to do.

Postindustrialists' assumptions about class conflict are also too sanguine. Emancipatory changes would almost certainly set off a firestorm of opposition from a wide variety of business interests. Organized labor is also likely to object, if only to defend its position within the existing industrial order. Indeed, postindustrialism offers a real dilemma to the labor movement. Delinking wages and social benefits from work time would undercut the centrality of wages as a source of income and thereby threaten the power base of the trade unions. It is important to keep in mind that where unions have fo-cused on wage struggles, as in the United States in the early twenti-eth century, or Australia and New Zealand more recently, they have backed away from universal social policies.[9] In the end, then, like social democracy, the viability of the postindustrial project would depend on the emergence of different political movements and structures than America has or is likely to develop in the near fu-ture.

## Can Conservatism Succeed?

Are we likely then to see the triumph of laissez-faire in social policy as many conservatives imagine? Undoubtedly, the decline of orga-nized labor, the discrediting of the state, and growing racial division have redounded to the short-term advantage of the opponents of public provision; as we saw in the mid-1990s, congressional Repub-licans used their new-found political strength to end the federal en-titlement to public assistance. If conservatives do not suffer a sud-den political setback, they are likely to eventually move on the rest of their agenda, including the partial privatization of social security and Medicare and the elimination of what remains of the War on Poverty. Where government is already too involved to be easily dis-engaged, conservatives will push to replace the direct provision of social services with vouchers, possibly finding allies on the left who also object to the overbureaucratization associated with the welfare state.

But for social-policy conservatives to succeed several things would have to happen. Either their predictions about the salutary effects of laissez-faire (that private entrepreneurs and philanthropists will step in when government steps back; that welfare mothers will find jobs; that all Americans will save more and work harder) will have to come true, or Americans will have to learn to live with a greater degree of inequality and more visible poverty. There is no question that if people were to work longer hours (or start businesses, or cut back sharply on their expenses); if working families were to put more money in private retirement and medical savings accounts; if the well-off were to tithe to their churches and spend their weekends at soup kitchens, then it is possible that the government might withdraw the safety net.[10] Privatization might also be politically self-reinforcing. Broad participation in private pension and private health-insurance programs could undercut public support for socializing these risks and costs, ending whatever mass support still existed for universalism or an active government. The result would be a narrowly targeted, discretionary welfare state administered locally, one which would likely prove even more vulnerable to retrenchment.

The problem here is that there is little evidence that conservative policies actually work, and good reasons to believe that welfare cutbacks will result in a substantial increase in poverty and homelessness. Contrary to supply-side predictions, for example, the laissez-faire policies of the 1980s worsened economic conditions for many. Aside from the boon to the well-off from tax cuts, the Reagan administration's economic and labor policies alone increased income inequality.[11] Supply-side tax cutting simply made the problem worse—increasing the tax burden of the bottom 95% while lightening taxes on the top 1%—*without* triggering the promised investment boom.[12] And if the American states engage, as liberals fear they will, in an interstate "race to the bottom" by sharply cutting the programs that support the most vulnerable groups, the situation will only worsen.

Conservative proposals to "empower" the poor, which have been associated with the Kemp faction within the Republican party, do not seem particularly promising either. To succeed, empowerment would have to mean more than rolling back Great Society reforms and stripping benefits from those who depend on them; it would have to involve spending substantial amounts of money so that people could purchase the educational and training services that they need to make their way into the economic mainstream. But while some advocates of empowerment support new government expenditures, this idea runs against the current conservative preoccupation with cutting taxes.[13] Supply-side conservatives counter that cutting taxes will "grow the economy," thus helping all families. For their own reasons, social conservatives agree: they suggest that tax cuts will allow families to work fewer hours and spend more time at home with their children. But supply-side policies have not worked in the past, and the idea that working families will cut back their hours if federal income taxes are reduced ignores two facts: many families are in precarious economic situations, and they are not in control of how many hours they spend on the job.[14]

Some conservatives want to cut welfare programs not to save money, but to end "the culture of poverty" that they believe has trapped the poor in a "cycle of dependency." But there is, in fact, little evidence that government programs affect poor people's behavior significantly. Welfare has not pulled many people out of the labor market or encouraged them to go on welfare. Changes in family structure, not benefit levels, explain why most people turn to public assistance and why some succeed in leaving it.[15] Nor does the evidence support the claim that AFDC breaks up families. Changing attitudes about women, premarital sex, divorce, and the family appear to be far more important.[16] There is also little proof that welfare dependency is transmitted intergenerationally.[17] If government is not at the root of the problem, then cutting back government is not likely to solve it.

Moreover, the welfare dependent are a very small subset of the poor, and theories of poverty and redemption based on their experience tell us little about most poor Americans. By any reasonable definition, the underclass targeted by conservative social policy is far smaller in numbers (somewhere between 1.8 million and 2.5 million persons) than usually imagined.[18] Looked at over time, the population of poor people consists of a small number of persistently poor and a large number of people who move in and out of poverty, hovering just above or below the poverty line as their family circumstances and job prospects change.[19] Nearly half of poor Americans live in intact families.[20] Fewer than 1 in 20 poor people are black ghetto residents.[21] Even welfare clients defy the stereotypes: only a minority of families who have received AFDC benefits since the program expanded have depended on it for a long time.[22] And contrary to the received wisdom, dysfunctional behavior among minorities is *decreasing* in frequency: more minority youth are graduating from high school; a smaller proportion of minority teenagers are having children out of wedlock; fewer blacks commit crimes or have crimes committed against them; drug use is *declining*.[23]

Workfare is not likely to change many lives for the better either, because enforced work is not likely to improve either the attitudes of the poor (if attitudes are a problem), or their expectations that something positive will come from that work without changes in job markets, remedial education, and job training. Rather, making welfare mothers take low-wage jobs is only likely to generalize the problem of working poverty, as people with little education and burdensome family responsibilities will be forced into the low-wage, low-skilled jobs that already prevent millions of working Americans from escaping poverty.

Even the welfare dependent poor targeted by conservatives are not likely to see their lives change by a "cold bath" in the labor market. As some conservatives admit, young, unmarried, uneducated mothers with young children "suffer from so many disadvantages that employment clearly would be difficult for them."[24] As income becomes even more tightly linked to education, their prospects are only likely to worsen. The working and middle classes may feel better once no one is given a "free ride," but that is not likely to improve the distribution of income or opportunity in America. Moreover, once these changes are in place, it will be that much harder for conservatives to use the issue against liberals. At that point, the electorate may rediscover that it actually supports the principle of public provision and most of the programs designed to implement it.

## Liberalism Redux?

Public disenchantment with free-market solutions to economic insecurity is not likely, however, to revive the liberalism of the New Deal and Great Society reformers. Cyclical theories of American politics predict the periodic reemergence of a vibrant liberalism.[25] History lends some support to this view: Progressivism was followed two decades later by the New Deal, and the New Deal was followed thirty years later by the Great Society. On this calendar, we might expect a liberal revival presently. Particularly if economic conditions continue to stagnate and real wages decline, unions could be rehabilitated, and the public might look more favorably on government. A crisis might even force the issue, leading economic and political elites to seek to reverse the decline of government institutions in order to restore public order and economic competitiveness.

Paradoxically, the decline of the Democratic party might accelerate this trend. As more conservative Democrats become Republicans (as happened at the beginning of the 104th Congress) and the party shrinks back to its core northern-urban constituency, it might use its time in the wilderness to rethink and clarify its message, as the Republicans did to good effect in the 1960s. The Democratic party could even prosper—if it returned with an ideologically coherent liberalism that spoke to popular concerns, perhaps melding economic populism with greater respect for the culture and values of mainstream America. As we have seen, the public has a rather pragmatic attitude about activist social policies, including health care, day care, social security, and unemployment insurance. It is imaginable that if conservative efforts to substantially reduce the federal role succeed, liberals might find themselves *by default* the leaders of a broad, diverse, cross-class, multiracial coalition in support of public provision.

The problem is that many of the background conditions that previously sustained liberalism have eroded. The decomposition of working-class politics (such as it was); the willingness of economic elites to cooperate in the dismantling of the interventionist state; the deepening racial divide; changes in the world economy—all make the reconstruction of a national welfare state committed to social equality and racial justice deeply problematic. Even if the Democratic party were to clarify its message, it is unclear that the social or institutional basis exists to carry it. The Democrats might prosper as defenders of the public against the ravages of the market, but it is worth keeping in mind that the ability of the Democratic party to make any real difference at all in the struggle over social policy appears to depend on its ability to mobilize a clearly class-aligned base rather than a motley collection of interest groups and movements acting defensively, supported by corporate elites who think progressive policies are better for business.[26]

Without other, bigger changes in the political-institutional environment, the more likely outcome, I think, is a political stalemate in which conservatives periodically come to power and then are rejected after making or proposing too-severe cuts, replaced by moderates who use public policy to cushion the worst effects of the market. In such a political environment, reformers might make some gains. Recently adopted legislation guaranteeing the portability of employees' health insurance is one example. The federal government might also offer tax credits to employers who give jobs to former welfare clients, as Clinton has proposed, or increase incentives for individuals to save for their retirement and for medical emergencies. All these things are important, but it is hard to imagine reviving New Deal-Great Society liberalism on this basis.

## A New Liberalism?

What are the prospects for a different liberalism that might escape the orbit of the New Deal and Great Society and reconfigure the politics of social policy in the next century?

Recently, observers sympathetic to the liberal agenda, such as E. J. Dionne, have suggested that progressives might profit by making the case for an affirmative government that would serve not particular groups but the nation as a whole by helping individuals, families, and local communities survive in the new, global economy. Reformers would, in effect, redefine and generalize the class struggle, though no one has put it precisely in this way. The goals of government would still be liberal, that is, to promote economic opportunity, personal freedom, and social justice, but public policies would not be designed to advance the claims of, or redress wrongs done to, "special" interests—whether defined by race, gender, or sexual orientation. Rather, reformers would recommit government to serving everyone, or at least the vast majority of Americans who have been put at risk by an impersonal and often predatory world market.[27]

Just as the populists defended rural Americans against capitalist industry, a revived liberalism would defend America against footloose, multinational corporations. Though protectionism sometimes figures in this scenario, these liberals do not intend to revive economic nationalism. Rather, they want to see the U.S. government cooperate with international organizations and other nation-states to force international market actors to meet certain minimal standards of behavior. Government would focus not on income maintenance, but on winning new rules for international trade, while making social investments in education and training, and formulating economic policies that promote technological change. Presumably, these policies would help American workers to better survive in the new, high-technology global economic order. A shared commitment to "American values," including personal responsibility, hard work, and equal opportunity, would help cement the majority's commitment to such a program.

A populist liberalism of this sort makes a good deal of political and policy sense as a way of appealing to economically insecure voters and simultaneously reinventing government for the twenty-first century. But as currently formulated, it still does not solve the problems that have caused reformers so much trouble in prior epochs.

First, populist liberalism does not directly address the political power of the multinational corporations that it hopes to regulate. If the behavior of powerful market actors in the global economy is at the root of the problems faced by working families, then reformers will have to decide how to deal with it. How far are they willing to go to appease corporations who might oppose reform? As we have seen, Franklin Roosevelt, Kennedy, Johnson, and Clinton went to considerable lengths to secure business support, crafting social-policy initiatives to minimize opposition from employers and other

economic interests worried about the tax, wage, and price effects of
a too-generous welfare state. In the preceding chapters, I suggested
that in the 1930s and 1960s less presidential solicitude for these interests could have resulted in more generous social policies, and
that by better serving those who might have benefited from a more
active government, perhaps done more to cement popular support
for liberalism.

But those chapters also indicated the political logic of this busi-
ness-friendly strategy. For the most part, political and institutional
structures have seriously impeded efforts to adopt more explicitly
class-redistributional policies. Any effort to change course now
would confront the same obstacles in an even more debilitating (for
reformers) political environment. Only a major ideological and political assault on corporate power would have a chance of changing
the balance of forces, and that would of course alienate the entire
business community, on whom a democratic capitalist society so
heavily depends for growth, jobs, and incomes.

Alternatively, it is possible to imagine recruiting some capitalists
for reform, as Roosevelt tried with the largest industrial firms in
1933, and as Clinton hoped to do with high-technology companies,
Wall Street bankers, and large insurers in 1993. Their corporate interests could be taken into account, providing, where necessary, tax
credits and public subsidies, advantageous regulatory and social
policies, and other market-oriented measures. But the history re-
counted here does not invite optimism. As we have seen, concessions to business bought Roosevelt very little space to maneuver.
Even after Roosevelt had demonstrated that he wanted to save
rather than undo American capitalism, business fought change, resisting the expansion of unions, lobbying against social spending,
and generally fighting a rearguard effort to stop reform. Similarly,
Clinton found that his corporate allies' conditions for cooperation,
particularly Wall Street's demand that the budget deficit be reduced, sharply limited his ability to adopt the social investment policies that would have addressed the interests of his working- and
middle-class supporters. Even his concessions to the largest insurers did not guarantee their support for health insurance reform. Indeed, one could argue that much of the Clinton plan's complexity
resulted from the White House's effort to reform the American
health-care system while protecting the economic interests of the
most important private players in it.

Proponents of a more active government will also have to deal
again with race. Most current efforts to reinvent liberalism evade
the issue or suggest that reformers should explicitly repudiate the
idea that government owes a special debt to African Americans. The
political advantages of such a position in a society in which 83% of

the population is, or classifies itself as, "white" is obvious. On this argument, racial targeting has been the problem, and a social policy more attentive to the majority's needs would be far more popular; it might even renew the public's faith in government.[28] But this view misstates the problem: the Great Society was far less targeted than its critics contend. Its social programs were not only or even principally about race: the aged got far more from Congress than blacks ever did. Nor has affirmative action, arguably the most inflammatory of the race-based policies, had the effects that the public imagines. While some qualified whites have undoubtedly lost jobs or been denied admission to the college of their choice because of it, the available evidence does not support the claim that affirmative action has equalized opportunity, let alone that whites *as a group* now suffer from "reverse discrimination."[29]

Nonetheless, conservative efforts to link the Great Society to racial preferences have succeeded. Liberals blame conservatives for making that effort, but conservatives would not have succeeded had race not already been such an indelible part of the American political experience—for both African Americans and whites. Often, white political leaders have found race a useful political weapon to use against blacks. Indeed, Kenneth O'Reilly makes a compelling case that only two presidents in American history—Abraham Lincoln and Lyndon Johnson—resisted the temptation to resort to explicit or implicit racism in order to appeal to white voters and southern power brokers.[30]

As we saw, Roosevelt's record on race during the New Deal was particularly disappointing. Conceivably, had he successfully confronted southern racism in the 1930s, Roosevelt might have been more successful in his effort to realign the party system, clearing the way for the adoption of a truly liberal agenda in the 1940s and 1950s. Instead, by accommodating racism, the New Deal undercut efforts both to nationalize politics and to create a universal welfare state that might well have generated more popular support. Roosevelt was of course aware of the problem. After having secured the passage of the Social Security and Wagner acts, he made several attempts to loosen the South's grip on the Democratic party and Congress, challenging the Democratic party's rules that gave the South a de facto veto over the selection of the party's presidential candidate and, in 1938, mounting a frontal assault on the most reactionary southern Democrats.[31] But as I noted earlier, even as he mounted this challenge, Roosevelt sought southern conservative support, accommodating in policy the interests of whites nervous about the racial implications of New Deal liberalism.

Kennedy's record on civil rights was almost as disappointing. Even though blacks had been essential to his 1960 victory over

Nixon (providing the margin of victory in cities in key northern industrial states) and despite the public's growing impatience with
southern racism, the White House kept the civil rights movement at
arm's length. Deeply worried about southern support in Congress,
Kennedy delayed using federal power to protect civil rights activists
and procrastinated on new civil rights legislation until the last possible moment.[32]

In both cases, it is not at all clear what these compromises accomplished. Roosevelt's concessions to the South bought him little.
Southern agricultural interests opposed the New Deal after having
won benefits from it. In the second half of the decade, their congressional representatives joined Republicans in the conservative
coalition that stopped the New Deal in its tracks. Kennedy's back-
room negotiations with southern political elites produced little of
consequence. And when Kennedy finally responded to public revul-
sion at the actions of the Birmingham police by introducing his long-
delayed civil rights legislation, southern conservatives in Congress
kept it from coming to a vote.

Here too, liberals will have to decide just how far they are willing to stretch their "big tent," and what concessions they are willing
to make to those interests who resist racial liberalism. Concretely,
reformers must decide how to address the needs of black constituents who are disproportionately poor and unemployed, while
assuring the white majority that it also takes its economic anxieties
seriously. As attractive as it sounds, class-based affirmative action,
the currently popular proposal to square this circle, will not solve
the problem: special needs will still require special and expensive
solutions. It is quite likely, for example, that a frontal assault on
ghetto poverty would require a massive public investment in the nation's cities. This would be very expensive, and unimaginable without increasing taxes or radically reordering spending priorities, including sharp cuts in the defense budget.

This brings us finally to foreign policy and the impact that
American interventionism has had on domestic politics. I argued in
chapter 5 that Johnson's commitment to the war in Vietnam finally
stopped the Great Society. Not only did the White House spend
scarce political capital and finally throw away the fiscal surplus that
had made social policy innovation seem feasible, the administration's
war policies increased business's leverage over the administration.
Eventually, Johnson was forced to sacrifice his plans to expand the
War on Poverty in order to secure corporate support for the tax surcharge made necessary by the war in Asia. But while the war's impact on domestic reform was dramatic in the mid-1960s, it was not
exceptional: both the Roosevelt and Kennedy administrations faced
the same dilemma and paid a similar, though not quite as exorbitant,

price for choosing guns over butter. In both cases, the decision to intervene also meant a decision to abandon domestic reform in order to secure support from congressional conservatives and business elites for the administration's foreign policy. Though Roosevelt had already been beaten back by the conservative coalition in 1938, the White House's search for congressional support for European intervention in 1939 led Roosevelt to abandon entirely any hope that he might revive his domestic agenda. Military priorities then led the administration to even closer relations with corporate elites during World War II, as Roosevelt looked to business to administer the war machine. Though on a smaller scale, the same trade-off occurred in the Kennedy administration. In Kennedy's case, every misstep in pursuit of his anticommunist foreign policy, from the Bay of Pigs to the disastrous summit encounter with Khrushchev, increased White House dependence on business support.[33]

Since the war in Vietnam, liberals have been divided on this issue. Some have wanted the U.S. government to take an aggressive role in the world, not only to protect American workers but to do more to see that workers elsewhere are not exploited, that the global environment is protected, and that democracy flourishes in once-authoritarian regimes. Other liberals have called for the government to refocus its attention on problems at home. On paper, a "home" strategy is enormously promising. It would allow simultaneously for substantial reductions in the defense budget—which might be used to pay for social reform and alleviate the need to raise taxes—and appeal to the nationalist sentiments of displaced blue- and white-collar workers. There are three problems with it, however. First, and most obvious, it is hard to know how America can simultaneously withdraw from current global commitments and retain its influence over global events. Some have suggested the government can use access to the American market as a lever, replacing the threat of military intervention with economic sanctions. While theoretically possible, this would by no means be easy. America would not only face retaliation from abroad, but it is certain that the multinational corporations who operate in the world market and who insist on free access to it would use *their* enormous political leverage to reverse this course. Second, American corporations and their allies within the defense establishment have an enormous stake in American military preparedness. Even after the end of the Cold War, it has proved extremely difficult for Congress to resist demands to maintain the defense budget. In different ways, both problems return us to the question of businesses' political influence.

But there is another issue here as well. Presidents are drawn to foreign policy because they enjoy greater latitude and freedom from institutional and interest constraints in that domain. Even though different foreign policy decisions would have altered the trajectory of American social policy, it is not hard to see how Roosevelt, Kennedy, and Johnson were led to the choices that they made. To reinvent liberalism, liberals will have to confront the political-economy of interventionism as well.[34]

# Conclusion

What, finally, does this history of the American welfare state tell us about the questions that animated this study? The most striking conclusion is just how much political and institutional structures have done to frustrate the development of a more generous, comprehensive welfare state in the United States—how few choices reformers really had.

Standing outside the system, it is relatively easy to find fault with how American reformers went about building the welfare state. Even when large political and economic shocks temporarily lowered the political-institutional barriers to change, reformers chose to extend rather than supplant market principles and institutions, helping to recreate the very same structures and organizations that imprisoned them. In the Progressive period, the decision to build targeted, maternalist programs rather than universal programs made it that much more difficult for middle-class Americans to identify a widely shared public interest in economic security—an interest that might have simultaneously guided and legitimated state intervention into the market. In the 1930s and 1940s, the decision to build a federated welfare state and *not* pursue full employment institutionalized the economic foundations of corporate power, left American workers unusually dependent on market sources of income and the decisions of private employers, and reproduced political divisions within the working class. In the 1960s, the decision to launch a War on Poverty and to extend social protection to the aged without substantially increasing the state's redistributional or regulatory capacities left the American welfare state extremely vulnerable to political attack. In the 1970s, the failure to do more to protect working and middle-class standards of living from changes in the global economy made matters worse, feeding the backlash against the welfare state.

Still, it is hard to ignore how rational and reasonable these choices were given the political environment in which they were made, an environment that included a comparatively weak and, recently, declining labor movement, deep racial divisions, a frag-

151

mented state, and business elites hostile to reform and eager to use that state structure to veto unwanted policies.

Arguably, mistakes have been made. I emphasized two: Roosevelt's early concessions to business and ongoing concessions to the South in the 1930s and Johnson's too-ready embrace of tax-cut Keynesianism and his willingness to sacrifice the Great Society to the pursuit of an unwinnable war. These choices did matter, and it is possible to imagine how different decisions would have changed the shape of American liberalism.

But it is not clear that different decisions would have changed radically the overall trajectory of the American welfare state. In each case, the pursuit of alternatives would have involved substantial risks, perhaps even the collapse of reform entirely. Progressive reformers turned to protective policies because they could count on broadly based opposition from both business and labor to statist reforms that regulated relations between workers and employers. Congressional conservatives would have fought any challenge to the South's interest in racial domination. Surely, the business community would have used its not inconsiderable political influence to fight any attempt to build social democracy in the United States. Even at the height of the Great Society, liberals adopted a limited policy agenda in part because redistributional tax reform and broadly based labor-market policies seemed politically unfeasible.

Here it is useful to remember the findings reported in chapter 1. Comparative evidence suggests that reformers are likely to enjoy considerable discretion only under certain very specific conditions—for example, a high level of political organization on the part of those who would benefit from reform, agreement among the potential beneficiaries on the elements of a common political strategy, and a political structure that does not overly burden those who advocate change. Absent these preconditions, reformers are likely to face enormous collective action problems that make rational only the most limited reforms.

One could push the argument back a step and argue that reformers could have made other choices had other political actors also chosen differently. Clearly, the political strategy of organized labor has been a large part of the problem: American unions have responded to their institutional weaknesses by adopting political and economic strategies that have emphasized organization building, collective bargaining, and political moderation rather than state-led social reform. In the early twentieth century, though unions often lobbied for specific policies that would aid workers, the American Federation of Labor (AFL) refused to embrace the principle that state power should be used to correct market failures or redistribute income to workers. Instead, it adopted a voluntarist approach to work-

ers' problems that favored the private pursuit of labor's economic interests by organizing, bargaining, and controlling access to craft jobs,
establishing union-managed unemployment relief funds, and restricting immigration—not lobbying for a social insurance state.

In the 1930s, with the collapse of collective bargaining and the
rise of the more radical Congress of Industrial Organizations (CIO)
unions, organized labor did more fully embrace government action,
but the labor movement turned back to collective bargaining in the
1940s, lobbying for public policies that augmented union efforts on
behalf of workers, including fiscal policies to stimulate growth, public sector spending to make labor markets tighter (and, as a result,
collective bargaining easier), and labor policies to maintain the organizational clout of existing unions. By the mid-1950s, this mixed
benefit strategy rather than social democracy had become the dominant strategy of both wings of the labor movement, reinforcing the
market-conforming orientation of New Deal liberalism.

A strong case can be made that this strategy ultimately helped
undermine the labor movement by dividing it from unorganized
workers—the majority of the American labor force—and ironically
leaving workers too dependent on a fickle state. A decision by the
AFL to abandon voluntarism for social democracy in the early twentieth century might have changed the balance of political forces at a
key moment in the development of modern social policy. A decision
in the 1930s to provide independent political representation for the
large pool of unattached, disaffected, working-class voters, including
African Americans, might have substantially augmented organized
labor's leverage within the party system.

Perhaps. But it is hard not to conclude that organized labor's
preference for private over public solutions and its indifference to
social democracy were also reasonable responses to a hostile political environment. Divisions within the labor movement by race, ethnicity, and skill—divisions that were often cultivated by employers—
served to undermine workers' ability to act collectively and pressure
government successfully. As Samuel Gompers understood, the American working class *was* difficult to organize. Native skilled workers
were the most likely candidates for union representation. And political solidarity *was* problematic in a political system in which ethnocultural motivations were paramount in electoral politics. The
wholesale disenfranchisement of blacks in the late nineteenth and
early twentieth centuries was particularly important because it removed a potential source of political support at a critical moment in
the development of the American welfare state.

American political history, the hostility of public institutions to
organized labor's claims at the height of industrialization, and the
obstacles to collective action subsequently posed by federated state

and party structures, compounded labor's political problems. As
Martin Shefter has argued, early democratization helped dampen
whatever enthusiasm American workers might have had for Marxist
socialism. With ready access to the political system, American
workers did not have to fight the kind of class battles for basic political rights that European labor movements had had to fight, and
consequently were not radicalized in the same way.[1] Even when
American workers were drawn to radical ideas and candidates, the
political system made it difficult to translate working-class support
for alternatives into political power. As the Populists and Socialists
found out, winner-take-all electoral arrangements frustrated efforts
to build radical movements by marginalizing third parties. Workers
who mounted these sorts of challenges, as often occurred at the
local level, had problems translating regional support into national
power. With industrial workers and particularly organized workers,
concentrated in the northeastern and midwestern cities, labor could
not hope to wield much power in Congress. Because they were well
organized throughout the nation, employers were in a far better position to influence national governance. Given this situation, a labor
movement that restricted itself to organizing skilled workers was
more likely to succeed through collective bargaining in early twentieth-century America than by mounting a political movement for the
advancement of the working class as a whole.

Nor did organized labor have an easy time finding allies in the
1930s. While the children of immigrants were ready for unions, decentralized political structures encouraged middle-class farmers not
to seek alliances with labor. It is important to remember that social
democracy succeeded in Sweden in part because the centralized
structure of the Swedish state forced the Agrarian party to bargain
with and finally come to terms with organized labor.[2] American
commerical farmers had another option: they could rely on congressional conservatives to resist reforms that redistributed from the
countryside to the city.

American labor could also expect massive resistance from employers who have been unusually antistatist and hostile to workers,
and who have found ready allies among southern conservatives and
commercial farmers who, for their own reasons, have wanted to
stop statist reform. Because they have rarely been able to overcome
this combined opposition, American unions have been unable to win
critical pro-labor legislation, even from Democrats.

The unions have also been correct to fear the impact that liberal
reforms might have on union members. In the 1960s, organized
labor thought that public-works programs for the poor might take
jobs away from union workers, and they opposed the Great Society's foray into public service employment unless those efforts were

limited to the inner-city poor. Without a concerted effort to protect union jobs, antipoverty programs (including current efforts to push welfare clients into the labor market) would probably have had the effect that unions feared. It is more helpful, then, to see the unions' decision to support liberals within the Democratic party as a rational calculation about what could be won through state institutions, rather than, as some would have it, the product of ideological delusions or political and personal corruption. Within the context of existing political and social structures, labor's choices made sense—if only for organized labor.

The political choices of other actors have been equally constrained by the political environment and equally reasonable in it. Maternalism made sense for Progressive women and the Progressive movement: women-centered reform revalued women's role, and it advanced the political careers of women activists. Maternalism also helped legitimate the idea of a collective, statist response to problems of industrialism and capitalism. Significant new agencies *were* created and new laws passed between 1906 and 1920. Maternalist rhetoric convinced many judges to accept protective laws as constitutional that otherwise might have been held to violate due process and freedom of contract norms.[3]

At the same time, middle-class reformers have generally had reasons to keep their distance from organized labor. Conflicts between the unions and the middle classes have been based both in self-interest and in very different perspectives on politics and reform. Drawing more heavily on a salaried professional-managerial class than small property owners, American middle-class movements have not been wrong to prefer a non-partisan administrative state that would mediate between business and labor, to a corporatist or even union-dominated state that would serve only the best organized interests. It has also made economic sense for the more affluent middle classes to choose private market solutions over public goods and universal access to state-run programs. Better educated, better situated, and more affluent, the middle classes have had a very different relationship with market capitalism than workers have. Whether this had made them a credible "third force," better able to represent the public interest is debatable, but it has left them with very different interests.

Finally, because all actors' strategic decisions have been interrelated, all would have had to adjust their expectations for significant change to occur. It would have been futile, for example, in the 1940s for the unions to try to build a social-democratic coalition within a Democratic party that could not overcome southern opposition to progressive civil-rights and labor legislation. With that option foreclosed, the unions had little choice but to turn to other solutions, even though doing so effectively brought to an end whatever hope New Dealers had had that American liberalism might become more like European social democracy.[4]

Not that these strategies were optimal; far from it. Organized labor's political moderation only encouraged business interests to defend more strongly laissez-faire: because American workers did not threaten the established order, American business elites had fewer reasons to support state actors' efforts to create cooperative institutions. And without a stronger state, business interests were less likely to believe that government could craft cooperative solutions that might have worked. The underdevelopment of public institutions precluded state-sponsored cartelization as an option and encouraged American businesses to engage in permanent industrial conflict rather than seek corporatist solutions. In fact, the absence of centralized, proactive public institutions and class-wide organizations that could articulate and enforce class-wide pacts led both business and labor to retreat toward the defense of their short-term economic interests rather than seek cooperative political solutions to social problems. Many members of the middle class have also found themselves facing diminishing prospects without the social protections and economic policies that they might otherwise have enjoyed.

These strategic choices have also led reformers to rely more heavily on market actors and market processes and, as a result, to build a welfare state unable to adequately confront the problems it addresses. This has caused a vicious circle in which policy failure and the perception of unfairness have eroded popular support, declining popular support has made social programs vulnerable to retrenchment, and retrenchment has eroded the government's ability to solve problems—all without yielding new solutions. From the point of view of progressive reform, the failure of a too-small welfare state to meet people's needs has created the worst of worlds because it has convinced many that government cannot work for them and paved the way for a symbolic politics of blame rather than a sustained effort to restructure government to make it more effective.

Finally, this analysis suggests where reformers might best concentrate their efforts in the future. In the long run, the defense of public provision and the effort to build a more comprehensive welfare state rests more on reformers' ability to change the background institutions and alter the balance of power between competing political forces than on a campaign to defend the welfare state. This may seem perverse, but it follows directly from what we have seen. Political and institutional structures need to be changed if reformers are to do more. These changes should involve everything from changes in election laws—including campaign finance reform—to changes in the labor laws to make union organization easier. Institutional reforms must be tried too, including changes in the relationship between the executive and legislative branches to better approximate unitary government, and greater public access to the electronic media. Proposals of this sort can be multiplied endlessly. But in all cases, the goal would be the same: increasing the likelihood that reformers would choose differently by increasing the odds that they might actually succeed.

# Notes

## Introduction

1. On public assistance for poor families, see Timothy M. Smeeding, "Why the U.S. Antipoverty System Doesn't Work Very Well," *Challenge* (January–February 1992):30–35. On public programs to combat joblessness, see Richard B. Freeman, "How Labor Fares in Advanced Economies," in Richard B. Freeman, ed., *Working Under Different Rules* (New York: Russell Sage Foundation, 1994), 20–25; Lawrence Mishel and Jared Bernstein, *The State of Working America, 1992–93* (Armonk, N.Y.: M. E. Sharpe, 1993), 448. On medical care, see Joseph White, *Competing Solutions: American Health Care Proposals and International Experience* (Washington, D.C.: Brookings Institution, 1995), 232.

2. By structure, I mean the relatively permanent institutional and organizational factors that give order to social life.

3. See, for example, the essays in Todd Schafer and Jeff Faux, eds., *Reclaiming Prosperity: A Blueprint for Progressive Economic Reform* (Armonk, N.Y.: M. E. Sharpe, 1996).

## One. The Problem

1. Total public expenditures on social welfare purposes were 21% of the gross domestic product in 1992. See U.S. Bureau of the Census, *Statistical Abstract of the United States: 1995*, 115th ed. (Washington, D.C.: 1995), 374.

2. Organization for Economic Cooperation and Development, *New Orientations for Social Policy* (Paris: OECD, 1994), 59–61. Note that the OECD reports that Australia spends an even lower GDP share on social purposes, but that the Australian figures exclude program expenditures by the six states and two territories of that nation. OECD, *New Orientations,* 59. Even compared with other "liberal" or, in Richard Titmuss's terms, "residual" welfare states, such as Great Britain, Canada, Australia, and New Zealand, where the state is expected to do less, the United States stands out. The American government spends a smaller share of the nation's GDP on social purposes and on labor-market programs, and provides single-parent families with less cash assistance. On the concept of a "liberal" welfare state, see Gosta Esping-Andersen, *The Three Worlds of Welfare Capitalism*

(Princeton, N.J.: Princeton University Press, 1990). On "residualism," see Richard M. Titmuss, *Social Policy* (New York: Pantheon, 1974). For specific data, see OECD, *New Orientations*, 59–61; Organization for Economic Cooperation and Development, *Labour Market Policies for the 1990s* (Paris: OECD, 1990), 52–53.

3. See Gosta Esping-Andersen, *Politics Against Markets: The Social Democratic Road to Power* (Princeton, N.J.: Princeton University Press, 1985); Esping-Andersen, *Three Worlds of Welfare Capitalism*. See also Richard Rose, "How Exceptional Is the American Political Economy?" *Political Science Quarterly* 104 (1989):91–115.

4. U.S. Bureau of the Census, *Statistical Abstract of the United States, 1995* (Washington, D.C.: 1995), 115, 357. In combination, the total population covered by Medicare and Medicaid and active duty military personnel account for 27% of the U.S. population.

5. Philip K. Robins, "Federal Support for Child Care: Current Policies and a Proposed New System," *Focus* (Summer 1988):1–9.

6. Sheila B. Kamerman and Alfred J. Kahn, "What Europe Does for Single-parent Families," *The Public Interest* 93 (Fall 1988):84–86; Alfred J. Kahn and Sheila B. Kamerman, *Income Transfers for Families With Children: An Eight Country Study* (Philadelphia: Temple University Press, 1983); Sheila B. Kamerman and Alfred J. Kahn, "Social Policy and Children in the United States and Europe," in John L. Palmer and Isabel V. Sawhill, eds., *The Vulnerable* (Washington, D.C.: The Urban Institute, 1988), 351, 363–64; "Bottom of the Heap," *Economist* (December 11, 1993):28, cited in Seymour Martin Lipset, *American Exceptionalism: A Doubled-Edged Sword* (New York: W. W. Norton, 1996), 28.

7. Joseph Hogan and Andrew Graham, "The United States," in Andrew Graham with Anthony Seldon, eds., *Government and Economies in the Postwar World* (London: Routledge, 1990), 225–252; Douglass A. Hibbs, *The American Political Economy* (Cambridge, Mass: Harvard University Press, 1987); Andrew Martin, "The Politics of Economic Policy in the United States," *Sage Professional Paper* (Beverly Hills, Calif.: Sage Publications, 1973), 40.

8. See OECD, *Labour Market Policies;* Harold Wilensky and Lowell Turner, *Democratic Corporatism and Policy Linkages* (Berkeley, Calif.: Institute of International Studies, 1987); Goran Therborn, *Why Some Peoples Are More Unemployed Than Others* (London: Verso, 1986); Jeffrey A. Hart, *Rival Capitalists: International Competitiveness in the United States, Japan, and Western Europe* (Ithaca, N.Y.: Cornell University Press, 1992), chap. 5; Thomas Janoski, *The Political Economy of Unemployment* (Berkeley, Calif.: University of California Press, 1990).

9. Paul Osterman, *Employment Futures: Reorganization, Dislocation, and Public Policy* (New York: Oxford University Press, 1988), chap. 5.

10. OECD, *Labour Market Policies, 52–53.* In the United States, labor-market spending is targeted either by design through programs such as the Job Corps, summer youth employment, and the Targeted Jobs Tax credit, or inadvertently, because programs like the Employment Service have been used to administer work tests for public assistance programs.

11. Michael K. Brown, "Remaking the Welfare State: A Comparative

Perspective," in Michael K. Brown, ed., *Remaking the Welfare State: Retrenchment and Social Policy in America and Europe* (Philadelphia: Temple University Press, 1988), 6, 10; Desmond S. King, *The New Right: Politics, Markets and Citizenship* (London: Macmillan, 1987).

12. Richard B. Freeman, "How Labor Fares in Advanced Economies," in Richard B. Freeman, ed., *Working Under Different Rules* (New York: Russell Sage Foundation, 1994), 2–5; Robert Haveman, Barbara Wolfe, and Victor Halberstadt, "The European Welfare State in Transition," in John L. Palmer, ed., *Perspectives on the Reagan Years* (Washington, D.C.: The Urban Institute, 1986), 166.

13. As a result, the GDP share spent on social purposes has drifted steadily downward in comparison with the typical European case. The U.S. GDP share as a percentage of the median OECD GDP share went from 74% in 1970 to 68% in 1980 and remained there. OECD, *New Orientations*, 59–61. See also Rose, "How Exceptional," 91–115.

14. Paul Pierson, *Dismantling the Welfare State? Reagan, Thatcher, and the Politics of Retrenchment* (New York: Cambridge University Press, 1994).

15. On the impact of political culture generally, see Gabriel A. Almond and Sidney Verba, *The Civic Culture* (Boston: Little, Brown, 1963); J. P. Nettle, "The State as a Conceptual Variable," *World Politics* 20 (1968): 559–92. On the impact of political culture in America, see Louis Hartz, *The Liberal Tradition in America* (New York: Harcourt, Brace & World, 1955). For a clear statement about the causal relationship between values and welfare state development, see Anthony King, "Ideas, Institutions, and the Policies of Governments: A Comparative Analysis, Part I and II," *British Journal of Political Science* 3 (1973):291–313, 409–423.

16. See, for example, Daniel Levine, *Poverty and Society: The Growth of the American Welfare State in International Comparison* (New Brunswick, N.J.: Rutgers University Press, 1988), 11.

17. King, "Ideas, Institutions, and the Politics of Governments," 418–420.

18. For evidence on the cross-national variation in public attitudes toward the welfare state, and the distinctiveness of American culture, see Richard M. Coughlin, "Social Policy and Ideology: Public Opinion in Eight Nations," *Comparative Social Research* 2 (1979):3–40; Herbert McClosky and John Zaller, *The American Ethos* (Cambridge, Mass.: Harvard University Press, 1984); Robert Y. Shapiro and John T. Young, "Public Opinion and the Welfare State: The United States in Comparative Perspective," *Political Science Quarterly* 104 (1989):59–87, esp. 77–78; Benjamin I. Page and Robert Y. Shapiro, *The Rational Public: Fifty Years of Trends in Americans' Policy Preferences* (Chicago: University of Chicago Press, 1992), 124.

19. On the methodological problem, Gary King, Robert O. Keohane, and Sidney Verba, *Designing Social Inquiry: Scientific Inference in Qualitative Research* (Princeton, N.J.: Princeton University Press, 1994), 191.

20. Colin Gordon, *New Deals: Business, Labor, and American Politics, 1920–1935* (New York: Cambridge University Press, 1994), 8, 19.

21. Robert D. Putnam, *Making Democracy Work: Civic Traditions in Modern Italy* (Princeton, N.J.: Princeton University Press, 1993).

22. Esping-Andersen, *Politics Against Markets*, Chapter 8.

23. See Ann Shola Orloff, *The Politics of Pensions: A Comparative Analysis of Britain, Canada, and the United States, 1880–1940* (Madison: University of Wisconsin Press, 1993), 90.

24. Lipset, *American Exceptionalism*, 72, 101.

25. In the mid-1980s, 47.7% thought government should, 45.4% thought it should not. See Tom W. Smith, "The Welfare State in Cross-National Perspective," *Public Opinion Quarterly* 51 (Fall 1987):416.

26. Times Mirror Center for the People and the Press, *The Pulse of Europe: A Survey of Political and Social Values and Attitudes* (Washington, D.C.: 1991), sect. 7.

27. Shapiro and Young, "Public Opinion and the Welfare State," 71.

28. R. Kent Weaver and William T. Dickens, eds., *Looking Before We Leap: Social Science and Welfare Reform* (Washington, D.C.: Brookings Institution, 1995), 113. See also Yeheskel Hasenfeld and Jane A. Rafferty, "The Determinants of Public Attitudes Toward the Welfare State," *Social Forces* 67 (June 1989):1028. Even after the Republican takeover of Congress, a majority (59%) did not want to spend less on welfare. "GAO Says JOBS Plan Not Working," *Los Angeles Times* (December 19, 1994), A24.

29. Hasenfeld and Rafferty, "The Determinants of Public Attitudes," 1028; Robert Y. Shapiro, Kelly D. Patterson, Judith Russell, and John T. Young, "Employment and Social Welfare," *Public Opinion Quarterly* 51 (Summer 1987):273.

30. Shapiro, Patterson, Russell, and Young, "Employment and Social Welfare," 274–75; John Dobie and Keith Melville, "The Public's Social Welfare Mandate," *Public Opinion* 11 (January–February 1989), 48.

31. Shapiro, Patterson, Russell and Young, "Employment and Social Welfare," 274–75.

32. Page and Shapiro, *The Rational Public*, 164–65; Robert Y. Shapiro, Kelly D. Patterson, Judith Russell, and John T. Young, "Public Assistance," *Public Opinion Quarterly* 51 (1987), 127.

33. On the importance of notions of desert and equity to support for the American welfare state, see Fay Lomax Cook and Edith J. Barrett, *Support for the American Welfare State: The Views of Congress and the Public* (New York: Columbia University Press, 1992). On public opinion about welfare and work, see Shapiro, Patterson, Russell, and Young, "Employment and Social Welfare," 279–80.

34. This literature is enormous. The interested reader can consult the following review essays for guidance: Michael Shalev, "Class Politics and the Western Welfare State," in Shimon E. Spiro and Ephraim Yuchtman-Yaar, eds., *Evaluating the Welfare State* (New York: Academic Press, 1983), 27–40; Theda Skocpol and Edwin Amenta, "States and Social Policies," *American Review of Sociology* 12 (1986):131–57; Gosta Esping-Andersen and Kees van Kersbergen, "Contemporary Research on Social Democracy," *Annual Review of Sociology* 18 (1992):187–208; Edwin Amenta, "The State of the Art in Welfare State Research on Social Spending Efforts in Capitalist Democracies since 1960," *American Journal of Sociology* 99 (November 1993):750–63. See also John D. Stephens, *The Transition from Capitalism to Socialism* (Urbana: University of Illinois Press, 1979); J. Rogers Hollingsworth

and Robert A. Hanneman, "Working-Class Power and the Political Economy of Western Capitalist Societies," *Comparative Social Research* 5 (1982): 61–80; Walter Korpi, *The Democratic Class Struggle* (London: Routledge & Kegan Paul, 1983). On the United States in particular, see Michael Shalev and Walter Korpi, "Working Class Mobilization and American Exceptionalism," *Economic and Industrial Democracy* 1 (1980):31–61.

35. Pierson, *Dismantling the Welfare State?*, 29–30.

36. Orloff and Skocpol, "Why Not Equal Protection?," 736–39. Support for the American Socialist party in 1912 was 6% of the popular vote compared with 6.4% for the British Labour party in 1910. See Richard Oestreicher, "Urban Working-Class Political Behavior and Theories of American Electoral Politics, 1870–1940," *Journal of American History* 74 (March 1988):1270.

37. See, for example, Theda Skocpol, "Bringing the State Back In," in Peter Evans, Dietrich Rueschmeyer, and Theda Skocpol, eds., *Bringing the State Back In* (Cambridge: Cambridge University Press, 1985), 3–37; Peter Hall, *Governing the Economy* (New York: Oxford University Press, 1986); G. John Ikenberry, *Reasons of State: Oil Politics and the Capacities of American Government* (Ithaca, N.Y.: Cornell University Press, 1988); James March and Johan Olsen, *Rediscovering Institutions* (New York: Free Press, 1989); Sven Steinmo, Kathleen Thelen, and Frank Longstreth, eds., *Structuring Politics* (New York: Cambridge University Press, 1992).

38. Theda Skocpol, "Political Response to Capitalist Crisis: Neo-Marxist Theories of the State and the Case of the New Deal," *Politics and Society* 10 (1980):155–201; Skocpol, "Bringing the State Back In," 9, 16; Martin Shefter, "Party, Bureaucracy, and Political Change in the United States," in Louis Maisel and Joseph Cooper, eds., *Political Parties: Development and Decay* (Beverly Hills, Calif.: Sage, 1978), 211–65; Martin Shefter, "Trade Unions and Political Machines: The Organization and Disorganization of the American Working Class in the Late Nineteenth Century," in Ira Katznelson and Aristede Zolberg, eds., *Working Class Formation: Nineteenth Century Patterns in Europe and the United States* (Princeton, N.J.: Princeton University Press, 1986), 197–276; Ira Katznelson, "Working-Class Formation and the State: Nineteenth-Century England in American Perspective," in Evans, Rueschmeyer and Skocpol, eds., *Bringing the State Back In*, 257–84; generally, see the essays in Steinmo, Thelen, and Longstreth, eds., *Structuring Politics*.

39. Ann Shola Orloff, "The Political Origins of America's Belated Welfare State," in Margaret Weir, Ann Shola Orloff, and Theda Skocpol, eds., *The Politics of Social Policy in the United States* (Princeton, N.J.: Princeton University Press, 1988), 37–80.

40. See Victoria C. Hattam, *Labor Visions and State Power* (Princeton, N.J.: Princeton University Press, 1992); William G. Ross, *A Muted Fury: Populists, Progressives, and Labor Unions Confront the Courts, 1890–1937* (Princeton, N.J.: Princeton University Press, 1993); Orloff and Skocpol, "Why Not Equal Protection?," 742–43; Orloff, *The Politics of Pensions*, 16–19, 269–70; Skocpol, *Protecting Soldiers and Mothers: The Political Origins of Social Policy in the United States* (Cambridge, Mass.: Harvard University Press, 1992), chapter 5.

41. Theda Skocpol and Kenneth Finegold, "State Capacity and Economic Intervention in the Early New Deal," *Political Science Quarterly* 97 (Summer 1982):255–78; Skocpol and Ikenberry, "The Political Formation," 92–98; Theda Skocpol, "The Legacies of New Deal Liberalism," in Douglas MacLean and Claudia Mills, eds., *Liberalism Reconsidered* (Totowa, N.J.: Rowman and Allanheld, 1983), 91; Margaret Weir, "The Federal Government and Unemployment: The Frustration of Policy Innovation from the New Deal to the Great Society" in Weir, Orloff, and Skocpol, eds., *The Politics of Social Policy*, 151–52.

42. Margaret Weir, *Politics and Jobs* (Princeton, N.J.: Princeton University Press, 1992), 66–67.

43. Michael Goldfield, "Worker Insurgency, Radical Organization, and New Deal Labor Legislation," *American Political Science Review* 83 (December 1989):1257–82.

44. While state courts were more hostile, even they "moved consistently toward approval of a wide range of reform legislation." Melvin I. Urofsky, "State Courts and Protective Legislation during the Progressive Era: A Reevaluation," *The Journal of American History* 72 (June 1985): 63–64 (quote appears on p. 64).

45. This argument is best developed in accounts of the Progressive era. See William Graebner, "Federalism and the Progressive Era: A Structural Interpretation of Reform," *Journal of American History* 64 (1977):331–57; David Brian Robertson, "The Bias of American Federalism: The Limits of Welfare-State Development in the Progressive Era," *The Journal of Policy History* 1 (1989):261–89.

46. See, for example, Fritz W. Sharpf, *Crisis and Choice in European Social Democracy* (Ithaca, N.Y.: Cornell University Press, 1991), 11–16; Weir, *Politics and Jobs;* Linda Gordon, *Pitied But Not Entitled: Single Mothers and the History of Welfare, 1890–1935* (New York: The Free Press, 1994); Alan Brinkley, *The End of Reform: New Deal Liberalism in Recession and War* (New York: Alfred A. Knopf, 1995).

47. See Eric Nordlinger, *On the Autonomy of the Democratic State* (Cambridge, Mass.: Harvard University Press, 1981).

48. On Sweden, see Esping-Andersen, *Politics Against Markets*, chapter 3; on Austria, Esping-Andersen and van Kersbergen, "Contemporary Research on Social Democracy," 202.

49. Bob Jessop, *State Theory: Putting the Capitalist State in Its Place* (Cambridge, England: Polity Press, 1990).

50. Gordon, *New Deals*, 9; Jessop, *State Theory*, 260.

51. Kathleen Thelen and Sven Steinmo, "Historical Institutionalism in Comparative Politics," in Steinmo, Thelen, and Longstreth, eds., *Structuring Politics*, 17.

## Two. An Unusually Inhospitable Environment for Reform

1. See James Weinstein, *The Corporate Ideal in the Liberal State, 1900–1918* (Boston: Beacon Press, 1968); Cathie Jo Martin, "Business and the Politics of Social Welfare Innovation" (Paper delivered at the Annual

Meeting of the American Political Science Association, Chicago, Ill., August 30–September 3, 1995).

2. Francis G. Castles, *The Social Democratic Image of Society* (London: Routledge, 1978); John D. Stephens, *The Transition from Capitalism to Socialism* (Urbana: University of Illinois Press, 1979); Lars Bjorn, "Labor Parties, Economic Growth, and the Redistribution of Income in Five Capitalist Democracies," *Comparative Social Research* 2 (1979):93–128; Walter Korpi, *The Democratic Class Struggle* (London: Routledge & Kegan Paul, 1983); Walter Korpi, "Power, Politics, and State Autonomy in the Development of Social Citizenship," *American Sociological Review* 54 (June 1989):309–28; Gosta Esping-Andersen, *Politics Against Markets* (Princeton, N.J.: Princeton University Press, 1985); Gosta Esping-Andersen, *The Three Worlds of Welfare Capitalism* (Princeton, N.J.: Princeton University Press, 1990).

3. The relationship between working-class power and *social* spending is reported in Stephens, *The Transition from Capitalism to Socialism,* and discussed in Francis Castles and R. D. McKinlay, "Public Welfare Provision, Scandinavia, and the Sheer Futility of the Sociological Approach to Politics," *British Journal of Political Science* 9 (1979):157–71; Francis G. Castles, "How Does Politics Matter?: Structure or Agency in the Determination of Public Policy Outcomes," *European Journal of Political Research* 9 (1981):119–32. Cameron reported that left control of government was "a powerful source of the discrepancy in the growth of *total* government spending" (my emphasis). David R. Cameron, "Does Government Cause Inflation? Taxes, Spending, and Deficits," in Leon N. Lindberg and Charles S. Maier, eds., *The Politics of Inflation and Economic Stagnation* (Washington, D.C.: Brookings Institution, 1985), 239. Huber et al. report a significant link between left rule and total government spending in Evelyne Huber, Charles Ragin, and John D. Stephens, "Social Democracy, Christian Democracy, Constitutional Structure, and the Welfare State," *American Journal of Sociology* 99 (November 1993):711–49. But these authors conclude that left rule does not encourage transfer spending, and they support Pampel and Williamson's conclusion that "class variables have weak effects, often in the direction opposite to that of predictions" on the size of *social* spending. Fred C. Pampel and John B. Williamson, "Welfare Spending in Advanced Industrial Democracies, 1950–1980," *American Journal of Sociology* 93 (May 1988):1440. Heidenheimer et al. suggest that the relationship between the growth of transfer payments and the presence of socialist governments varies across the range of possible outcomes: the relationship is strongest at the lower extreme where socialist parties and labor movements are weak or absent. In these cases, transfer payments are likely to be small. But the relationship is unreliable and weak at the upper range and nonexistent in the midrange, where political power is more evenly balanced between left and right. See Arnold J. Heidenheimer, Hugh Heclo, and Carolyn Teich Adams, *Comparative Public Policy,* 3rd ed. (New York: St. Martin's Press, 1990), chapter 7. Huber, Ragin, and Stephens suggest that this reflects the left's interest in state interventions that widen the scope of nonmarket allocations and that have explicitly redistributional effects (Huber, Ragin, and Stephens, "Social Democracy," 715). This conclusion is sup-

ported by research by Korpi and Esping-Andersen, which indicates that working-class power has been most clearly associated with the "structure" and "quality" of social benefits, rather than their size. See John Myles, *Old Age in the Welfare State* (Boston: Little, Brown, 1984), 85–89; Korpi, "Power, Politics, and State Autonomy," 323; Esping-Andersen, *The Three Worlds,* 137–38. For two more recent summaries of these issues, see Gosta Esping-Andersen and Kees van Kersbergen, "Contemporary Research on Social Democracy," *Annual Review of Sociology* 18 (1992):187–208; Edwin Amenta, "The State of the Art in Welfare State Research on Social Spending in Capitalist Democracies since 1960," *American Journal of Sociology* 99 (November 1993):750–63.

4. Esping-Andersen, *The Three Worlds,* 129–33.

5. Ann Shola Orloff, *The Politics of Pensions: A Comparative Analysis of Britain, Canada, and the United States, 1880–1940* (Madison: University of Wisconsin Press, 1993), 66–72.

6. Peter Flora and Jens Alber, "Modernization, Democratization, and the Development of Welfare States in Western Europe," in Peter Flora and Arnold J. Heidenheimer, eds., *The Development of Welfare States in Europe and America* (New Brunswick, N.J.: Transaction, 1981), 37–80.

7. See Douglas E. Ashford, *The Emergence of Welfare States* (Oxford: Basil Blackwell, 1986); Daniel Levine, *Poverty and Society: The Growth of the American Welfare State in International Comparison* (New Brunswick, N.J.: Rutgers University Press, 1988).

8. Hicks and Misra find that the impact of "left rule" varies over time: it had significant effects on social spending (health care and income maintenance) levels between 1974 and 1982, but not between 1960 and 1974. See Alexander Hicks and Joya Misra, "Political Resources and the Growth of Welfare in Advanced Capitalist Democracies, 1960–1982," *American Journal of Sociology* 99 (November 1993): 696, 699.

9. Harold Wilensky, "Leftism, Catholicism, and Democratic Corporatism: The Role of Political Parties in Recent Welfare State Development," in Flora and Heidenheimer, eds., *The Development of Welfare States,* 345–82.

10. On centrist reformers, see Stephens, *The Transition from Capitalism to Socialism;* Wilensky, "Leftism, Catholicism, and Democratic Corporatism;" Francis Castles, *The Impact of Parties* (Beverly Hills, Calif.: Sage, 1982); Esping-Andersen, *The Three Worlds;* Huber, Ragin, and Stephens, "Social Democracy." Note however the contrary finding in Hicks and Misra, "Political Resources," 692.

11. Castles, *The Social Democratic Image;* Esping-Andersen, *Politics Against Markets;* Margaret Weir and Theda Skocpol, "State Structures and the Possibilities for 'Keynesian' Responses to the Great Depression in Sweden, Britain, and the United States," in Peter Evans, Dietrich Rueschmeyer, and Theda Skocpol, eds., *Bringing the State Back In* (New York: Cambridge University Press, 1985), 107–63.

12. Harold L. Wilensky, *The Welfare State and Equality* (Berkeley: University of California Press, 1975), 53.

13. Frances Fox Piven and Richard A. Cloward, *Regulating the Poor,* 2nd ed. (New York: Vintage, 1993).

14. Wilensky, *The Welfare State and Equality,* 53.

15. Castles and his co-authors argue that these alliances may be more important than left rule. Sten G. Borg and Francis G. Castles, "The Influence of the Political Right on Public Income Maintenance Expenditure and Equality," *Political Studies* 29 (December 1981):621. See also Castles and McKinlay, "Public Welfare Provision," 168; Castles, *The Social Democratic Image of Society.*

16. Gunnar Myrdal, *Beyond the Welfare State* (New Haven, Conn.: Yale University Press, 1960), 54. For a more recent survey, see Stephanie G. Gould and John L. Palmer, "Outcomes, Interpretations, and Policy Implications," in John L. Palmer, Timothy Smeeding, and B. B. Torrey, eds., *The Vulnerable* (Washington, D.C.: The Urban Institute, 1988).

17. Wilensky, *The Welfare State and Equality,* 53. See also Harold L. Wilensky, *The 'New Corporatism': Centralization, and the Welfare State* (Beverly Hills, Calif.: Sage Publications, 1976), 35.

18. Wilensky, *The Welfare State and Equality,* 53.

19. Michael Shalev and Walter Korpi, "Working Class Mobilization and American Exceptionalism," *Economic and Industrial Democracy* 1 (1980):31–61; Mike Davis, *Prisoners of the American Dream* (London: Verso, 1986); Mike Goldfield, *The Decline of Organized Labor in the United States* (Chicago: University of Chicago Press, 1987). See also Gary Marks, "Variations in Union Political Activity in the United States, Britain, and Germany from the Nineteenth Century," *Comparative Politics* 22(October 1989):83–104.

20. U.S. Bureau of the Census, *Statistical Abstract of the United States 1993* (Washington, D.C.: 1993), 436. For comparative data, see Richard B. Freeman, "Labour Market Institutions and Economic Performance," *Economic Policy* (April 1988):66.

21. On employer resistance, see Michael Goldfield, *The Decline of Organized Labor in the United States* (Chicago: University of Chicago Press, 1987). On government policies, see Christopher L. Tomlins, *The State and the Unions: Labor Relations, Law, and the Organized Labor Movement in America, 1880–1960* (Cambridge: Cambridge University Press, 1985). On the size of the American economy, see Michael Wallerstein, "Union Organization in Advanced Industrial Democracies," *American Political Science Review* 83 (June 1989):481–502.

22. Aristede R. Zolberg, "How Many Exceptionalisms?" in Ira Katznelson and Aristede R. Zolberg, eds., *Working-Class Formation: Nineteenth Century Patterns in Western Europe and the United States* (Princeton, N.J.: Princeton University Press, 1986), 442.

23. Ira Katznelson, *City Trenches: Urban Politics and the Patterning of Class in the United States* (Chicago: University of Chicago Press, 1981), 10–12, 65–67; Gwendolyn Mink, *Old Labor and New Immigrants in American Political Development: Union, Party, and State, 1875–1920* (Ithaca, N.Y.: Cornell University Press, 1986), chap. 2; Shalev and Korpi, "Working Class Mobilization," 43–45.

24. Richard Oestreicher, "Urban Working-Class Political Behavior and Theories of American Electoral Politics, 1870–1940," *Journal of American History* 74 (March 1988):1261. On the "ethnocultural" identities of Ameri-

can workers, see Paul Kleppner, *The Cross of Culture: A Social Analysis of Midwestern Politics, 1850–1900* (New York: The Free Press, 1970); Walter Dean Burnham, "The Politics of Heterogeneity," in Richard Rose, ed., *Electoral Participation: A Comparative Handbook* (New York: Free Press, 1974), 653–725; Paul Kleppner, *The Third Electoral System: 1853–1892* (Chapel Hill: University of North Carolina Press, 1979); James Sundquist, *Dynamics of the Party System: Alignment and Realignment of Political Parties in the United States* (Washington, D.C.: Brookings Institution, 1983).

25. Robert R. Alford, *Party and Society* (Chicago: Rand McNally, 1963).

26. Thomas Bryne Edsall with Mary Edsall, *Chain Reaction* (New York: W. W. Norton, 1991).

27. African Americans stayed out or were shut out of unions, were forced to accept the lowest paid jobs, and were recruited as strike breakers. Philip S. Foner, *Organized Labor and the Black Worker, 1619–1981* (New York: International Publishers, 1982); David Montgomery, *The Fall of the House of Labor* (Cambridge: Cambridge University Press, 1987).

28. Michael Goldfield, "The Color of Politics in the United States: White Supremacy as the Main Explanation for the Peculiarities of American Politics from Colonial Times to the Present," in Dominick La Capra, ed., *The Bounds of Race* (Ithaca, N.Y.: Cornell University Press, 1991), 131–32; Nelson Lichtenstein, "From Corporatism to Collective Bargaining: Organized Labor and the Eclipse of Social Democracy in the Postwar Era," in Steve Fraser and Gary Gerstle, eds., *The Rise and Fall of the New Deal Order, 1930–1980* (Princeton, N.J.: Princeton University Press, 1989), 136–37.

29. Jill Quadagno, *The Color of Welfare: How Racism Undermined the War on Poverty* (New York: Oxford University Press, 1994), 62.

30. Goldfield, "The Color of Politics," 132. On the concept of institutional leverage, see Margaret Weir, Ann Shola Orloff, and Theda Skocpol, "Understanding American Social Politics" in Margaret Weir, Ann Shola Orloff, and Theda Skocpol, eds., *The Politics of Social Policy in the United States* (Princeton, N.J.: Princeton University Press, 1988), 20.

31. On business and Progressivism, see Robert H. Wiebe, *Businessmen and Reform: A Study of the Progressive Movement* (Chicago: Quadrangle Books, 1962); Gabriel Kolko, *The Triumph of Conservatism* (Chicago: Quadrangle Books, 1967); Weinstein, *The Corporate Ideal;* Edward Berkowitz and Kim McQuaid, *Creating the Welfare State: The Political Economy of Twentieth Century Reform* (New York: Praeger, 1980). On business support for workmen's compensation, see James Weinstein, "Big Business and the Origins of Workmen's Compensation," *Labor History* 8 (1967):156–74.

32. Jill S. Quadagno, "Welfare Capitalism and the Social Security Act of 1935," *American Sociological Review* 49 (October 1984):641–42.

33. Kim McQuaid, *Uneasy Partners, Big Business in American Politics, 1945–1990* (Baltimore, Johns Hopkins University Press, 1994), 131–33; Kim McQuaid, *Big Business and Presidential Power, From FDR to Reagan* (New York: William Morrow, 1982), 233–54.

34. Kolko, *The Triumph of Conservatism;* Weinstein, *The Corporate*

*Ideal;* G. William Domhoff, *Who Rules America Now?* (New York: Simon and Schuster, 1983); Thomas Ferguson, "Party Realignment and American Industrial Structure: The Investment Theory of Political Parties in Historical Perspective," in Paul Zarembka, ed., *Research in Political Economy* 6 (Greenwich, Conn.: JAI Press, 1983), 1–82; Quadagno, "Welfare Capitalism"; J. Craig Jenkins and Barbara G. Brents, "Social Protest, Hegemonic Competition, and Social Reform: A Political Struggle Interpretation of the Origins of the American Welfare State," *American Sociological Review* 54 (1989):891–909.

35. Colin Gordon, *New Deals: Business, Labor, and American Politics, 1920–1935* (New York: Cambridge University Press, 1994), 19.

36. See Robert H. Salisbury, "Why No Corporatism in America?" in Philippe C. Schmitter and Gerhard Lehmbruch, eds., *Trends Toward Corporatist Intermediation* (Beverly Hills, Calif.: Sage, 1979), 213–30; Graham K. Wilson, "Why Is There No Corporatism in the United States?" in Gerhard Lehmbruch and Philippe C. Schmitter, eds., *Patterns of Corporatist Policy-making* (Beverly Hills, Calif.: Sage, 1982), 219–36.

37. Decisions by organizations like the United States Chamber of Commerce to work with Democrats and liberals have sparked membership revolts led by small business interests that have forced that organization's leaders to pull back. For example, in 1935 the Chamber membership officially rejected the public position of its president, Henry Harriman, who had recommended both working with Roosevelt and cautious support of the New Deal. Robert M. Collins, *The Business Response to Keynes* (New York: Columbia University Press, 1981), 36–40. In 1993, the Chamber's leadership faced a major revolt, led by smaller business interests, after it began negotiating with the Clinton administration over health care reform. Jeanne Saddler and Kevin G. Salwen, "U.S. Chamber of Commerce Splits Again over Issue of Health Insurance Mandates," *Wall Street Journal* (February 17, 1993), A3.

38. David Vogel, "Why Businessmen Distrust Their State," *British Journal of Political Science* 8 (January 1978):45–78; Theda Skocpol and Edwin Amenta, "Did Capitalists Shape Social Security?" *American Sociological Review* 50 (1985):572–75; Val Burris, "The Political Partisanship of American Business: A Study of Corporate Political Action Committees," *American Sociological Review* 52 (December 1987):732–44; Alan Neustadtl and Dan Clawson, "Corporate Political Groupings: Does Ideology Unify Business Political Behavior?" *American Sociological Review* 53 (April 1988):172–90; Dan Clawson and Alan Neustadtl, "Interlocks, PACs, and Corporate Conservatism," *American Journal of Sociology* 94 (January 1989):749–43; Edwin Amenta and Sunita Parikh, "Capitalists Did Not Want the Social Security Act: A Critique of the 'Capitalist Dominance' Thesis," *American Sociological Review* (1990):124–29; Sanford Jacoby, "American Exceptionalism Revisited: The Importance of Management," in Sanford Jacoby, ed., *Masters to Managers: Historical and Comparative Perspectives on American Employers* (New York: Columbia University Press, 1991), 173–241; Sanford M. Jacoby, "Employers and the Welfare State: The Role of Marion B. Folsom," *Journal of American History* 80 (September 1993): 528. On the link between smallness and corporatism, see Peter J. Katzen-

stein, *Small States in World Markets* (Ithaca, N.Y.: Cornell University Press, 1985).

39. Daniel Nelson, *Unemployment Insurance: The American Experience, 1915–1935* (Madison: University of Wisconsin Press, 1969); Theda Skocpol, *Protecting Soldiers and Mothers: The Political Origins of Social Policy in the United States* (Cambridge, Mass.: Harvard University Press, 1992), 184.

40. Paul Pierson, "The Scope and Nature of Business Power: Employers and the American Welfare State, 1900–1935" (Paper delivered at the Annual Meeting of the American Political Science Association, Chicago, Ill., August 30–September 3, 1995), 2. See also Skocpol and Amenta, "Did Capitalists Shape Social Security?" 572, and Amenta and Parikh, "Capitalists Did Not Want the Social Security Act," 124–26. On business opposition to tax increases during the depression, see Herbert Stein, *The Fiscal Revolution in America* (Chicago: University of Chicago Press, 1969), 82–90.

41. Ed Berkowitz and Kim McQuaid, "Businessman and Bureaucrat: The Evolution of the American Social Welfare System, 1900–1940," *Journal of Economic History* 38 (March 1978):128; G. William Domhoff, "The Wagner Act and Theories of the State: A New Analysis Based on Class-Segment Theory," *Political Power and Social Theory* 6 (1987):167.

42. Sar A. Levitan and Martha R. Cooper, *Business Lobbies: The Public Good and the Bottom Line* (Baltimore: Johns Hopkins University Press, 1984), 103–04; McQuaid, *Big Business and Presidential Power*, 233–54.

43. Kolko, *The Triumph of Conservativism*, chap. 6.

44. Jill Quadagno, *The Transformation of Old-Age Security* (Chicago: University of Chicago Press, 1988), 112–14; Gordon, *New Deals*, chap. 7.

45. There is a large literature on how party systems affect interest representation. Generally, see Allessandro Pizzorno, "Interests and Parties in Pluralism," in Suzanne D. Berger, ed., *Organizing Interests in Western Europe* (New York: Cambridge University Press, 1981), 249–86. For comparative materials, see Kay Lawson, *The Comparative Study of Political Parties* (New York: St. Martin's Press, 1976); Martin Shefter, "Party, Bureaucracy, and Political Change in the United States," in Louis Maisel and Joseph Cooper, eds., *Political Parties: Development and Decay* (Beverly Hills, Calif.: Sage, 1978), 211–65. The impact of electoral arrangements is discussed in Frances Fox Piven and Richard A. Cloward, *Why Americans Don't Vote* (New York: Vintage, 1989). See also their discussion in Piven and Cloward, *Regulating the Poor*, 433–40.

46. Piven and Cloward suggest that in two-party systems, party platforms will tend to avoid conflictual issues because party managers are interested in holding together large and diverse coalitions. Piven and Cloward, *Regulating the Poor*, chap. 12.

47. On the logic of distributive politics, see Theodore J. Lowi, "American Business, Public Policy, Case-Studies, and Political Theory," *World Politics* 16(1964):677–715.

48. Ira Katznelson, *City Trenches* (Chicago: University of Chicago Press, 1981), 62–67; Ira Katznelson, "Working-Class Formation and the State: Nineteenth-Century England in American Perspective," in Evans, Rueschmeyer, and Skocpol, eds., *Bringing the State Back In*, 273.

49. By centralization, I mean the degree to which government's juris-dictional and administrative authority is consolidated. This definition is bor-rowed from Alexander M. Hicks and Duane H. Swank, "Politics, Institu-tions, and Welfare Spending in Industrialized Democracies, 1960–1982," *American Political Science Review* 86 (September 1992), 661. On central-ization generally, see Paul Pierson, "Fragmented Welfare States: Federal In-stitutions and the Development of Social Policy," *Governance* 8 (October 1995):449–78.

50. David R. Cameron, "The Expansion of the Public Economy: A Comparative Analysis," *American Political Science Review* 72 (1978): 1243–61; Castles, ed., *The Impact of Parties;* Wilensky, *The "New Corpo-ratism," Centralization and the Welfare State;* Wilensky, "Leftism, Catholi-cism, and Democratic Corporatism." Huber et al. find that those "aspects of constitutional structure that disperse political power and offer multiple points of influence on the making and implementation of policy are inimical to welfare state expansion . . ." (Huber, Ragin, and Stephens, "Social Democracy," 722, 735). But Hicks and Misra report that centralization has a "more equivocal effect" on welfare expansion than this account suggests. See Hicks and Misra, "Political Resources," 698, 700 fn.

51. Hicks and Swank, "Politics, Institutions, and Welfare Spending," 658.

52. Castles, *The Social Democratic Image of Society,* 72. See also Cameron, "The Expansion of the Public Economy."

53. For an early and influential discussion of the impact of federalism on "stateness" see J. P. Nettle, "The State as a Conceptual Variable," *World Politics* 20 (1968):559–92.

54. Dahl and Lijphart have both argued that unitary governments should spend more on social programs because they provide opponents of reform with fewer opportunities to block it, and encourage the formation of encompassing organizations (unions and parties) on the left. Robert Dahl, *Dilemmas of Pluralist Democracy* (New Haven, Conn.: Yale University Press, 1982); Arend Lijphart, *Democracies* (New Haven, Conn.: Yale Uni-versity Press, 1984).

55. On the concept of structural power, see Charles E. Lindblom, *Poli-tics and Markets: The World's Political-Economic Systems* (New York: Basic Books, 1977); Fred Block. "The Ruling Class Does Not Rule: Notes on the Marxist Theory of the State," *Social Revolution* 33 (1977):6–28.

56. Seymour Martin Lipset, *American Exceptionalism: A Double-Edged Sword* (New York: W. W. Norton, 1996), 42.

57. Jerald Hage and Robert A. Hanneman, "The Growth of the Wel-fare State in Britain, France, Germany, and Italy: A Comparison of Three Paradigms," *Comparative Social Research* (1980):69. In a related study, they report that the left's ability to shape outcomes depends on the struc-ture of the state and the responses of state actors. Jerald Hage, Robert Hanneman, and E. T. Gargan, *State Responsiveness and State Activism: An Examination of the Social Forces and State Strategies that Explain the Rise in Social Expenditure in Britain, France, Germany, and Italy* (London: Unwin Hyman, 1989).

58. Ellen Immergut, *The Political Construction of Interests: National*

*Health Insurance Politics in Switzerland, France and Sweden, 1930–1970* (New York: Cambridge University Press, 1992).

59. Huber, Ragin, and Stephens, "Social Democracy," 722. Note in this regard that American federalism has been far more debilitating than the kind of parliamentary federalism found in Canada. Christopher Leman, "Patterns of Policy Development: Social Security in the United States and Canada," *Public Policy* 25 (1977):261–91.

60. Interestingly, Immergut's study suggests that the combination of decentralized structures and active representative institutions encourages opponents of reform *not* to compromise. Immergut, *The Political Construction of Interests*, 64–65.

61. Cathie Jo Martin, "Business and the Politics of Social Welfare Innovation" (Paper delivered at the Annual Meeting of the American Political Science Association, Chicago, Ill., August 30–September 3, 1995).

62. Hicks and Misra, "Political Resources;" Manfred G. Schmidt, "The Welfare State and the Economy in Periods of Economic Crisis," *European Journal of Political Research* 11 (1983):1–26; Fritz W. Scharpf, "Economic and Institutional Constraints of Full Employment Strategies: Sweden, Austria, Germany," in John Goldthorpe, ed., *Order and Conflict in Contemporary Capitalism* (Oxford: Clarendon, 1984), 257–90; Alexander Hicks and W. David Patterson, "On the Robustness of the Left Corporatist Model of Economic Growth," *Journal of Politics* 51 (1989):662–75.

63. Joel Rogers, "Divide and Conquer: Further 'Reflections on the Distinctive Character of American Labor Laws,'" *Wisconsin Law Review* 1 (1990):1–147.

64. Rogers, "Divide and Conquer," 26–27, 59–65.

65. Peter B. Evans and John D. Stephens, "Development and the World Economy," in Neil J. Smelser, ed., *Handbook of Sociology* (Beverly Hills, Calif.: Sage, 1988), 750.

66. Wilensky, *The Welfare State and Equality*, 53–54.

67. Margaret Weir and Theda Skocpol, "State Structures and the Possibilities for 'Keynesian' Responses to the Great Depression in Sweden, Britain, and the United States," in Evans, Rueschmeyer, and Skocpol, eds., *Bringing the State Back In,* 107–63.

68. On the impact of federalism in the United States, see David B. Robertson and Dennis R. Judd, *The Development of American Public Policy* (Glenview, Ill.: Scott, Foresman, 1989); Margaret Weir, Ann Shola Orloff, and Theda Skocpol, "Introduction: Understanding American Social Policies," in Weir, Orloff, and Skocpol, eds., *The Politics of Social Policy,* 20–27.

69. David Brian Robertson, "The Bias of American Federalism: The Limits of Welfare-State Development in the Progressive Era," *Journal of Policy History* 1 (1989):261–89; Gordon, *New Deals*, 20–21.

70. Colleen A. Dunlavy, "Political Structure, State Policy, and Industrial Change: Early Railroad Policy in the United States and Prussia," in Sven Steinmo, Kathleen Thelen, and Frank Longstreth, eds., *Structuring Politics* (New York: Cambridge University Press, 1992), 114–54.

71. William Graebner, "Federalism and the Progressive Era: A Structural Interpretation of Reform," *Journal of American History* 64 (1977): 331–57.

72. Walter Dean Burnham, *Critical Elections and the Mainsprings of American Politics* (New York: W. W. Norton, 1970).

73. Dietrich Rueschemeyer, Evelyne Huber Stephens, and John D. Stephens, *Capitalist Development and Democracy* (Chicago: University of Chicago Press, 1992), 122–32; J. Morgan Kousser, *The Shaping of Southern Politics: Suffrage Restriction and the Establishment of the One-Party South, 1880–1910* (New Haven, Conn.: Yale University Press, 1974); Lee J. Alston and Joseph P. Ferrie, "Labor Costs, Paternalism and Loyalty in Southern Agriculture: A Constraint on the Growth of the Welfare State," *Journal of Economic History* 45 (1985):95–117; Warren G. Whatley, "Labor for the Picking: The New Deal and the South," *Journal of Economic History* 43 (December 1983):905–29; V. O. Key, *Southern Politics in the State and Nation* (Knoxville: University of Tennessee Press, 1977), 667–68; Gary W. Cox and Mathew D. McCubbins, *Legislative Leviathan: Party Government in the House* (Berkeley: University of California Press, 1993); Richard Franklin Bensel, *Sectionalism and American Political Development* (Madison: University of Wisconsin Press, 1984), 233; Ira Katznelson, Kim Geiger, and Daniel Kryder, "Limiting Liberalism: The Southern Veto in Congress, 1933–1950," *Political Science Quarterly* 108 (Summer 1993):285–86.

## Three. Progressives

1. On the turn to maternalism, see Nancy F. Cott, "What's in a Name? The Limits of 'Social Feminism'; or, Expanding the Vocabulary of Women's History," *Journal of American History* 76 (December 1989):809–29; Seth Koven and Sonya Michel, "'Womanly Duties': Maternalist Politics and the Origins of Welfare States in France, Germany, Great Britain, and the United States, 1880–1920," *American Historical Review* 95 (October 1990): 1067–1108; Theda Skocpol and Gretchen Ritter, "Gender and the Origins of Modern Social Policies in Britain and the United States," *Studies in American Political Development* 5 (Spring 1991):36–93; Miriam Cohen and Michael Hanagan, "The Politics of Gender and the Making of the Welfare State, 1900–1940," *Journal of Social History* 24 (Spring 1991):469–84; Theda Skocpol, *Protecting Soldiers and Mothers: The Political Origins of Social Policy in the United States* (Cambridge, Mass.: Harvard University Press, 1992); Kathryn Kish Sklar, "The Historical Foundations of Women's Power in the Creation of the American Welfare State, 1830–1930," in Seth Koven and Sonya Michels, eds., *Mothers of a New World: Maternalist Politics and the Origins of Welfare States* (New York: Routledge, 1993), 43–94.

2. Gaston V. Rimlinger, *Welfare Policy and Industrialization in Europe, America, and Russia* (New York: John Wiley & Sons, 1971), 60–62, 120–21; Daniel Levine, *Poverty and Society: The Growth of the American Welfare State in International Comparison* (New Brunswick, N.J.: Rutgers University Press, 1988), 56–62, 78; Douglas E. Ashford, *The Emergence of the Welfare States* (Oxford: Basil Blackwell, 1986), 117; Peter Flora and Jens Alber, "Modernization, Democratization, and the Development of Welfare States in Western Europe," in Peter Flora and Arnold J. Heidenheimer,

eds., *The Development of Welfare States in Europe and America* (New Brunswick, N.J.: Transaction Books, 1981), 59.

3. On the definition of "modern," see T. H. Marshall, *Citizenship and Social Class* (Cambridge: Cambridge University Press, 1950), 24. Following Germany's breakthrough in the 1880s, Denmark established old-age pensions in 1891, health insurance in 1892, and unemployment insurance in 1907. Sweden passed health insurance legislation in 1891 and established old-age pensions in 1913. In 1908, Great Britain passed the Pensions Act, followed in 1911 by the National Insurance Act, creating health and unemployment insurance. Flora and Alber, "Modernization," 59.

4. Ann Shola Orloff, *The Politics of Pensions: A Comparative Analysis of Britain, Canada, and the United States, 1880–1940* (Madison: University of Wisconsin Press, 1993), 16–19, 269–70.

5. Daniel Nelson, *Unemployment Insurance: The American Experience, 1915–1935* (Madison: University of Wisconsin Press, 1969).

6. Peter Flora and Arnold J. Heidenheimer, "The Historical Core and Changing Boundaries of the Welfare State," in Peter Flora and Arnold J. Heidenheimer, eds., *The Development of Welfare States in Europe and America* (New Brunswick, N.J.: Transaction Books, 1981), 17–34.

7. Robert H. Wiebe, *Businessmen and Reform: A Study of the Progressive Movement* (Chicago: Quadrangle Books, 1962), 168–70.

8. Wiebe, *Businessmen and Reform*, 176–81.

9. Stephen Skowronek, *Building a New American State: The Expansion of National Administrative Capacities, 1877–1920* (Cambridge: Cambridge University Press, 1982), 3–10, 15; David B. Robertson and Dennis R. Judd, *The Development of American Public Policy* (Glenview, Ill.: Scott, Foresman, 1989), 17.

10. Lawrence Goodwyn, *Democratic Promise: The Populist Moment in America* (New York: Oxford University Press, 1976).

11. Richard Oestreicher, "Urban Working-Class Political Behavior and Theories of American Electoral Politics, 1870–1940," *Journal of American History* 74 (March 1988):1261. On the "ethnocultural" identities of American workers, see Paul Kleppner, *The Cross of Culture: A Social Analysis of Midwestern Politics, 1850–1900* (New York: The Free Press, 1970); Walter Dean Burnham, "The Politics of Heterogeneity," in Richard Rose, ed., *Electoral Participation: A Comparative Handbook* (New York: The Free Press, 1974), 653–725; Paul Kleppner, *The Third Electoral System: 1853–1892* (Chapel Hill: University of North Carolina Press, 1979); James Sundquist, *Dynamics of the Party System: Alignment and Realignment of Political Parties in the United States* (Washington: D.C.: Brookings Institution, 1983).

12. The class forces represented by the AALL is the subject of some historical controversy. The fact that the organization was heavily dependent on wealthy donors has played an important role in the case for the "corporate liberal" interpretation of Progressivism. The AALL *was* heavily dependent on capitalist funding, but it also counted a large number of social workers, academics, and intellectuals; and in campaigns for compulsory, public-benefit programs, it often found itself in conflict with business groups who preferred to leave these things to the market, or to organize private

welfare efforts. The AALL's campaign for compulsory, government-run, state-level health insurance pitted the organization against both the insurance industry and many of the most important business lobbying groups, including the conversative National Association of Manufacturers and the corporate liberal National Civic Federation. See G. William Domhoff, *The Higher Circles* (New York: Random House, 1970), 207–18; Theda Skocpol and John Ikenberry, "The Political Formation of the American Welfare State in Historical and Comparative Perspective," *Comparative Social Research* 6 (1983):87–148; Theda Skocpol and Edwin Amenta, "Did Capitalists Shape Social Security?" *American Sociological Review* 50 (1985):572–75; G. William Domhoff, "Corporate-Liberal Theory and the Social Security Act: A Chapter in the Sociology of Knowledge," *Politics and Society* 15 (1986–87):297–330; Theda Skocpol, "A Brief Response," *Politics and Society* 15 (1986–1987):331–32; Skocpol, *Protecting Soldiers and Mothers,* 183–94.

13. Paula Baker, "The Domestication of Politics: Women and American Political Society, 1780–1920," in Linda Gordon, ed., *Women, the State, and Welfare* (Madison: University of Wisconsin Press, 1990), 71–72. On black women reformers, see Linda Gordon, "Black and White Visions of Welfare: Women's Welfare Activism, 1890–1945," *The Journal of American History* (September 1991):559–90.

14. Theda Skocpol, Marjorie Abend-Wein, Christopher Howard, Susan Goodrich Lehmann, "Women's Associations and the Enactment of Mothers' Pensions in the United States," *American Political Science Review* 87 (September 1993):697. For a skeptical view of the impact of the women's clubs on the spread of mothers' pensions, see the exchange in Cheryl Logan Sparks and Peter R. Walniuk; Theda Skocpol, "The Enactment of Mothers' Pensions: Civil Mobilization and Agenda Setting or Benefits of the Ballot," *American Political Science Review* 89 (September 1995):710–30. On the development of the women's movement in the late nineteenth century, see Karen J. Blair, *The Clubwoman as Feminist: True Womanhood Redefined, 1868–1914* (New York: Holmes & Meier, 1980); Baker, "Domestication," 70–74; William L. O'Neil, *Feminism in America: A History,* 2nd rev. ed. (New Brunswick, N.J.: Transaction, 1988), chap. 3; Sklar, "The Historical Foundations," 60–69; Skocpol, *Protecting Soldiers and Mothers,* chap. 6 and 421–22.

15. Linda Gordon, *Pitied But Not Entitled: Single Mothers and the History of Welfare* (New York: The Free Press, 1994), 55–64 (the Addams quote is on p. 61). For a careful analysis of the social democratic impulse among social feminists, see Wendy Sarvasy, "The Transition from War to Peace: Women's Citizenship, World War I, and a Feminist Welfare State" (Paper delivered at the Annual Meeting of the American Political Science Association, Washington, D.C., August 29–September 1, 1991).

16. Gordon, *Pitied,* 61.

17. Zolberg argues that the proportion of American skilled workers who could be considered in some sense socialist was roughly comparable to what was found in Great Britain or France at this time. Aristede R. Zolberg, "How Many Exceptionalism?" in Ira Katznelson and Aristede R. Zol-

berg, eds., *Working-Class Formation: Nineteenth Century Patterns in Western Europe in Western Europe and the United States* (Princeton, N.J.: Princeton University Press, 1986), 426–27.

18. Christopher Anglim and Brian Gratton, "Organized Labor and Old Age Pensions," *International Journal of Aging and Human Development* 25 (1987): 95.

19. Gwendolyn Mink, *Old Labor and New Immigrants in American Political Development* (Ithaca, N.Y.: Cornell University Press, 1986), 254.

20. Mink, *Old Labor*, 250.

21. Anglim and Gratton, "Organized Labor," 92.

22. Elizabeth Brandeis, *Labor Legislation*, Vol. 3 of John R. Commons and associates, *History of Labor in the United States, 1896–1932* (New York: Macmillan, 1935), 555–57.

23. Wiebe, *Businessmen and Reform*, 158.

24. Olive Banks, *Faces of Feminism: A Study of Feminism as a Social Movement* (New York: St. Martin's Press, 1981), 110–11.

25. See Michael Rogin, "Voluntarism: The Political Functions of an Anti-Political Discourse," *Industrial and Labor Relations Review* 15 (July 1962):521–35; Christopher L. Tomlins, *The State and the Unions: Labor Relations, Law, and the Organized Labor Movement in America, 1880–1960* (Cambridge: Cambridge University Press, 1985); Mink, *Old Labor;* Victoria C. Hattam, *Labor Visions and State Power* (Princeton, N.J.: Princeton University Press, 1992); William G. Ross, *A Muted Fury: Populists, Progressives, and Labor Unions Confront the Courts, 1890–1937* (Princeton, N.J.: Princeton University Press, 1993).

26. Wiebe, *Businessmen and Reform;* Gabriel Kolko, *The Triumph of Conservatism* (Chicago: Quadrangle Books, 1967).

27. Susan Lehrer, *Origins of Protective Labor Legislation for Women* (Albany: State University of New York Press, 1987), 189.

28. Wiebe, *Businessmen and Reform*, chap. 7.

29. Wiebe, *Businessmen and Reform*, 37–39.

30. Weinstein, *The Corporate Ideal in the Liberal State, 1900–1918* (Boston: Beacon Press, 1968); Edward Berkowitz and Kim McQuaid, *Creating the Welfare State: The Political Economy of Twentieth Century Reform* (New York: Praeger, 1980).

31. Weinstein, *The Corporate Ideal*, xii–xiii.

32. Mink, *Old Labor*, 184; Ronnie Steinberg, *Wages and Hours: Labor and Reform in Twentieth-Century America* (New Brunswick, N.J.: Rutgers University Press, 1982), 85; Skocpol, *Protecting Soldiers and Mothers*, 183–85.

33. Mink, *Old Labor*, 82–85. See also Jill S. Quadagno, "Welfare Capitalism and the Social Security Act of 1935," *American Sociological Review* 49 (October 1984):632–47; H. M. Gitelman, "Welfare Capitalism Reconsidered," *Labor History* 33 (Winter 1992):5–31; Stuart D. Brandes, *American Welfare Capitalism, 1880–1940* (Chicago: University of Chicago Press, 1976); Berkowitz and McQuaid, *Creating the Welfare State*, 18–21.

34. Berkowitz and McQuaid, *Creating the Welfare State*, 33–39; Levine, *Poverty and Society*, 152–58; James Weinstein, "Big Business and the Origins of Workmen's Compensation," *Labor History* 8 (September

1967):166–68; Robert F. Wesser, "Conflict and Compromise: The Workmen's Compensation Movement in New York, 1890s–1913," *Labor History* 12 (1971):345–72.

35. Mark H. Leff, "Consensus for Reform: The Mothers' Pension Movement in the Progressive Era," *Social Service Review* 47 (1973); Christopher Howard, "Sowing the Seeds of 'Welfare': The Transformation of Mothers' Pensions, 1900–1940," *Journal of Policy History* 4 (1992):198.

36. Lehrer, *Origins of Protective Labor Legislation for Women*, 197, 205–06.

37. Lehrer, *Origins of Protective Labor Legislation for Women*, 202.

38. Lehrer, *Origins of Protective Labor Legislation for Women*, 218, 222–24.

39. Lehrer, *Origins of Protective Labor Legislation for Women*, 187. Those who operated in unregulated and highly competitive environments fought particularly hard against protective legislation. Southern textile manufacturers led the fight against child labor reform. Berkowitz and McQuaid suggest that in Oregon, where employers operated in markets relatively isolated from national product markets, business interests actually supported wage and hour regulations for women workers. Berkowitz and McQuaid, *Creating the Welfare State*, 30–32.

40. Steinberg, *Wages and Hours*, 188–89. This seems to account for the willingness of employers to see the Keating-Owen child labor law passed in 1916. Southern textile producers appeared to have been the principal opponents of federal child labor legislation in the Senate. Arthur S. Link, *Woodrow Wilson and the Progressive Era, 1910–1917* (New York: Harper & Row, 1963), 226–27.

41. Michael B. Katz, *In the Shadow of the Poorhouse: A Social History of Welfare in America* (New York: Basic Books, 1986), 122.

42. Link, *Woodrow Wilson*, 16; Katz, *In the Shadow*, 162; Alan Dawley, *Struggles for Justice* (New York: Cambridge University Press, 1991), 135.

43. Woodrow Wilson, *The New Freedom* (Englewood Cliffs, N.J.: Prentice-Hall, 1961), 28–115; William Diamond, *The Economic Thought of Woodrow Wilson* (Baltimore: Johns Hopkins University Press, 1943), 122.

44. David Brian Robertson, "The Bias of American Federalism: The Limits of Welfare-State Development in the Progressive Era," *Journal of Policy History* 1 (1989):285.

45. William Graebner, "Federalism in the Progressive Era: A Structural Interpretation of Reform," *The Journal of American History* 64 (September 1977):332.

46. Robertson, "The Bias of American Federalism," 274; Graebner, "Federalism in the Progressive Era," 335, 339–40.

47. Graebner, "Federalism in the Progressive Era," 343–44, 349–50.

48. Robertson, "The Bias of American Federalism," 279–80.

49. Oestreicher reports 6.4%, Orloff 7.6%, Kesselman and Krieger 7.1%. Oestreicher, "Urban Working-Class Political Behavior," 1270; Orloff, *The Politics of Pensions*, 71; Mark Kesselman and Joel Krieger, eds., *European Politics in Transition* (Lexington, Mass.: D. C. Heath and Company, 1987), 86.

50. Robertson and Judd, *The Development of American Public Policy*, 72.

51. Seventeen of the thirty-seven states that had mandated workmen's compensation reform by 1919 had state-run plans that spent public monies on this form of social insurance. Robertson, "The Bias of American Federalism," 269–70.

52. Orloff claims that workmen's compensation and mothers' pensions were acceptable because they reworked "government functions already being carried out in the courts and added no significant amount of government spending." But that misstates what was at stake in workmen's compensation (replacing a court-based system with insurance). Moreover, Skocpol's account suggests that if they had had their way, the Progressive reformers would have spent considerably more on mothers' pensions than they did. Orloff, *The Politics of Pensions,* 239; Skocpol, *Protecting Soldiers and Mothers.* In response, see Paul Pierson, "The Scope and Nature of Business Power: Employers and the American Welfare State" (Paper delivered at the Annual Meeting of the American Political Science Association, Chicago, Ill., August 30–September 3, 1995), 24.

53. Melvin I. Urofsky, "State Courts and Protective Legislation during the Progressive Era: A Reevaluation," *The Journal of American History* 72 (June 1985):63–64. In *Lochner v. New York,* decided in 1905, the Supreme Court invalidated a New York law that had limited the hours of bakery workers to ten per day and sixty per week as an infringement on "liberty of contract." In *Adair v. United States,* decided in 1908, the Supreme Court declared that a Congressional statute protecting the rights of union members was an unconstitutional invasion of personal liberty and property rights.

54. Gordon, *Pitied,* 61.

55. Roy Lubove, *The Struggle for Social Security, 1900–1935* (Cambridge, Mass.: Harvard University Press, 1968).

56. Louis Leotta, "Abraham Epstein and the Movement for Old Age Security," *Labor History* 16 (Summer 1975), 362–63.

57. Two state federations, Washington State and North Dakota, did play leading roles, but most state federations opposed the proposal. Skocpol, *Protecting Soldiers and Mothers,* 210, 374, 401, 413–14; Berkowitz and McQuaid, *Creating the Welfare State,* 32.

58. Skocpol, *Protecting Soldiers and Mothers,* 401, 416–17.

59. Berkowitz and McQuaid, *Creating the Welfare State,* 37–41. Many states adopted workmen's compensation only slightly later than had the typical European government. Robert T. Kudlre and Theodore R. Marmor, "The Development of Welfare States in North America," in Peter Flora and Arnold J. Heidenheimer, eds., *The Development of Welfare States in Europe and America* (New Brunswick, N.J.: Transaction Books, 1981), 82.

60. The Charity Organization Societies and the Eastern philanthropies were most opposed to mothers' pensions. A few Jewish charities backed them. See Katz, *In the Shadow,* 127–28.

61. Skocpol, *Protecting Soldiers and Mothers,* 425.

62. Skocpol, Abend-Wein, Howard, and Lehmann, "Women's Associations," 698. See also Christopher Howard, "Sowing the Seeds of 'Welfare':

The Transformation of Mothers' Pensions, 1900–1940," *Journal of Policy History* 4 (1992):188–227.

63. Skocpol, *Protecting Soldiers and Mothers*, chap. 7.

64. Skocpol, *Protecting Soldiers and Mothers*, 8–10, 374.

65. Skocpol, *Protecting Soldiers and Mothers*, 46.

66. Katz, *In the Shadow*, 203.

67. Skocpol, *Protecting Soldiers and Mothers*, 418.

68. Link, *Woodrow Wilson*, 59; Walter I. Trattner, *Crusade for the Children: A History of the National Child Labor Committee and Child Labor Reform in America* (Chicago: Quadrangle Books, 1970), 34–42, 103, 127–32, 136.

69. For representative statements see Karen Offen, "Defining Feminism: A Comparative Historical Approach," *Signs* 14 (Autumn 1988): 119–57; Ann Orloff, "Gender in Early U.S. Social Policy," *Journal of Policy History* 3 (Summer 1991): 249–81; Skocpol, *Protecting Soldiers and Mothers*, 525–39 (the quote is on p. 2).

70. Gordon, *Pitied*, 37.

71. Skocpol, *Protecting Soldiers and Mothers*, 8–10.

72. Mimi Abramovitz, *Regulating the Lives of Women* (Boston: South End Press, 1988), 200–206.

73. Gordon, *Pitied*, 49, 63.

74. Steinberg, *Wages and Hours*, 62.

75. Rubinow estimated 860,000 beneficiaries. Cited in Barbara Nelson, "The Origins of the Two-Channel Welfare State: Workmen's Compensation and Mothers' Aid," in Gordon, *Women, the State, and Welfare*, 128. Skocpol's estimate is slightly different: in 1910, she reports, "about 35 percent of northern men 65 and over were federal military pensioners." It is not clear from this note whether the base includes black men. Skocpol, *Protecting Soldiers and Mothers*, 557, fn. 1.

76. Koven and Michel, "Womanly Duties," 1080.

77. Katz, *In the Shadow*, 143–44. See also Virginia Sapiro, "The Gender Basis of American Social Policy," *Political Science Quarterly* 101 (1986):223.

78. Skocpol, *Protecting Soldiers and Mothers*, 11.

79. On the establishment of two tracks in the Progressive period, see Diana M. Pearce, "Toil and Trouble: Women Workers and Unemployment Compensation," *Signs* 10 (Spring 1985):439–59; Barbara J. Nelson, "The Origins of the Two-Channel Welfare State: Workmen's Compensation and Mothers' Aid," in Gordon, *Women, the State, and Welfare*, 123–51; Gordon, *Pitied*. Sapiro goes further, arguing that aid was designed to enable women "to *care* for their families and not, by and large, to *provide* for them in the sense that is expected of a breadwinner." In this sense, these programs were really for children, *not* women. Sapiro, "The Gender Basis of American Social Policy," 231. See also Howard, "Sowing the Seeds of 'Welfare'," 214–17.

80. Steinberg, *Wages and Hours*, 207.

81. Gordon, *Pitied*, 38.

82. Koven and Michel, "Womanly Duties," 1107. Gordon takes an even more extreme position: First-wave feminism, she argues, contributed to the

'modernization' of male domination, its adaptation to new economic and social conditions . . . (because) these first feminists rarely advocated full equality between women and men and never promoted the abolition of traditional gender relations or the sexual division of labor . . . organized feminism was in part . . . a program to adapt the family and the civil society to the new economic conditions of industrial capitalism. . . .

Linda Gordon, "Family Violence, Feminism, and Social Control," in Gordon, ed., *Women, the State, and Welfare*, 187–88.

## Four. The New Deal

1. Michael B. Katz, *In the Shadow of the Poorhouse* (New York: Basic Books, 1986), part 2.
2. See G. William Domhoff, "Corporate-Liberal Theory and the Social Security Act: A Chapter in the Sociology of Knowledge," *Politics and Society* 15 (1986–1987):297–330; Thomas Ferguson, "Party Realignment and American Industrial Structure: The Investment Theory of Political Parties in Historical Perspective," in Paul Zarembka, ed., *Research in Political Economy* 6 (Greenwich, Conn.: JAI Press, 1983), 1–82; Gosta Esping-Andersen, *The Three Worlds of Welfare Capitalism* (Princeton, N.J.: Princeton University Press, 1990).
3. Robert R. Alford, *Party and Society* (Chicago: Rand McNally, 1963); Richard Oestreicher, "Urban Working-Class Political Behavior and Theories of American Electoral Politics, 1870–1940," *Journal of American History* 74 (March 1988):1257–86.
4. William E. Leuchtenburg, *Franklin D. Roosevelt and the New Deal, 1932–1940* (New York: Harper & Row, 1963):106, 111–12.
5. On the Townsend movement, see Abraham Holtzman, *The Townsend Movement: A Political Study* (New York: Bookman, 1963); Edwin Amenta and Yvonne Zylan, "It Happened Here: Political Opportunity, the New Institutionalism, and the Townsend Movement," *American Sociological Review* 56 (April 1991):250–65.
6. Oestreicher, "Urban Working-Class Political Behavior," 1264.
7. Linda Gordon, *Pitied But Not Entitled: Single Mothers and the History of Welfare, 1890–1935* (New York: The Free Press, 1994):223–35.
8. Leuchtenburg, *Franklin D. Roosevelt*, 116–17, the quote is on p. 117.
9. Frances Fox Piven and Richard Cloward, *Regulating the Poor* (New York: Vintage, 1971), 84.
10. Colin Gordon, *New Deals: Business, Labor, and Politics in America, 1920–1935* (New York: Cambridge University Press, 1994), 250–53.
11. Jill S. Quadagno, "Welfare Capitalism and the Social Security Act of 1935," *American Sociological Review* 49 (October 1984):641.
12. Paul Pierson, "The Scope and Nature of Business Power: Employers and the American Welfare State, 1900–1935" (Paper delivered at the

Annual Meeting of the American Political Science Association, Chicago, Ill., August 31–September 3, 1995).

13. Gordon, *Pitied*, 250.

14. Daniel Nelson, *Unemployment Insurance: The American Experience, 1915–1935* (Madison: University of Wisconsin Press, 1969), 156–61.

15. Katz, *In the Shadow*, 240–41; Jill Quadagno, *The Transformation of Old-Age Security* (Chicago: University of Chicago Press, 1988), 108–9.

16. The following account borrows liberally from Michael Goldfield's work on labor and race. See Michael Goldfield, "Race and the CIO: The Possibilities for Racial Egalitarianism During the 1930s and 1940s," *International Labor and Working-Class History* 44 (Fall 1993):1–32, and Michael Goldfield, "The Color of Politics in the United States: White Supremacy as the Main Explanation for the Peculiarities of American Politics from Colonial Times to the Present," in Dominick La Capra, ed., *The Bounds of Race* (Ithaca, N.Y.: Cornell University Press, 1991), 131–32. See also Robert H. Zieger, *American Workers, American Unions, 1820–1985* (Baltimore: Johns Hopkins University Press, 1986), 114–23; Mike Davis, *Prisoners of the American Dream* (London: Verso, 1986), 82–93.

17. Goldfield, "Race and the CIO," 5.

18. Ira Katznelson, Kim Geiger, and Daniel Kryder, "Limiting Liberalism: The Southern Veto in Congress, 1933–1950," *Political Science Quarterly* 108 (Summer 1993):298.

19. See Thomas Ferguson, "From Normalcy to New Deal: Industrial Structure, Party Competition, and American Public Policy in the Great Depression," *International Organization* 38 (Winter 1984):41–94; Thomas Ferguson, "Industrial Conflict and the Coming of the New Deal: The Triumph of Multinational Liberalism in America," in Steve Fraser and Gary Gerstle, eds., *The Rise and Fall of the New Deal Order* (Princeton, N.J.: Princeton University Press, 1989):3–31; G. William Domhoff, *The Powers that Be: Processes of Ruling Class Domination in America* (New York: Vintage Books, 1979), 103–104; J. Craig Jenkins and Barbara G. Brents, "Social Protest, Hegemonic Competition, and Social Reform: A Political Struggle Interpretation of the Origins of the American Welfare State," *American Sociological Review* 54 (December 1989):900.

20. Gordon, *New Deals*, 253–79.

21. Quadagno, "Welfare Capitalism," 636–38; Domhoff, "Corporate-Liberal Theory," 297–330.

22. Piven and Cloward, *Regulating the Poor*, 80–84.

23. Peter Swenson, "Arranged Alliance: Business and the New Deal's Cross-Class Coalition" (Paper delivered to the Annual Meeting of the American Political Science Association, Chicago, Ill., August 31–September 3, 1995), 25.

24. See Herbert Stein, *The Fiscal Revolution in America* (Chicago: University of Chicago Press, 1969), 82–90.

25. Quadagno, "Welfare Capitalism," 642–43.

26. On the opposition of welfare capitalists to national social insurance in the early 1930s, see Edward D. Berkowitz and Kim McQuaid, "Businessman and Bureaucrat: The Evolution of the American Social Welfare System, 1900–1940," *Journal of Economic History* 38 (March 1978), 128–29.

27. Edwin Amenta and Sunita Parikh, "Capitalists Did Not Want the Social Security Act: A Critique of the 'Capitalist Dominance' Thesis," *American Sociological Review* 56 (February 1991):124–29; Theda Skocpol and Edwin Amenta, "Did Capitalists Shape Social Security?" *American Sociological Review* 50 (August 1985):572–75.

28. Jess Gilbert and Carolyn Howe, "Beyond 'State vs. Society': Theories of the State and New Deal Agricultural Policies," *American Sociological Review* 56 (April 1991):209; Margaret Weir, *Politics and Jobs* (Princeton, N.J.: Princeton University Press, 1992), 48–50.

29. Katznelson, Geiger, and Kryder, "Limiting Liberalism," 284, 288–91.

30. On labor and social policy in the region, see Richard Franklin Bensel, *Sectionalism and American Political Development* (Madison: University of Wisconsin Press, 1984), chap. 4; Jill Quadagno, "From Old-Age Assistance to Supplemental Security Income: The Political Economy of Relief in the South, 1935–1972," in Margaret Weir, Ann Shola Orloff, and Theda Skocpol, eds., *The Politics of Social Policy in the United States* (Princeton, N.J.: Princeton University Press, 1988), 235–63; Kenneth Finegold, "Agriculture and the Politics of U.S. Social Provision: Social Insurance and Food Stamps," in Weir, Orloff, and Skocpol, eds. *The Politics of Social Policy,* 199–234; Lee J. Alston and Joseph P. Ferrie, "Labor Costs, Paternalism and Loyalty in Southern Agriculture: A Constraint on the Growth of the Welfare State," *Journal of Economic History* 45 (1985):95–117; Warren G. Whatley, "Labor for the Picking: The New Deal and the South," *Journal of Economic History* 43 (December 1983):905–29.

31. See Philip Harvey, *Securing the Right to Employment* (Princeton, N.J.: Princeton University Press, 1989), 104.

32. Bensel, *Sectionalism,* 233.

33. Katznelson, Geiger, and Kryder, "Limiting Liberalism," 284, 291–92.

34. J. Morgan Kousser, *The Shaping of Southern Politics: Suffrage Restriction and the Establishment of the One-Party South, 1880–1910* (New Haven, Conn.: Yale University Press, 1974).

35. V. O. Key, *Southern Politics in the State and Nation* (Knoxville: University of Tennessee Press, 1977), 667–68; Gary W. Cox and Mathew D. McCubbins, *Legislative Leviathan: Party Government in the House* (Berkeley: University of California Press, 1993); Lee J. Alston and Joseph P. Ferrie, "Paternalism in Agricultural Labor Contracts in the U.S. South: Implications for the Growth of the Welfare State," *American Economic Review* 83 (September 1993):860; Katznelson, Geiger, and Kryder, "Limiting Liberalism," 285.

36. Theda Skocpol and John Ikenberry, "The Political Formation of the American Welfare State in Historical and Comparative Perspective," *Comparative Social Research* 6 (1983), 126–33.

37. Katznelson, Geiger, and Kryder, "Limiting Liberalism," 293.

38. New York was the first state to establish a compulsory, statewide unemployment program (Wisconsin's 1932 law only required employers to establish individual-company unemployment reserves). See Nelson, *Unemployment Insurance,* chap. 8.

39. Gordon, *Pitied*, 49.

40. Edwin Amenta and Bruce G. Carruthers, "The Formative Years of U.S. Social Spending Policies: Theories of the Welfare State and the American States During the Great Depression," *American Sociological Review* 53 (October 1988): 664. Quadagno reports twenty-five old-age assistence programs in place in 1934. Quadagno, "Welfare Capitalism," 635.

41. Jill Quadagno, "Two Models of Welfare State Development: Reply to Skocpol and Amenta," *American Sociological Review* 50 (August 1985): 577. See also Quadagno, *The Transformation*, 15–16; Piven and Cloward, *Regulating the Poor*, 130–35.

42. Leuchtenburg, *Franklin D. Roosevelt*, 84–85.

43. Leuchtenburg, *Franklin D. Roosevelt*, 84.

44. Frank Freidel, *Franklin D. Roosevelt: A Rendezvous with Destiny* (Boston: Little, Brown, 1990), 85.

45. Leuchtenburg, *Franklin D. Roosevelt*, 146–47.

46. Leuchtenburg, *Franklin D. Roosevelt*, 45–54.

47. Kenneth D. Davis, *FDR, the New Deal Years, 1933–1937* (New York: Random House, 1986), 45–54, 50–53, 60–61, 111–15.

48. Leuchtenburg, *Franklin D. Roosevelt*, 122–25, 130.

49. Davis, *FDR, the New Deal Years*, 97–103, 120, 322–25.

50. Leuchtenburg, *Franklin D. Roosevelt*, 89.

51. Quadagno, "Welfare Capitalism," 639–41; Kim McQuaid, *Big Business and Presidential Power* (New York: William Morrow, 1982), 54–55; Davis, *FDR, the New Deal Years*, 449.

52. On business's impact on the parameters of the debate, see Quadagno, "Welfare Capitalism," 638–43; J. Craig Jenkins and Barbara G. Brents, "Social Protest, Hegemonic Competition, and Social Reform: A Political Struggle Interpretation of the Origins of the American Welfare State," *American Sociological Review* 54 (December 1989):900.

53. Edwin E. Witte, *The Development of the Social Security Act* (Madison: University of Wisconsin Press, 1962), 187–89; James Morone, *The Democratic Wish: Popular Participation and the Limits of American Government* (New York: Basic Books, 1990), 255–56.

54. Davis, *FDR, the New Deal Years*, 452.

55. Secretary of the Treasury Henry Morgenthau, Jr., made the case for these concessions on other grounds, including efficiency and practicality of administration, arguing for example that it would be difficult to administer an old-age benefit program for farm laborers, transient workers, and domestics, or an unemployment insurance program for small-business employees. But the administration and Morgenthau were clearly aware that conservatives, particularly southern representatives on the House and the Senate committees, wanted these changes for their own reasons. Davis, *FDR, the New Deal Years*, 459–61; Paul Douglas, *Social Security in the United States* (New York: McGraw-Hill, 1936), 102; Gordon, *Pitied*, 276. On the relationship between the South and the New Deal generally, see Frank Freidel, *F.D.R. and the South* (Baton Rouge: Louisiana State University Press, 1965); Nicol C. Rae, *Southern Democrats* (New York: Oxford University Press, 1994).

56. Leuchtenburg, *Franklin D. Roosevelt and the New Deal*, 184.

57. Stein, *The Fiscal Revolution*, 89; Otis L. Graham, Jr., *Toward a Planned Society* (New York: Oxford University Press, 1976), 22.

58. Leuchtenburg, *Franklin D. Roosevelt and the New Deal*, 170, 242.

59. Leuchtenburg, *Franklin D. Roosevelt and the New Deal*, 249.

60. Stein, *The Fiscal Revolution*, 460–61.

61. On the development of labor market policies in the United States, see Desmond King, *Actively Seeking Work? The Politics of Unemployment and Welfare Policy in the United States and Great Britain* (Chicago: University of Chicago Press, 1995); Harvey, *Securing the Right to Employment*.

62. Edward G. Carmines and James A. Stimson, *Issue Evolution: Race and the Transformation of American Politics* (Princeton, N.J.: Princeton University Press, 1989), 31.

63. Domhoff, "Corporate-Liberal Theory," 313.

64. Stein, *The Fiscal Revolution*, 83.

65. Gary M. Anderson and Robert D. Tollison, "Congressional Influence and Patterns of New Deal Spending, 1933–1939," *Journal of Law and Economics* 34 (April 1991): 170. See also Margaret Weir, *Politics and Jobs* (Princeton, N.J.: Princeton University Press, 1992), 48–50.

66. Piven and Cloward, *Regulating the Poor*, 112.

67. James Patterson, *Congressional Conservatism and the New Deal* (Lexington: University of Kentucky Press, 1967), 339–52.

68. Stein, *The Fiscal Revolution*, 460.

69. Paul K. Conklin, *The New Deal* (Arlington Heights, Ill.: Harlan Davidson, 1992), 99.

70. Steve Fraser, "The 'Labor Question,'" in Fraser and Gerstle, eds., *The Rise and Fall of the New Deal Order*, 55–84; James A. Hodges, *New Deal Labor Policy and the Southern Cotton Textile Industry 1933–1941* (Knoxville: University of Tennessee Press, 1986); Stanley Vittoz, *New Deal Labor Policy and the American Industrial Economy* (Chapel Hill: University of North Carolina Press, 1987).

71. Katznelson, Geiger, and Kryder, "Limiting Liberalism," 299.

72. Weir, *Politics and Jobs*, 44; Conklin, *The New Deal*, 100–01.

73. Harvey, *Securing the Right to Employment*, 110.

74. Harvey, *Securing the Right to Employment*, 107–9; Weir, *Politics and Jobs*, 46–47, 51; Graham, *Toward a Planned Society*, 87–88.

75. This was the Brannan Plan. See Gregory Hooks, "From an Autonomous to a Captured State Agency: The Decline of the New Deal in Agriculture," *American Sociological Review* 55 (February 1990):40–41.

76. Katz, *In the Shadow*, 219, 225–26, 228–29.

77. James T. Patterson, *America's Struggle Against Poverty* (Cambridge, Mass.: Harvard University Press, 1986), 59.

78. Katz, *In the Shadow*, 220.

79. Patterson, *America's Struggle*, 62–63.

80. The 25% estimate is from Katz, *In the Shadow*, 229; the 30% estimate is from Patterson, *America's Struggle*, 64.

81. Katz, *In the Shadow*, 228–30; Patterson, *America's Struggle*, 63–67.

82. These amendments eliminated the requirement that benefits pro-

vide "a reasonable subsistence" and removed a provision that allowed the federal government to vet the staffing of state welfare agencies. Robert C. Lieberman, "Race and the Development of American Institutions" (Paper delivered at the Annual Meeting of the American Political Science Association, Chicago, Ill., August 31–September 3, 1995), 38–42.

83. Patterson, *America's Struggle,* 67.

84. Davis, *FDR, the New Deal Years,* 461; Andrew Achenbaum, *Old Age in a New Land* (Baltimore: Johns Hopkins University Press, 1978), 134. On southern opposition generally, see Douglas, *Social Security,* 100.

85. David B. Robertson and Dennis R. Judd, *The Development of American Public Policy* (Glenview, Ill.: Scott, Foresman, 1989), 104–5; Lieberman, "Race and the Development of American Institutions," 38–42.

86. Harvey, *Securing the Right to Employment,* 110; Graham, *Toward a Planned Society,* 86–90.

87. Margaret Weir and Theda Skocpol, "State Structures and the Possibilities for 'Keynesian' Responses to the Great Depression in Sweden, Britain, and the United States," in Peter Evans, Dieter Rueschmeyer, and Theda Skocpol, eds., *Bringing the State Back In* (Cambridge: Cambridge University Press, 1985), 145.

88. Frances Fox Piven, "Structural Constraints and Political Development: The Case of the American Democratic Party," in Frances Fox Piven, ed., *Labor Parties in Post-Industrial Societies* (New York: Oxford University Press, 1992), 235–64.

89. On the two track system and its political implications, see Pearce, "Toil and Trouble," 439–59; Nelson, "The Origins of the Two-Channel Welfare State," 123–51; Jane Jenson, "Representations of Gender: Policies to 'Protect' Women Workers and Infants in France and the United States before 1914," in Gordon, ed., *Women, the State, and Welfare,* 152–77; Gordon, *Pitied,* 299–303.

90. Leuchtenburg, *Franklin D. Roosevelt,* 144, 231.

91. Leuchtenburg, *Franklin D. Roosevelt,* 24–27.

92. Leuchtenburg, *Franklin D. Roosevelt,* 144, 231.

93. James L. Sundquist, *Dynamics of the Party System* (Washington, D.C.: Brookings Institution, 1983), 227; Conklin, *The New Deal,* 96; Weir, *Politics and Jobs,* 51; Sidney M. Milkis, *The President and the Parties* (New York: Oxford University Press, 1993), 83–92; Leuchtenburg, *Franklin D. Roosevelt,* 267–69.

94. Freidel, *Franklin D. Roosevelt,* 98.

95. Freidel, *Franklin D. Roosevelt,* 144.

96. Leuchtenburg, *Franklin D. Roosevelt,* 117.

97. Gordon, *Pitied,* 242.

98. U.S. Bureau of the Census, *Historical Statistics of the United States, Colonial Times to 1970,* Bicentennial Ed., part 2 (Washington, D.C., 1975), 1083.

99. Leuchtenburg, *Franklin D. Roosevelt,* 91–92.

100. Leuchtenburg, *Franklin D. Roosevelt,* 147.

101. Davis, *FDR, the New Deal Years,* 50–53.

102. Freidel, *Franklin D. Roosevelt,* 128.

103. For a detailed account of Roosevelt's perceptions of how business

might finally accept New Deal inspired changes in the political economy, see Peter Swenson, "Arranged Alliance: Business Interests in the New Deal," *Politics and Society* 25 (March 1997): 66–116; Davis, *FDR, the New Deal Years,* 398.

104. Davis, *FDR, the New Deal Years,* 504.

105. Mark H. Leff, "Taxing the 'Forgotten Man': The Politics of Social Security Finance in the New Deal," *The Journal of American History* 70 (September 1983):359–81.

106. Davis, *FDR, the New Deal Years,* 543.

107. Leuchtenburg, *Franklin D. Roosevelt,* 165.

108. Davis, *FDR, the New Deal Years,* 504; Leuchtenburg, *Franklin D. Roosevelt,* 183–84.

109. Leuchtenburg, *Franklin D. Roosevelt,* 344–46.

110. Leuchtenburg, *Franklin D. Roosevelt,* 108.

111. Davis, *FDR, the New Deal Years,* 423, 429, 435.


## Five. Great Society

1. Margaret Weir, *Politics and Jobs* (Princeton, N.J.: Princeton University Press, 1992), 66–67.

2. Andrew Glyn, Alan Hughes, Alain Lipietz, and Ajit Singh, "The Rise and Fall of the Golden Age," in Stephen A. Marglin and Juliet B. Schor, eds., *The Golden Age of Capitalism: Reinterpreting the Postwar Experience* (New York: Oxford University Press, 1990), 47.

3. Lawrence Mishel and Jared Bernstein, *The State of Working America, 1992–1993* (Armonk, N.Y.: M. E. Sharpe, 1993), 33, 44, 134; Glyn, Hughes, Lipietz, and Singh, "The Rise and Fall," 76–84.

4. Kim McQuaid, *Uneasy Partners: Big Business in American Politics, 1945–1990* (Baltimore: Johns Hopkins University Press, 1994), 118–20.

5. See Roger Friedland, "Class, Power, and Social Control: The War on Poverty," in Maurice Zeitlin, ed., *Classes, Class Conflict, and the State* (Cambridge, Mass.: Winthrop, 1980), 193–216.

6. Edward Berkowitz and Kim McQuaid, *Creating the Welfare State* (New York: Praeger, 1980), 136; Beth Stevens, "Labor Unions, Employee Benefits, and the Privatization of the American Welfare State," *Journal of Policy History* 2 (1990):233–60; Frank R. Dobbin, "The Origins of Private Social Insurance: Public Policy and Fringe Benefits in America, 1920–1950," *American Journal of Sociology* 97 (March 1992):1416–50.

7. McQuaid, *Uneasy Partners,* 84–86; Martha Derthick, *Policymaking for Social Security* (Washington, D.C.: Brookings Institution, 1979), 132; W. Andrew Achenbaum, *Social Security: Visions and Revisions* (Cambridge: Cambridge University Press, 1986), 44.

8. McQuaid, *Uneasy Partners,* 118–20.

9. James L. Sundquist, *Politics and Policy: The Eisenhower, Kennedy, and Johnson Years* (Washington, D.C.: Brookings Institution, 1968), 47–48.

10. David Vogel, *Fluctuating Fortunes: The Political Power of Business in America* (New York: Basic Books, 1989), 23.

11. Philip H. Burch, Jr., *Elites in American History: The New Deal to Carter Administration* (New York: Holmes and Meier, 1980), 195.

12. Irving Bernstein, *Guns or Butter: The Presidency of Lyndon Johnson* (New York: Oxford University Press, 1996), 107; Vogel, *Fluctuating Fortunes*, 25.

13. Cathie Jo Martin, "Business and the New Economic Activism: The Growth of Corporate Lobbies in the Sixties," *Polity* 27 (Fall 1994):63–64.

14. Sundquist, *Politics and Policy*, 47; T. Levitt, "The Johnson Treatment," *Harvard Business Review* 45 (January 1967):116; Sol Linowitz, "The Growing Responsibility of Business in Public Affairs," *Management Review* 55 (September 1966):55; Henry Ford, "The Revolution in Public Expectations," *Public Relations Journal* 26 (October 1970):17.

15. James T. Patterson, *America's Struggle Against Poverty* (Cambridge, Mass.: Harvard University Press, 1986), 167; Derthick, *Policymaking*, 197–98; Henry Pratt, *Gray Agendas: Interest Groups and Public Pensions in Canada, Britain, and the United States* (Ann Arbor: University of Michigan Press, 1993), 84.

16. Robert H. Zieger, *American Workers, American Unions, 1920–1985* (Baltimore: Johns Hopkins University Press, 1986), 186.

17. See Frances Fox Piven and Richard A. Cloward, *Regulating the Poor*, 2nd ed. (New York: Vintage Books, 1993); Sanford F. Schram and J. Patrick Turbott, "Civil Disorder and the Welfare Explosion: A Two-Step Process," *American Sociological Review* 48 (1983):408–14; Michael B. Katz, *In the Shadow of the Poorhouse* (New York: Basic Books, 1986), 320 fn. 32; Alexander Hicks and Joya Misra, "Political Resources and the Growth of Welfare in Advanced Capitalist Democracies, 1960–1982," *American Journal of Sociology* 99 (November 1993):697.

18. Lee J. Alston and Joseph F. Ferrie, "Paternalism in Agricultural Labor Contracts in the U.S. South: Implications for the Growth of the Welfare State," *American Economic Review* 83 (September 1993):860; Jill Quadagno, "From Old-Age Assistance to Supplemental Security Income: The Political Economy of Relief in the South, 1935–1972," in Margaret Weir, Ann Shola Orloff, and Theda Skocpol, eds., *The Politics of Social Policy in the United States* (Princeton, N.J.: Princeton University Press, 1988), 252; Gavin Wright, *Old South, New South: Revolutions in the Southern Economy Since the Civil War* (New York: Basic Books, 1986), 268.

19. Quadagno, "From Old-Age Assistance to Supplemental Security Income," 254; Richard Franklin Bensel, *Sectionalism and American Political Development, 1880–1980* (Madison: University of Wisconsin Press, 1984), 241–42; David M. Potter, *The South and the Concurrent Majority* (Baton Rouge: Louisiana State University Press, 1972), 78–87.

20. Zieger, *American Workers*, 147–48, 185–86; Beth Stevens, "Blurring the Boundaries: How the Federal Government Has Influenced Welfare Benefits in the Private Sector," in Weir, Orloff, and Skocpol, eds., *The Politics of Social Policy*, 134–38; Mike Davis, *Prisoners of the American Dream* (London: Verso, 1986), 108–20; Kim Moody, *An Injury to All: The Decline of American Unionism* (London: Verso, 1988), chap. 3; Joel Rogers, "Divide and Conquer: Further 'Reflections on the Distinctive Character of American Labor Laws,'" *Wisconsin Law Review* (1990):1–147.

21. Zieger, *American Workers*, 114–23; Davis, *Prisoners*, 82–93.

22. Hugh Mosley, "Corporate Social Benefits and the Underdevelopment of the American Welfare State," *Contemporary Crises* 5 (1981): 152.

23. The percentage of nonagricultural workers in unions declined from a postwar peak of 34.7% in 1954 to 28.9% in 1964. See Michael Goldfield, *The Decline of Organized Labor in the United States* (Chicago: University of Chicago Press, 1987), 10.

24. The unions forged an alliance with the liberal National Farmers Union, and the White House tried to build a farm-labor coalition by exchanging votes for the repeal of 14(b) for votes for a farm bill raising price supports. Bernstein, *Guns or Butter*, 310.

25. Zieger, *American Workers*, 174–79, 186; Donald G. Nieman, *Promises to Keep: African-Americans and the Constitutional Order, 1776 to the Present* (New York: Oxford University Press, 1991), 123; Jill Quadagno, *The Color of Welfare: How Racism Undermined the War on Poverty* (New York: Oxford University Press, 1994), 23.

26. Jill Quadagno, "Social Movements and State Transformation: Labor Unions and Racial Conflict in the War on Poverty," *American Sociological Review* 57 (October 1992):616–34.

27. Quadagno, *The Color of Welfare*, 69–71.

28. Zieger, *American Workers*, 177–79 (the quote is on 177).

29. Quadagno, *The Color of Welfare*, 77–78.

30. Michael Goldfield, "Race and the CIO: The Possibilities for Racial Egalitarianism During the 1930s and 1940s," *International Labor and Working-Class History* 44 (Fall 1993):19.

31. Thomas Bryne Edsall with Mary Edsall, *Chain Reaction: The Impact of Race, Rights, and Taxes on American Politics* (New York: W. W. Norton, 1991), 37, 59; Benjamin I. Page and Robert Y. Shapiro, *The Rational Public: Fifty Years of Trends in American Policy Preferences* (Chicago: University of Chicago Press, 1992), 71–75.

32. Quadagno, *The Color of Welfare*, 66; Jill Quadagno, "Race, Class, and Gender in the U.S. Welfare State: Nixon's Failed Family Assistance Plan," *American Sociological Review* 55 (February 1990):21–22.

33. Carl M. Brauer, "Kennedy, Johnson, and the War on Poverty." *The Journal of American History* 69 (June 1982):112; Nicholas Lemann, "The Unfinished War," *The Atlantic Monthly* (January 1989):58.

34. Thomas Ferguson and Joel Rogers, *Right Turn: The Decline of the Democrats and the Future of American Politics* (New York: Hill and Wang, 1986), 167.

35. Sar A. Levitan and Martha R. Cooper, *Business Lobbies: The Public Good and the Bottom Line* (Baltimore: Johns Hopkins University Press, 1984), 103–4.

36. Bernstein, *Guns or Butter*, 156.

37. Kim McQuaid, *Big Business and Presidential Power: From FDR to Reagan* (New York: William Morrow, 1982), 254.

38. Quadagno, "Race, Class, and Gender," 23–35.

39. Quadagno, *The Color of Welfare*, 129–31.

40. According to the Gallup poll, 72% of southern whites opposed the

desegregation of public accommodations in 1964. Bernstein, *Guns or Butter,* 44.

41. Most Western European countries set their economic policies to reduce unemployment to the 2%-3% range. Instead, the CEA announced that the federal government would consider a 4% jobless rate to be a "reasonable and prudent full employment target." See Richard B. Duboff, "Full Employment: The History of a Receding Target," *Politics and Society* 7 (1977):10.

42. Sundquist, *Politics and Policy,* 48; James T. Patterson, *Grand Expectations: The United States, 1945-1974* (New York: Oxford University Press, 1996), 463-65.

43. McQuaid, *Uneasy Partners,* 111.

44. Bernstein, *Guns or Butter,* 28.

45. McQuaid, *Big Business and Presidential Power,* 213; Margaret Weir, "The Federal Government and Unemployment: The Frustration of Policy Innovation from the New Deal to the Great Society," in Weir, Orloff, and Skocpol, eds., *The Politics of Social Policy in the United States,* 172-73; Brauer, "Kennedy, Johnson, and the War on Poverty," 108; Patterson, *Grand Expectations,* 468.

46. Patterson, *Grand Expectations,* 473-77; Herbert S. Parmet, *The Democrats: The Years After FDR* (New York: Oxford University Press, 1976), 172; Nieman, *Promises to Keep,* 164, 169-70; Quadagno, *The Color of Welfare,* 63, 92.

47. Patterson, *Grand Expectations,* 482.

48. Brauer, "Kennedy, Johnson, and the War on Poverty," 102.

49. Patterson, *America's Struggle Against Poverty,* 134-35; Brauer, "Kennedy, Johnson, and the War on Poverty," 108.

50. Bernstein, *Guns or Butter,* 92-94.

51. Brauer, "Kennedy, Johnson, and the War on Poverty," 108.

52. Katz, *In the Shadow,* 265.

53. Nieman, *Promises to Keep,* 185.

54. Patterson, *Grand Expectations,* 539.

55. Patterson, *Grand Expectations,* 535, 586; Patterson, *America's Struggle Against Poverty,* 141; Bernstein, *Guns or Butter,* 97-98.

56. McQuaid, *Big Business and Presidential Power,* 228, 232, 238-47; Patterson, *America's Struggle Against Poverty,* 141.

57. Weir, "The Federal Government and Unemployment," 186.

58. Weir, *Politics and Jobs,* 70.

59. Henry J. Aaron, *Politics and the Professors: The Great Society in Perspective* (Washington, D.C.: Brookings Institution, 1978), 20.

60. McQuaid, *Big Business and Presidential Power,* 228.

61. Laurie J. Bassi and Orley Ashenfelter, "The Effect of Direct Job Creation and Training Programs on Low-Skilled Workers," in Sheldon Danziger and Daniel H. Weinberg, eds., *Fighting Poverty: What Works and What Doesn't* (Cambridge, Mass.: Harvard University Press, 1986), 134-35.

62. Sven Steinmo and Jon Watts, "It's the Institutions, Stupid! Why Comprehensive National Health Insurance Always Fails in America," *Journal of Health Politics, Policy and Law* 20 (Summer 1995):348-50.

190                                                    Notes to pages 95–103

63. Patterson, *Grand Expectations,* 607.
64. Bernstein, *Guns or Butter,* 360–63.
65. Bernstein, *Guns or Butter,* 170.
66. McQuaid, *Big Business and Presidential Power,* 240–54.
67. On the South's response to the Great Society, see William G. Meyer, *The Changing American Mind: How and Why American Public Opinion Changed Between 1960 and 1988* (Ann Arbor: University of Michigan Press, 1993), 26–27; Patterson, *Grand Expectations,* 557; Edsall and Edsall, *Chain Reaction,* 37; Page and Shapiro, *The Rational Public,* 74–75; Bernstein, *Guns or Butter,* 391.
68. Edsall and Edsall, *Chain Reaction,* 61–64.
69. Bernstein, *Guns or Butter,* 414, 529.
70. Patterson, *Grand Expectations,* 649–50.
71. Bernstein, *Guns or Butter,* 433–35; Weir, *Politics and Jobs,* 93, Edsall with Edsall, *Chain Reaction,* 65.
72. Bernstein, *Guns or Butter,* 527.
73. Katz, *In the Shadow,* 265–66.
74. Martha F. Davis, *Brutal Need: Lawyers and the Welfare Rights Movement, 1960–1973* (New Haven, Conn.: Yale University Press, 1993).
75. Mimi Abramovitz, *Regulating the Lives of Poor Women: Social Welfare Policy From Colonial Times to the Present* (Boston: South End Press, 1988), 335; Achenbaum, *Social Security,* 56; Patterson, *America's Struggle,* 171.
76. Social spending rose from 9.9% of GDP in 1960 to 18.7% in 1975. See OECD, *The Future of Social Protection* (Paris: 1988), 10.
77. Lawrence Mishel and David M. Frankel, *The State of Working America* (Armonk, N.Y.: M. E. Sharpe, 1991), 171.
78. Committee on Ways and Means, U.S. House of Representatives, Overview of Entitlement Programs, *1993 Green Book* (Washington, D.C.: 1993), 1313.
79. John E. Schwarz, *America's Hidden Success: A Reassessment of Twenty Years of Public Policy* (New York: W. W. Norton, 198), 43.
80. Katz, *In the Shadow,* 264.
81. Patterson, *Grand Expectations,* 540.
82. Robert D. Plotnick, "Government Assistance for the Poor, 1965–1972," in Robert D. Plotnick and Felicity Skidmore, *Progress Against Poverty: A Review of the 1964–1974 Decade* (New York: Academic Press, 1975), 66.
83. Robert D. Plotnick, "Poverty and the Public Cash Transfer System, 1965–1972," in Plotnick and Skidmore, *Progress Against Poverty,* 147.
84. Paul A. Jargowsky and Mary Jo Bane, "Ghetto Poverty in the United States, 1970–1980," in Christopher Jencks and Paul E. Peterson, eds., *The Urban Underclass* (Washington, D.C.: Brookings Institution, 1991), 252–53.
85. The term is John Kenneth Galbraith's. See McQuaid, *Uneasy Partners,* 123.
86. Patterson, *Grand Expectations,* 539; Bernstein, *Guns or Butter,* 103.
87. Bernstein, *Guns or Butter,* 155.
88. Bernstein, *Guns or Butter,* 105–06, 386.

89. Bernstein, *Guns or Butter*, 344.

90. Patterson, *Grand Expectations*, 597–98.


## Six. Backlash

1. OECD, *New Orientations for Social Policy* (Paris: OECD, 1994), 59–61.

2. Paul Pierson, *Dismantling the Welfare State? Reagan, Thatcher, and the Politics of Retrenchment* (New York: Cambridge University Press, 1994), 67.

3. Gary Burtless, "Public Spending on the Poor: Historical Trends and Economic Limits," in Sheldon H. Danziger, Gary D. Sandefur, and Daniel H. Weinberg, eds., *Confronting Poverty: Prescriptions for Change* (Cambridge, Mass.: Harvard University Press, 1994), 57.

4. Samuel Bowles, David M. Gordon, and Thomas E. Weisskopf, *After the Wasteland: A Democratic Economics for the Year 2000* (Armonk, N.Y.: M. E. Sharpe, 1990), 159. For peak-year rates, see Bennett Harrison and Barry Bluestone, *The Great U-Turn: Corporate Restructuring and the Polarizing of America* (New York: Basic Books, 1988), 7.

5. Thomas A. Kochan, Harry C. Katz, and Robert B. McKersie, *The Transformation of American Industrial Relations* (New York: Basic Books, 1986), 65–78; Harrison and Bluestone, *The Great U-Turn*, chap. 2.

6. Samuel Bowles and Herbert Gintis, "The Crisis of Liberal-Democratic Capitalism: The Case of the United States," *Politics and Society* 11 (1982):73.

7. Bowles and Gintis, "The Crisis of Liberal-Democratic Capitalism," 73.

8. Social-welfare expenditures accounted for 12% of total workers' consumption spending in 1948. Bowles and Gintis, "The Crisis of Liberal-Democratic Capitalism," 76.

9. Patrick J. Akard, "Corporate Mobilization and Political Power: The Transformation of U.S. Economic Policy in the 1970s," *American Sociological Review* 57 (October 1992):597–615; Sar A. Levitan and Martha R. Cooper, *Business Lobbies* (Baltimore: Johns Hopkins University Press, 1984), 34–40; M. Margaret Conway, "PACs and Congressional Elections in the 1980s," in Alan Cigler and Burt Loomis, eds., *Interest Group Politics* (Washington, D.C.: Congressional Quarterly, 1986), 73.

10. Philip Harvey, *Securing the Right to Employment* (Princeton, N.J.: Princeton University Press, 1989), 110–12; William C. Berman, *America's Right Turn: From Nixon to Bush* (Baltimore: Johns Hopkins University Press, 1994), 26, 46.

11. Thomas Ferguson and Joel Rogers, *Right Turn: The Decline of the Democrats and the Future of American Politics* (New York: Hill and Wang, 1986), 109; Kim McQuaid, *Uneasy Partners: Big Business in American Politics, 1945–1990* (Baltimore: Johns Hopkins University Press, 1994), 156–57.

12. Thomas Bryne Edsall, *The New Politics of Inequality* (New York: W. W. Norton, 1984), chap. 3; Berman, *America's Right Turn*, 70–71.

13. Kochan, Katz, and McKersie, *The Transformation of American Industrial Relations*, 48.

14. For 1954, see U.S. Bureau of the Census, *Historical Statistics of the United States, Colonial Times to 1970*, Bicentennial ed., part 2 (Washington, D.C.: 1975), 178; for 1994, see U.S. Bureau of the Census, *Statistical Abstract of the United States: 1995*, 115th edition (Washington, D.C.: 1995), 443.

15. Michael Goldfield, *The Decline of Organized Labor in the United States* (Chicago: University of Chicago Press, 1987), 15.

16. Marick F. Masters, Robert S. Atkin, and John Thomas Delaney, "Unions, Political Action, and Public Policies: A Review of the Past Decade," *Policy Studies Journal* 18 (Winter 1989–1990), 474.

17. Goldfield, *The Decline of Organized Labor*, 20–21.

18. Edsall, *The New Politics of Inequality*, 161–62.

19. Edsall, *The New Politics of Inequality*, 164–69.

20. Edsall, *The New Politics of Inequality*, 142–43.

21. Edsall, *The New Politics of Inequality*, 164, 170.

22. Berman, *America's Right Turn*, 117.

23. Pierson, *Dismantling the Welfare State?*, 103, 126.

24. Jennifer L. Hochschild, *Facing up to the American Dream: Race, Class, and the Soul of the Nation* (Princeton, N.J.: Princeton University Press, 1995).

25. William Julius Wilson, *The Truly Disadvantaged: The Inner City, the Underclass, and Public Policy* (Chicago: University of Chicago Press, 1986), 129–32.

26. Benjamin I. Page and Robert Y. Shapiro, *The Rational Public: Fifty Years of Trends in American Policy Preferences* (Chicago: University of Chicago Press, 1992), 69–71, 77–79; Lawrence Bobo and Ryan A. Smith, "Antipoverty Policy, Affirmative Action, and Racial Attitudes," in Danziger, Sandefur, and Weinburg, eds., *Confronting Poverty*, 376.

27. Page and Shapiro, *The Rational Public*, 78.

28. Herbert S. Parmet, *The Democrats: The Years after FDR* (New York: Oxford University Press, 1976), 13, 22, 60.

29. Thomas Bryne Edsall with Mary Edsall, *Chain Reaction* (New York: W. W. Norton, 1991), 41.

30. Allen J. Matusow, *The Unraveling of America: A History of Liberalism in the 1960s* (New York: Harper & Row, 1984), 426–28; James L. Sundquist, *Dynamics of the Party System*, rev. ed. (Washington, D.C.: Brookings Institution, 1983), 394. See also Philip E. Converse, Warren E. Miller, Jerrold G. Rusk, and Arthur C. Wolfe, "Continuity and Change in American Politics: Parties and Issues in the 1968 Election," *American Political Science Review* 63 (December 1969):1083–1105.

31. Fay Lomax Cook and Edith J. Barrett, *Support for the American Welfare State: The Views of Congress and the Public* (New York: Columbia University Press, 1992).

32. Shanto Iyengar, "Framing Responsibility for Political Issues: The Case of Poverty," *Political Behavior* 12 (1990):19–40; Martin Gilens, "'Race Coding' and White Opposition to Welfare," *American Political Science Review* 90 (September 1996):593–604.

33. Seymour Martin Lipset, *American Exceptionalism: A Doubled-Edged Sword* (New York: W. W. Norton, 1996), 133.

34. Lawrence Bobo and Ryan A. Smith, "Antipoverty Policy, Affirmative Action, and Racial Attitudes," in Danziger, Sandefur, and Weinberg, eds., *Confronting Poverty*, 372, 388, 391.

35. Gary Orfield, "Race and the Liberal Agenda: The Loss of the Integrationist Dream, 1965–1974," in Margaret Weir, Ann Shola Orloff, and Theda Skocpol, eds., *The Politics of Social Policy in the United States* (Princeton, N.J.: Princeton University Press, 1988), 334; Page and Shapiro, *The Rational Public*, 74; William G. Mayer, *The Changing American Mind: How and Why American Public Opinion Changed Between 1960 and 1988* (Ann Arbor: University of Michigan Press, 1993), 25–26, 369–72. Note, however, that even this opposition was complex: in the late 1970s, large majorities supported "affirmative action in industry (provided there are no rigid quotas)" for women, blacks, and Hispanics. Page and Shapiro, *The Rational Public*, 97–98.

36. Robert Shapiro and J. T. Young, "Public Opinion and the Welfare State: The United States in Comparative Perspective," *Political Science Quarterly* 104 (1989):61; Bobo and Smith, "Antipoverty Policy," 371–72.

37. Edsall with Edsall, *Chain Reaction*, 152.

38. Lipset, *American Exceptionalism*, 139.

39. Lester M. Salamon and Alan J. Abramson, "Governance: The Politics of Retrenchment," in John L. Palmer and Isabel V. Sawhill, eds., *The Reagan Record: An Assessment of America's Changing Domestic Priorities* (Cambridge, Mass.: Ballinger, 1982), 49–52.

40. Pierson, *Dismantling the Welfare State?*, 36, 169.

41. Aaron Wildavsky, *The New Politics of the Budgetary Process* (Glenview, Ill.: Scott, Foresman, 1988), 236–58; Rudolph G. Penner and Alan J. Abramson, *Broken Purse Strings: Congressional Budgeting, 1974–1988* (Washington, D.C.: The Urban Institute, 1989); Allen Schick, *The Capacity to Budget* (Washington, D.C.: The Urban Institute, 1990); Steven E. Schier, *A Decade of Deficits* (Albany: State University of New York Press, 1992).

42. On these changes, see Ruy A. Texieira, *The Disappearing American Voter* (Washington, D.C.: Brookings Institution, 1993); Larry J. Sabato, *The Rise of the Political Consultants* (New York: Basic Books, 1981); William Greider, *Who Will Tell the People: The Betrayal of American Democracy* (New York: Simon and Schuster, 1992); Benjamin Ginsberg, "Money and Power: The New Political Economy of American Elections," in Thomas Ferguson and Joel Rogers, eds., *The Political Economy* (Armonk, N.Y.: M. E. Sharpe, 1984), 163–79.

43. Orfield, "Race and the Liberal Agenda," 347–51.

44. John C. Donovan, *The Politics of Poverty* (Washington, D.C.: University Press of America, 1980); Felicity Skidmore, "Growth in Social Programs, 1964–1974," in Robert D. Plotnick and Felicity Skidmore, *Progress Against Poverty: A Review of the 1964–1974 Decade* (New York: Academic Press, 1975), 8–9.

45. John Myles, *Old Age in the Welfare State: The Political Economy of Public Pensions*, rev. ed. (Lawrence: University Press of Kansas, 1989), 17, 23, 129; Jill Quadagno, *The Color of Welfare: How Racism Undermined the War on Poverty* (New York: Oxford University Press, 1994); Paul

C. Light, *The President's Agenda* (Baltimore: Johns Hopkins University Press, 1991), 50, 75–77; Burtless, "Public Spending on the Poor," 40.

46. David Frum, *Dead Right* (New York: Basic Books, 1994), 39, 47 (the quote is on 47).

47. Irwin Garfinkel and Sara S. McLanahan, *Single Mothers and Their Children* (Washington, D.C.: The Urban Institute, 1986), 129; D. Lee Bawden and John L. Palmer, "Social Policy: Challenging the Welfare State," in Palmer and Sawhill, eds., *The Reagan Record*, 185–86.

48. Pierson, *Dismantling the Welfare State?*, 16–17, 156–57.

49. Committee on Ways and Means, U.S. House of Representatives, *1991 Green Book* (Washington, D.C.: 1991), 657; Quadagno, *The Color of Welfare*, 162; Michael Katz, *In the Shadow of the Poorhouse* (New York: Basic Books, 1986), 287; Pierson, *Dismantling the Welfare State?*, 119–20.

50. Mickey Kaus, *The End of Equality* (New York: Basic Books, 1992), 131, 255–56, fn. 38; Joel F. Handler, *The Poverty of Welfare Reform* (New Haven, Conn.: Yale University Press, 1995), 77.

51. Revenues were reduced by $749 billion over five years; military spending increased in current dollars from $180.5 billion in FY 1981 to $333.7 billion in FY 1989, a real increase of 49.7%. On the politics of the budgetary process, see Wildavsky, *The New Politics of the Budgetary Process*, 228; on Kemp-Roth, see Sven Steinmo, *Taxation and Democracy: Swedish, British, and American Approaches to Financing the Modern State* (New Haven, Conn.: Yale University Press, 1993), 163. According to Murray Weidenbaum, the chair of Ronald Reagan's Council of Economic Advisers in 1981, the president understood and welcomed this outcome. See Sidney Blumenthal, "The Sorcerer's Apprentices," *The New Yorker* 69 (July 19, 1993):30–31. See also William Greider, "The Education of David Stockman," *The Atlantic Monthly* 248 (December 1981):27–54.

52. Clyde Wilcox, *Onward Christian Soldiers: The Religious Right in American Politics* (Boulder, Col.: Westview Press, 1996), 5–8, 126.

53. Elizabeth Drew, *Showdown: The Struggle Between the Gingrich Congress and the Clinton White House* (New York: Simon and Schuster, 1996), 300, 318; Dan Balz and Ronald Brownstein, *Storming the Gates: Protest Politics and the Republican Revival* (Boston: Little, Brown, 1996), 39, 248.

54. Drew, *Showdown*, 326–27.

55. Mimi Abramovitz, "Why Welfare Reform Is a Sham," *The Nation* (September 1988), 238–39; "Proposed AFDC Cuts Would Save Little, Study Says," *Los Angeles Times* (February 14, 1999), A41; "Workfare Plan Falls Short as Relief Rolls Lengthen," *Los Angeles Times* (March 5, 1991), A1; Kaus, *The End of Equality*, 255, fn. 38.

56. Judith M. Gueron and Edward Pauly, *From Welfare to Work* (New York: Russell Sage Foundation, 1991), 143; Handler, *The Poverty of Welfare Reform*, 81.

57. Wisconsin had adopted "bridefare," giving bonuses to clients who married and cutting benefits for recipients who had additional out-of-wedlock children while on welfare. "Learnfare" penalized parents whose children did not attend school. Some states had also sought to cut payments to

parents who failed to pay their rent or have their children immunized. "California Plan to Cut Welfare May Prompt Others to Follow," *New York Times* (December 18, 1991), A1; Balz and Brownstein, *Storming the Gates*, 261.

58. Balz and Brownstein, *Storming the Gates*, 284–93.

59. Blacks held 45% of the job-training slots created by the War on Poverty's manpower programs and 61% of all Job Corps positions. Margaret Weir, *Politics and Jobs* (Princeton, N.J.: Princeton University Press, 1992), 84–86.

60. Gerald D. Jaynes and Robin M. Williams, Jr., eds., *A Common Destiny: Blacks and American Society* (Washington, D.C.: National Academy of Sciences, 1989), 62.

61. Joseph A. Pechman, *Who Paid The Taxes, 1966–85* (Washington, D.C.: Brookings Institution, 1985), 73–75; Steinmo, *Taxation and Democracy*.

62. Theda Skocpol, "Targeting Within Universalism: Politically Viable Policies to Combat Poverty in the United States," in Christopher Jencks and Paul E. Peterson, eds., *The Urban Underclass* (Washington, D.C.: Brookings Institution, 1991), 411–36.

63. James T. Patterson, *America's Struggle Against Poverty* (Cambridge, Mass.: Harvard University Press, 1986), chap. 13.

64. Samuel Bowles, "The Post-Keynesian Capital-Labor Stalemate," *Socialist Review* 65 (1982):45–72.

65. Lawrence Mishel and Jared Bernstein, *The State of Working America, 1992–93* (Armonk, N.Y.: M. E. Sharpe, 1993), 402.

66. See Theda Skocpol, *Boomerang: Clinton's Health Security Effort and the Turn against Government in U.S. Politics* (New York: W. W. Norton, 1996); Haynes Johnson and David S. Broder, *The System: The American Way of Politics at the Breaking Point* (Boston: Little, Brown, 1996).

67. In addition to Skocpol, *Boomerang*, and Johnson and Broder, *The System*, the following account draws on Lawrence D. Brown, "Dogmatic Slumbers: American Business and Health Policy," *Journal of Health Politics, Policy and Law* 18 (Summer 1993):339–57; Cathie Jo Martin, "Together Again: Business, Government, and the Quest for Cost Control," *Journal of Health Politics, Policy and Law* 18 (Summer 1993):359–93; Hilary Stout and Rick Wartzman, "Why Clinton's Effort to Woo Big Business to Health Plan Failed," *Wall Street Journal* (February 11, 1994):A1; Julie Kosterlitz, "Stress Fractures," *National Journal* (February 19, 1994):412–17; Cathie Jo Martin, "Stuck in Neutral: Big Business and the Politics of National Health Reform," *Journal of Health Politics, Policy and Law* 20 (Summer 1995): 431–36; Sven Steinmo and Jon Watts, "It's the Institutions, Stupid! Why Comprehensive National Health Insurance Always Fails in America," *Journal of Health Politics, Policy and Law* 20 (Summer 1995):329–72; David W. Brady and Kara M. Buckley, "Health Care Reform in the 103rd Congress: A Predictable Failure," *Journal of Health Politics, Policy and Law* 20 (Summer 1995):447–62.

68. Skocpol, *Boomerang*, 55.

69. Johnson and Broder, *The System*, 194–95.

70. Jeanne Saddler and Kevin G. Salwen, "U.S. Chamber of Commerce Splits Again over Issue of Health Insurance Mandates," *Wall Street Journal* (February 17, 1993), A3; Julie Kosterlitz, "Stress Fractures," *National Journal* (February 19, 1994):412–17.

71. Steinmo and Watts, "It's the Institutions, Stupid!," 362.

72. Joseph White, *Competing Solutions: American Health Care Proposals and International Experience* (Washington, D.C.: Brookings Institution, 1995), 201.

73. Johnson and Broder, *The System,* 11, 35–40.


## Seven. Future of Reform

1. On these trends, see Scott Lash and John Urry, *The End of Organized Capitalism* (Madison: University of Wisconsin Press, 1987). See also the essays in William E. Peterson and Alastair H. Thomas, eds., *The Future of Social Democracy: Problems and Prospects of Social Democratic Parties in Western Europe* (New York: Oxford University Press, 1986).

2. Jennifer Hochschild, *Facing up to the American Dream: Race, Class, and the Soul of the Nation* (Princeton, N.J.: Princeton University Press, 1995).

3. See the essays collected in Robert E. Goodin and Julian Le Grand, eds., *Not Only the Poor: The Middle Classes and the Welfare State* (London: Allen and Unwin, 1987).

4. Mickey Kaus, *The End of Equality* (New York: Basic Books, 1992), 122–23.

5. Theda Skocpol, "Targeting Within Universalism: Politically Viable Policies to Combat Poverty in the United States," in Christopher Jencks and Paul E. Peterson, eds., *The Urban Underclass* (Washington, D.C.: Brookings Institution, 1991), 411–36.

6. The two classic postindustrial accounts are Daniel Bell, *The Coming of Post-Industrial Society* (New York: Basic Books, 1973) and Alain Touraine, *The Postindustrial Society* (New York: Random House, 1971). The two postindustrial accounts with the clearest implications for social policy are Michael J. Piore and Charles F. Sabel, *The Second Industrial Divide: Possibilities for Prosperity* (New York: Basic Books, 1984) and Fred Block, *Postindustrial Possibilities: A Critique of Economic Discourse* (Berkeley: University of California Press, 1990). The most radical formulation in this vein is André Gorz, *Paths to Paradise: On the Liberation from Work* (Boston: South End Press, 1985).

7. Robert Reich, *The Next American Frontier* (New York: Times Books, 1983), 246.

8. The implications of these changes for government and politics are explored in Claus Offe, *Disorganized Capitalism* (Cambridge, Mass.: MIT Press, 1985); Joshua Cohen and Joel Rogers, "Secondary Associations and Democratic Governance," *Politics and Society* 20 (December 1992): 393–472.

9. John Mathews, *Age of Democracy: The Politics of Post-Fordism* (New York: Oxford University Press, 1989), 118–19.

10. For essays in this vein, see Stuart M. Butler, ed., *Agenda for Em-*

*powerment* (Washington: The Heritage Foundation, 1990); the quote is on page vi.

11. Lawrence Mishel and David M. Frankel, *The State of Working America, 1990–91* (Armonk, N.Y.: M. E. Sharpe, 1990), 31.

12. At the federal level, despite reductions in the personal income tax, the income tax became less progressive after 1977: the sharpest reductions were concentrated on the very rich between 1977 and 1985. The average personal income tax for the top 1% fell 3.6% between 1977 and 1990. 1986 tax reform restored some progressivity to the law, particularly for the poorest households, but it did not reverse previous trends. It also recaptured whatever gains the middle class had made prior to 1986. Mishel and Frankel, *The State of Working America,* 53–55.

13. David Ellwood, "Welfare and Work: A Symposium," *The New Republic* (October 1986):18–23.

14. Robert Rector, "The 'ABC' Child Care Bill: An Attempt to Bureaucratize Motherhood," in Butler, ed., *Agenda for Empowerment,* 151–66.

15. Sar A. Levitan, *Programs in Aid of the Poor* (Baltimore: Johns Hopkins University Press, 1990), 55.

16. While there is some evidence that high AFDC benefits may have encouraged some mothers to end bad marriages, there is little evidence that welfare played more than a minor role in changing overall family patterns. There was, in particular, little relation between the level of benefits and the number of families headed by women. See David Ellwood, *Poor Support* (New York: Basic Books, 1988), 57–65. See also Christopher Jencks, *Rethinking Social Policy* (Cambridge, Mass.: Harvard University Press, 1992), 130–35. There is evidence that high AFDC benefits allowed single mothers to set up their own households (as opposed to living with their parents) and made divorced mothers more cautious about remarrying. See Jencks, "How Poor Are the Poor?" *The New York Review of Books* (May 9, 1985):45. Note however that the proportion of female-headed families is rising everywhere in the West, regardless of welfare-state structure.

17. The percentage of single mothers collecting welfare actually declined from 63% in 1972 to 45% in 1988. Christopher Jencks, "Is the American Underclass Growing?" in Christopher Jencks and Paul Peterson, eds., *The Urban Underclass* (Washington, D.C.: Brookings Institution, 1991), 60. Only 19% of black daughters and 26% of white daughters in highly dependent welfare families became highly dependent themselves. Nearly half (47%) of the black daughters who grew up in highly welfare dependent families received *no* welfare as adults. Committee on Ways and Means, U.S. House of Representatives, *1991 Green Book* (Washington, D.C.: 1991), 643–44. ("High welfare dependency" means that at least 25% of average family income over a seven-year period came from cash welfare payments.)

18. The 1.8 million figure is based on poor people living in "extreme poverty areas," that is, neighborhoods with poverty rates of more than 40% in the 100 largest cities. The 2.5 million figure is based on people living in neighborhoods with a high incidence of social problems, including frequency of female-headship, welfare receipt, low male labor-force participa-

tion rates, and high school-dropout rates. See Isabel V. Sawhill, "An Overview," *The Public Interest* 96 (Summer 1989):3–15; Ronald B. Mincy, "Underclass Variations by Race and Place: Have Large Cities Darkened Our Picture of the Underclass?" (Washington, D.C.: The Urban Institute, 1991), tables 1 and 3A. Mead estimates that his target group of long-term but employable poor is 4%–5% of the poor, or (my calculation) 1.3 to 1.7 million people. Lawrence Mead, *The New Politics of Poverty* (New York: Basic Books, 1992), 14. Research indicates that approximately 600,000 persons were homeless in the late 1980s. See Martha R. Burt and Barbara E. Cohen, *America's Homeless: Numbers, Characteristics, and Programs That Serve Them* (Washington, D.C.: The Urban Institute, 1989).

19. To be sure, at any given point in time, the long-term poor (people in the midst of an eight-year or longer "poverty spell") constituted 60% of the poverty population. But the point-in-time approach overrepresents the long-termers. Most people who become poor at some point in their lives are poor for a brief period (1–2 years). Mary J. Bane and David T. Ellwood, "The Dynamics of Dependence: The Routes to Self-Sufficiency," Working Paper, 1983. Cited in William Julius Wilson, *The Truly Disadvantaged: The Inner City, the Underclass, and Public Policy* (Chicago: University of Chicago Press, 1986), 176 and 219, fn. 61. In fact, 60.3% of persons beginning a poverty spell between 1970 and 1982 spent less than three (continuous) years poor. See Lawrence Mishel and Jared Bernstein, *The State of Working America, 1992–93* (Armonk, N.Y.: M. E. Sharpe, 1993), 282. These authors conclude that there is a "good deal of turnover in the poverty population; chronic poverty is the exception, not the rule." Mishel and Bernstein, *The State of Working America, 1992–93*, 283.

20. Only half (52.4%) of the poverty population in 1989 lived in female-headed families. U.S. House of Representatives, *1991 Green Book*, 1146, table 11.

21. In 1980, only 7% of the poverty population lived in those areas of the 100 largest cities where 40% or more of the residents were poor. David Ellwood, *Poor Support*, 193. Jargowsky and Bane report that there were 2.4 million ghetto poor (people living in SMSA's with 40% or more poverty rates) in 1980, or about 9% of all poor persons. Paul A. Jargowsky and Mary Jo Bane, "Ghetto Poverty in the United States, 1970–1980," in Jencks and Peterson, eds., *The Urban Underclass*, 269.

22. Again, the perspective taken matters. On the one hand, over an extended period, most of the people who received AFDC benefits did so for short "spells." Only half of persons beginning their first AFDC spell stayed 5 or more years; 30% stayed 8 or more years; half stayed less than 5 years. See U.S. House of Representatives, *1991 Green Book*, 640. The median continuous AFDC spell was 2.2 years. Levitan, *Programs in Aid of the Poor*, 55. Even this may exaggerate the problem: a "one-year" spell actually measures participation for at least one month in a given year. Nonetheless, the evidence shows that the longer someone stayed on welfare, the less likely they were to leave it. Robert Moffitt, "Incentive Effects of the U.S. Welfare System," Institute for Research on Poverty, Special Report Series, SR #48 (March 1991):41–42.

23. Generally, see Paul E. Peterson, "The Urban Underclass and the

Poverty Paradox," in Jencks and Peterson, eds., *The Urban Underclass*, 21. On teenage motherhood, see Jencks, "Is the American Underclass Growing?" in Jencks and Peterson, eds., *The Urban Underclass*, 84. After 1981, all three forms of violent crime among blacks—murder, aggravated assaults, and robberies—decreased in frequency. Jencks, "Is the American Underclass Growing?" 77.

24. Mead, *The New Politics of Poverty*, 125. Ellwood agrees: long-term AFDC recipients are typically less educated (usually high school dropouts), never-married mothers, with little previous work experience. Ellwood, *Poor Support*, 148.

25. See, for example, Kevin Phillips, *The Politics of Rich and Poor* (New York: HarperCollins, 1990).

26. On this point, see Brown's research, which shows that Democratic control of state legislatures only improves the prospects for social welfare legislation "where the dominant cleavage of social group support for the parties is drawn along class-related lines." Otherwise, partisan control has little effect. Robert D. Brown, "Party Cleavages and Welfare Effort in the American States," *American Political Science Review* 89 (March 1995):31.

27. For an interesting argument along these lines, see E. J. Dionne, Jr., *They Only Look Dead: Why Progressives Will Dominate the Next Political Era* (New York: Simon and Schuster, 1996).

28. Thomas Bryne Edsall with Mary D. Edsall, *Chain Reaction: The Impact of Race, Rights, and Taxes on American Politics* (New York: W. W. Norton, 1991); E. J. Dionne, Jr., *Why Americans Hate Politics* (New York: Touchstone, 1991), 95. See also Wilson, *The Truly Disadvantaged*.

29. Andrew Hacker, *Two Nations: Black and White, Separate, Hostile, Unequal* (New York: Charles Scribner's Sons, 1992), chaps. 7 and 8.

30. Kenneth O'Reilly, *Nixon's Piano: Presidents and Racial Politics From Washington to Clinton* (New York: The Free Press, 1995).

31. Paul K. Conklin, *The New Deal* (Arlington Heights, Ill.: Harlan Davidson, 1992), 95–96.

32. Donald G. Nieman, *Promises to Keep: African-Americans and the Constitutional Order, 1776 to the Present* (New York: Oxford University Press, 1991), 164–70.

33. Kim McQuaid, *Uneasy Partners* (Baltimore: Johns Hopkins University Press, 1994), 108–11, 116.

34. See David Gray Adler and Larry N. George, eds., *The Constitution and the Conduct of American Foreign Policy* (Lawrence: University Press of Kansas, 1996).

## Conclusion

1. Martin Shefter, "Party, Bureaucracy, and Political Change in the United States," in Louis Maisel and Joseph Cooper, eds., *Political Parties: Development and Decay* (Beverly Hills, Calif.: Sage, 1978), 211–65.

2. Margaret Weir and Theda Skocpol, "State Structures and the Possibilities for 'Keynesian' Responses to the Great Depression in Sweden, Britain, and the United States," in Peter B. Evans, Dietrich Rueschemeyer,

and Theda Skocpol, eds., *Bringing the State Back In* (Cambridge: Cambridge University Press, 1985), 143.

3. Theda Skocpol, *Protecting Soldiers and Mothers: The Political Origins of Social Policy in the United States* (Cambridge, Mass.: Harvard University Press, 1992).

4. Ira Katznelson, Kim Geiger, and Daniel Kryder, "Limiting Liberalism: The Southern Veto in Congress, 1933–1950," *Political Science Quarterly* 108 (Summer 1993):301.

# Index